THE POLITICS
OF BROADCAST REGULATION

Second Edition

THE POLITICS OF BROADCAST REGULATION

Second Edition

Erwin G. Krasnow, General Counsel,
National Association of Broadcasters

Lawrence D. Longley, Lawrence
University

Foreword by Newton Minow

ST. MARTIN'S PRESS   NEW YORK

Library of Congress Catalog Card Number: 77-86292
Copyright © 1978 by St. Martin's Press, Inc.
All Rights Reserved.
Manufactured in the United States of America.
21098
fedcb
For information, write St. Martin's Press, Inc.,
175 Fifth Avenue, New York, N.Y. 10010

cover design: Joe Notovitz

cloth ISBN: 0-312-62651-7
paper ISBN: 0-312-62652-5

Preface to the
Second Edition

When are five years a lifetime? When they occur between the first and second editions of a book that attempts to keep track of developments in the fields of broadcasting and regulation. The problem lies with both of those worlds. Broadcasting (and all of the communications universe) has grown enormously in size and impact since we last addressed the subject. And regulation, which once grew increasingly complicated by the decade, now seems to do so by the day.

The first edition of this book noted the emergence of citizens groups, the courts, and the White House as factors of increasing importance in the formulation of regulatory policies governing the broadcasting industry. During the past five years each of these participants has continued to play a significant role. The citizens movement has broadened its participation in FCC, court, and congressional proceedings. The courts, taking an activist role, have reversed FCC decisions on such important issues as indecent language, newspaper-broadcast crossownership, ex parte (or off-the-record) contacts, pay cable restrictions, and program format changes of radio stations. The White House, too, has been active. The Watergate tapes documented the attempts of the Nixon administration to muzzle the electronic media. And although the White House Office of Telecommunications, created by President Nixon's Executive Reorganization Plan No. 1 of 1970, has been deprived of independent existence by President Carter's Reorganization Plan No. 1 of 1977, it will be reincarnated in the Department of Commerce.

The other major participants in the making of regulatory policy—Congress, the FCC, and the industry—have continued to be active as well. The House Communications Subcommittee has conducted a series of hearings on the first overall revision of the Communications Act since its passage in 1934. The FCC, under the leadership of former Chairman Richard E. Wiley, has instituted changes in the way the agency conducts its business. And the broadcast industry has faced increasing challenges by such competing industry interests as cable television, land mobile radio, and copyright holders.

During the mid-1970s citizens band (CB) radio became the FCC's fastest-growing service and is now the largest single radio service administered by the commission. CB radio burgeoned from a selective two-way medium of person-to-person communications into a generalized communications medium in which the user "broadcasts" personal or business messages to virtually anyone who chooses to respond.

The second edition of this book differs from its predecessor in several major respects. There are expanded discussions of the roles of all the major participants in the broadcast decision-making process, reflecting changes in each participant's strategy and effectiveness. For example, there is a new section detailing how Congress affected the making of broadcast policy from 1970 to 1977. Chapter eight, on comparative license renewal challenges, describes the events occurring after the landmark Citizens Communications Center decision. A new case study has been added on the extraordinary growth of CB radio in the mid-1970s. The rise of CB radio has raised profound questions about the ability of the FCC to deal with rapid technological innovation.

Countless individuals have influenced both the original and the revised editions of this book, including virtually everyone that we have dealt with in the course of our work: Krasnow in Washington, D.C. in his communications law practice; Longley in his political science research. However, we wish to single out certain individuals for their special willingness to share their insights into various aspects of the politics of broadcast regulation. Among those deserving credit are Corry Azzi, Robert Booth, Michael Botein, Stuart Brotman, Richard Brown, Dean Burch, Dan Calibraro, Barry Cole, Leroy Collins, Kenneth Cox, Phil Cross, Everett Dillard, J. Leiper Freeman, Henry Geller, George J. Graham, Jr., James Graham, Chong-do Hah, Oren Harris, Sydney Head, E. William Henry, Susan Hill, Rosel Hyde, Mark Johnson, Tom Keller, John M. Kittross, Howard Kitzmiller, Linda Lacey, Brian Lamb, Robert E. Lee, Avery Leiserson, Lawrence Lichty, Don R. LeDuc, Lee Loevinger, Jack Loftus, Newton Minow, Steve Millard, Vincent Mosco,

Dawson Nail, Mal Oettinger, Max Paglin, Alan Pearce, William Pearl, James Popham, Carlos Roberts, Harry Shooshan III, Christopher Sterling, Herbert Terry, Sol Taishoff, Jack Wayman, Donald West, Richard E. Wiley, and Nicholas Zapple.

We have not mentioned the titles of the persons who have added to our understanding of the inner workings of the FCC, Congress, the courts, and the White House because in most instances, these individuals have held a variety of positions during the time this book was written. For example, many members of the FCC later worked within Congress, the White House, the broadcasting industry, or citizens groups.

We would be remiss if we did not acknowledge our debt to Mary Townsager and Elaine Romano for their editorial skill. Finally, we would like to express our appreciation to the members of our families—Judy, Michael, and Catherine Krasnow and Becky Longley—for providing the encouragement, sympathy, and patience necessary for this book's completion.

Be advised that the book you hold in your hands represents our best shot at a moving target.

Erwin G. Krasnow, Washington, D.C.
Lawrence D. Longley, Appleton, Wisconsin

Foreword

The Federal Communications Commission is one of the most important and least understood government agencies. Issues of momentous concern to every citizen come to the FCC, but its responsibilities, limitations, and activities are known only to a small segment of the press, the bar, and the engineering fraternities. True, it is accountable directly to the Congress and there are frequent congressional reviews of its decisions and deliberations. True, the courts are constantly reviewing—and increasingly reversing—commission cases and regulations. True, the President appoints the chairman and commissioners, thereby exercising some supervisory control. But despite these continuing links with all three branches of the federal government, the FCC remains unfamiliar to most citizens.

Since the early 1970s I have conducted a seminar each year at the Northwestern University Medill School of Journalism. Graduate students of journalism and law students attend, and we probe the issues confronted by the FCC from the perspectives of both law and journalism. Guest lecturers have included network presidents, commentators, producers, and regulators. We study why broadcasting is the only medium of expression under direct governmental regulation. Hard, sensitive, baffling problems arise in interpreting the First Amendment in a world of rapid technological changes. I often end class sessions by asking students to pretend they have just been appointed to the FCC by the President and must vote on a particular case or issue. It does not surprise me that often the vote is close.

That is one reason why I welcomed this book on its first publication and was able to use it so effectively in my class. Very few scholars have paid enough attention to the *politics* of the federal regulatory agencies. Professor William L. Cary of Columbia University Law School, former chairman of the Securities and Exchange Commission, led the way a decade ago in his classic book, *Politics and the Regulatory Agencies*. In that work Cary (who, fortunately for me, was my law professor when I was a student) perceptively analyzed the relationship between regulation and the political process from a scholarly as well as professional perspective. Now Erwin G. Krasnow, an active member of the FCC bar, who currently serves as general counsel to the National Association of Broadcasters, and Lawrence D. Longley, a political scientist with expertise in interest group politics, have pooled their talents to apply the analysis more specifically to the record of one agency—the FCC.

Their efforts have produced an uncommonly useful book which probes some very hard cases. Their revised and updated second edition is an even better book than before. By focusing on selected case histories—of FM broadcasting, of UHF television, of proposed limits on broadcast commercial time, of license renewal policies, and of citizens band radio—the authors have shown us how the regulatory process actually works, how it is influenced by political realities, and how decisions are really made.

Pressures are intense in the regulation of broadcasting. The industry is strong, vocal, and has many powerful friends. Citizens groups, a relatively recent interested party, now have acquired some muscle and sophistication in dealing with the regulatory world. The White House is becoming more concerned about regulatory decisions because of its new-found awareness that FCC decisions have both national and international implications. And the Congress and courts have the last word.

Let me give but one example from personal experience of the pressures encountered in broadcast regulation. When I was at the FCC, I was one of a few commissioners who wanted to place some limits on the amount of commercial time allowed on radio and television. We strongly believed that some rules were long overdue. We proposed that the commercial time rules established by the broadcasters themselves through the National Association of Broadcasters be enforced. I finally mustered a majority on the commission to support this proposal. After I left, my successor, Bill Henry, was besieged by the industry. The Congress reacted almost immediately, and as described in detail in chapter seven, the House of Representatives made it clear to the FCC that it regarded this area as off limits. Thus, we remain the only nation in the world with no rules on how many commercials a broadcaster may run, and our best broadcasters are reduced to the law of the jungle. Yet the FCC is blamed as a spineless tool of the broadcasting lobby, when in fact its efforts to regulate were frustrated by the Congress.

Authors Krasnow and Longley document similar examples in this work. They conclude, quite properly, that although the FCC may initiate policy, the fate of such policy is often determined by others. A good example which I know something about is the formulation of policy in the early 1960s concerning international communications satellites. Here we were able to get Comsat launched quickly and thus preserved American leadership in the world. But we succeeded only because the FCC compromised with various competing economic interests and theories, governmental and private agencies, and because we turned to the President and the Congress for the final word. This required an understanding of the political process; in fact, the essence of that process almost always requires compromise. Sometimes, such compromise does not serve the best interest of the public, but under our system of government, I do not know a better alternative.

The authors have penetrated beneath the surface to give their readers an accurate understanding of how the regulation of broadcasting really works. The idea of active practitioners like Erwin Krasnow working in harness with academic authorities like Lawrence Longley is a good one. The union of their efforts is in the best interests of their readers.

How do I know? I can best answer by quoting a favorite poem of President Kennedy. It is a poem written by a bullfighter, Domingo Ortega, as translated by Robert Graves:

> Bullfight critics ranked in rows
> Crowd the enormous Plaza full;
> But he's the only one who knows—
> And he's the one who fights the bull.

NEWTON N. MINOW

Contents

Introduction: The Lay of the Land

Broadcasting in America has emerged from its first half century as a critical and central element of society, shaping values and opinions to an extent unrivaled by all other forms of media. Yet entrepreneurial entry to this medium, as opposed to newspapers, magazines, or films, is not open to all but is rather strictly regulated by a government agency. Crucial decisions as to who may broadcast what programs are made by an "independent regulatory commission"—the Federal Communications Commission. Because the FCC operates in a supercharged political atmosphere, studying the manner in which the commission regulates broadcasting can be highly revealing of how our democratic system of government operates.

Curiously, although numerous studies of the FCC and the other independent regulatory agencies exist, few works deal with the political aspects of regulation. Almost two decades ago Marver Bernstein observed that "remarkably little empirical work has been done to describe and analyze the *political* context of particular regulatory programs."[1] His assessment still holds true. In fact, as late as 1972 Bernstein concluded:

> Our thinking about the regulatory process and the independent commissions remains impressionistic, and the need for empirical research is largely unfulfilled. As a consequence, we fall back on our value preferences concerning the role of government in economic life, on the biases of our professional affiliations, and on assertions by others that support our personal conceptions and conclusions.[2]

The lack of such empirical research may be due in part to the considerable confusion surrounding the concept of politics. Definitions of this term are so plentiful and varied that its application to broadcast regulation lacks precision. Harold Lasswell once commented that political science "is the study of influence and the influential" and "the influential are those who get the most of what there is to get." He encouraged analysis of political activities centering on "who gets what, when and how."[3] This focus provides a useful operational definition of politics: *Politics consists of those activities leading to decisions about the allocations of desired goods.* In the context of broadcast regulation those activities can range from legal briefs prepared by citizen groups to the appointment of a special task force by the White House on a key communications problem. They may also include an FCC proposal to regulate advertising time or a court of appeals decision to strike down commission standards for the renewal of broadcast licenses.[4] Such decisions usually result in allocations of desired goods, with only some of the participants getting what they want.

Despite persistent calls for an emphasis on the political aspects of policy making by agencies such as the FCC, most of the existing literature on broadcast regulation has emphasized instead such topics as the history and development of the FCC and the broadcasting industry, the agency's legal and administrative status, and the legal problems resulting from the combination of rule-making and adjudicative functions in the same body. The political context of particular regulatory programs is generally omitted or mentioned only perfunctorily. Questions such as "who gets what, when and how" out of the process are rarely considered—and never systematically. We propose to deal specifically with these questions. Their answers are central to the politics of broadcast regulation.

The first chapter of this book will examine the basic characteristics and the environmental context of the regulatory process, and then trace the historical development of broadcast regulation. Chapters two and three will examine the role of the various participants in the making of policy and will be followed, in chapter four, by an analytical consideration of the structure and characteristics of the regulatory process.

Chapters five through nine consist of five case studies of broadcast regulatory policies:

1. The questionable decision of the FCC, in 1945, to shift the frequency allocation for FM broadcasting from the 44 megacycle range to the 88–108 megacycle band
2. The development of the All-Channel Receiver Bill of 1962 as a desperate attempt to resolve the decade-old problems of a crippled Ultra High Frequency (UHF) television service

3. The abortive effort of the FCC in 1963 to set commercial time limits for broadcast licensees
4. The commission's attempts in the 1970s to establish policy on license renewal challenges
5. The efforts of the FCC, beginning in the mid-1970s, to develop policies designed to reduce congestion and clutter in citizens band radio

We chose these five case studies largely because they are clear instances of controversy over specific policy options. They also provide diverse examples of the political environment in which the FCC operates—examples which, taken together, support the formulation of generalizations and hypotheses about the broadcast regulatory process. These cases span the full history of the commission (FM having emerged as an issue in the early 1930s), and indeed policies governing each of the five areas continue to be developed today. In addition, the studies involve diverse broadcast interests— FM, TV, advertisers, manufacturers, citizens groups, license renewal applicants, and consumers—and they cover a broad range of issues, including frequency allocation, equipment requirements, the role of public participation, and technological innovation and its control. The comparative analysis of different types of decisions over an extended period allows for a broad analysis of parallels in decision-making approaches and serves to minimize the importance of coincidental events, the special tactics of a particular coalition of opponents, or the attitudes of a specific administration.

Most important, we feel that the politics of broadcast regulation is seen best in actual instances of political conflict. In the five cases studied here such conflict is evident, and political gains and losses resulting from policy decisions are quite marked.

In the final chapter we take a closing look at the politics of broadcast regulation by analyzing the five case studies as a group and reaching some conclusions about the regulatory process in broadcasting.

Notes

[1] Marver H. Bernstein, "The Regulatory Process: A Framework for Analysis," *Law and Contemporary Problems*, 26 (Spring 1961), 341 (emphasis added).

[2] Marver H. Bernstein, "Independent Regulatory Agencies: A Perspective on Their Reform," *The Annals*, 400 (March 1972), 21.

[3] Harold D. Lasswell, "Politics: Who Gets What, When, How," in *The Political Writings of Harold D. Lasswell* (Glencoe, Ill.: The Free Press, 1951), pp. 295, 309.

[4] These examples are discussed in detail in chapters seven and eight.

PART ONE
THE REGULATORY PROCESS

1

Broadcasting and the Regulatory Process

The Federal Communications Commission is a creature of Congress, staffed at its highest levels by White House appointees, subject at every moment to judicial review, and faced with daily pressures from the industries it regulates, other branches of government, and the public whose interest it was created to protect. Yet the regulation of American broadcasting is often portrayed as if it takes place within a cozy vacuum of administrative "independence." In reality, the making of broadcast policy by the FCC, an ostensibly independent agency, is an immensely political process—not, incidentally, as an aberration, but by its very nature. The FCC operates within a political system involving various participants, including the regulated industries, the public, the White House, the courts, the Congress, and the commission itself. It should be noted that these participants are neither monolithic nor unchanging entities but aggregations of human beings operating in various structured roles. Too frequently, these participants, and the description of their activities by such terms as "government regulation," are viewed in a way that suggests an impersonal mechanical operation. Realistically, there is no such thing as "government regulation"; there is only regulation by government officials.[1] The essence of the politics of broadcast regulation lies in the complex interactions among these diverse participants, not only in their day-to-day confrontations, but also in the more enduring adjustments and readjustments of their relationships.

To a great extent these relationships are determined by law—by statutes which themselves are the formal heritage of past political disputes. Such laws, however, are seldom crystal clear; the result of earlier political conflict may have been, and often is, legislation and rules drafted with deliberate ambiguity—broad general mandates which permit the politics of today to determine the rules and standards of tomorrow.

Thus a major task of the FCC (and other regulatory agencies) is not only to conform to the letter of the law but, beyond that, to attune its behavior to the requirements imposed by its political environment. To retain some flexibility and freedom of choice in its policy making, the commission must try to gain political support over opposition. This process is more subtle than normally suggested by concepts such as "legislative control of administration" or "administrative representation of interests." William W. Boyer aptly describes agency policy making as "environmental interaction": For effective policy initiation an administrator must attempt to perceive and anticipate the behavior of participants in the process and the environment reflected by them. Only thus can he hope accurately to assess the political ecology within which he must make his policy decisions.[2] Besides such assessments and adjustments a regulator also may seek to shape that environment by means of public speeches, private meetings, statements, testimony, and the like—calls for deregulation of the broadcasting industry or condemnation of television programing as a "vast wasteland." Thus "environmental interaction" is a two-way street: An administrator is constrained by his perceptions of environmental forces while at the same time he is himself influencing or even partially creating those very forces.

The Historical Context of Broadcast Regulation

The regulation of broadcasting as we know it today is to a large degree the product of its history. For example, the basic statute under which the FCC currently operates is virtually identical to the legislative charter given to the Federal Radio Commission in 1927. The very questions on the proper role of regulation posed during the 1920s and 1930s continue to be debated in the late 1970s. Only in 1976 did the House Communications Subcommittee initiate a comprehensive review of the Communications Act—the first such review since its passage in 1934.

Secretary Hoover and the Radio Conferences. The growth of large-scale broadcasting in the early 1920s found the Congress and the Executive Branch almost totally unprepared to meet new obligations in this field. Until 1927 the only law passed by Congress dealing with radio was the Radio Act of 1912, which was designed primarily for ship-to-ship and maritime communications. In 1921 Secretary of Commerce Herbert Hoover designated 833 kc. as the frequency for broadcasting (allowing but one station in a reception area), and in the summer of 1922 he added 750 kc. as a second broadcast frequency. Acting under what he believed to be congressional authority conferred by the 1912 maritime legislation, Hoover attempted to establish rules of broadcasting frequencies, hours of broadcast, and limits of power. In 1922 he convened the first of a series of industry conferences to discuss ways of controlling the use of these frequencies. After two months of study and investigation the First Radio Conference unanimously decided that regulation by private enterprise alone would not be effective and recommended the passage of legislation authorizing government control over the allocation, assignment, and use of broadcasting frequencies.

Representative Wallace H. White of Maine sponsored a measure designed to put the recommendations of the conference into effect by authorizing Secretary Hoover, assisted by an advisory committee, to act as a "traffic cop of the air." Congress, however, failed to enact this legislation. Hoover then called a Second Radio Conference in 1923 to work out ways of reducing the mounting interference to radio reception caused by the crowding of stations. Shortly before the conference Hoover's attempts to regulate were seriously undermined when the United States Court of Appeals for the District of Columbia Circuit ruled that the secretary of commerce lacked legal authority to withhold licenses from broadcast stations.[3] The court concluded that Congress had never intended to delegate such authority to the secretary of commerce.

While Congress continued to study the problem by holding periodic hearings, Hoover continued to call industry conferences. At the Third National Radio Conference in 1924, Hoover commented: "I think this is probably the only industry of the United States that is unanimously in favor of having itself regulated."[4] The industry had come to demand such controls as the increase in stations continued unchecked. By November 1925 more than 578 stations were on the air and applications had been filed for 175 more. With every channel filled, most stations were experiencing considerable interference from other stations and had been forced to work out complex time-sharing schemes.

Despite the evident need Secretary Hoover's regulatory initiatives were repeatedly thwarted. The final blows came in 1926 when a series of court rulings deprived him of any authority to regulate radio frequencies, power, or hours of operation. Hoover then limited the Department of Commerce to the role of a registration bureau and intensified his pleas for self-regulation.

The Federal Radio Commission as "Traffic Cop." The chaotic conditions resulting from reliance on voluntary measures in 1926 brought strong demands from the public and the radio industry that Congress take action. Until then, Congress had held several hearings but the House and the Senate had been unable to agree on legislation. The House had wanted the secretary of commerce to retain the authority to issue licenses, subject to appeal to a Federal Radio Commission, while the Senate favored the establishment of a permanent radio commission.

Addressing himself to the pending Federal Radio Act in 1926, Senator Clarence C. Dill of Washington, chairman of the Senate Interstate Commerce Committee, argued that the influence of radio on the social, political, and economic life of the American people and the complex problems of its administration

> demand that Congress establish an entirely independent body to take charge of the regulation of radio communications in all its forms. . . . The exercise of this power is fraught with such possibilities that it should not be entrusted to any one man nor to any administrative department of the Government. This regulatory power should be as free from political interference or arbitrary control as possible.[5]

(Nearly forty-five years later the President's Advisory Council on Executive Organization—popularly referred to as the Ash Council—recommended that the bipartisan collegial form of organization be retained for the FCC for the identical reasons mentioned by Senator Dill in 1926.[6])

Finally, in March 1926, Representative White's bill to authorize the secretary of commerce as "traffic cop of the air"—substantially the same bill he introduced in 1923—passed the House by a vote of 218 to 123. However, the measure soon ran into difficulties in the Senate, which continued to favor a permanent, independent radio commission. Early in 1927 a Senate-House conference committee hammered out a compromise which would establish a Federal Radio Commission on an experimental basis for one year.

This legislation that was finally enacted, the Radio Act of 1927, reflected an accommodation of interests between the House and Senate by setting up a curious division of responsibilities between the secretary of commerce and the new Federal Radio Commission. The Radio Act provided that applications for station licenses, renewals, and changes in facilities be referred by the Department of Commerce to the Federal Radio Commission, and it gave the FRC broad administrative and quasi-judicial powers over these applications. The secretary of commerce continued to have such powers as fixing the qualifications of operators, inspecting station equipment, and assigning call letters. After the expiration of one year, however, the secretary of commerce was to take over all powers—except the power to revoke licenses—with the FRC continuing purely as a part-time appellate body, dealing with appeals from the decisions of the secretary of commerce. An important feature of the Radio Act (which, however, received little attention at the time) was the requirement in Sections 9 and 11 that "the licensing authority should determine that the public interest, convenience, or necessity would be served by the granting [of a station's license]."

The act created a Radio Commission of five members appointed by the President with the advice and consent of the Senate. The President was required to nominate one commissioner from each of five geographical zones. One of the commissioners was to be designated by the President as its initial chairman, with subsequent chairmen being elected by the commission itself. Having structured the FRC so carefully, Congress then launched the infant commission with a serious handicap—it failed to give it any money! The commission was nevertheless able to function due to a clause in the Radio Act allowing it to utilize the unexpended balance in the appropriation made to the Department of Commerce under the item "wireless communications laws." The original members of the commission were forced to do their own clerical work, and, for the first four years, engineers had to be borrowed from other agencies.

The FRC faced other virtually insuperable problems: its temporary status as an experimental body with powers expiring after one year, the danger of internal strife because of each commissioner's appointment from a geographical zone, the great vagueness of the act and the lack of a specific mandate from Congress, the slowness of Senate confirmation of the commissioners, constant court challenges to its decisions, and the "prior rights" of stations already on the air. Llewellyn White summarized these problems in vivid terms:

> The F.R.C. had found the job cut out for it quite literally killing. One hearing alone required 170,000 affidavits. One out of ten decisions had to be fought through the courts. Congress had allowed the Commission a staff of twenty, including engineers and office workers. Two of the five Commissioners were not confirmed for nearly a year, one resigning in disgust after seven months' backbreaking work without pay.[7]

In addition to administrative bottlenecks the FRC faced monumental technical problems. As of 1927 there were 732 stations blanketing all 90 radio channels. At least 129 stations were broadcasting off their assigned channels, and 41 were broadcasting on channels reserved for Canadian use. In practice there were no restrictions concerning power or hours of operation. Adding to the confusion was the presence of completely unregulated amateurs on the broadcast band. In an effort to wipe the slate clean, the FRC announced that it would adopt "a completely new allocation of frequencies, power, and hours of operation for all of the existing 732 broadcast stations." The Radio Act encouraged this attempt at a fresh start by providing that all existing licenses were to expire sixty days after its enactment. The act further stated that "no license should be construed to create any right, beyond the terms, conditions, and periods of the license." The commission soon found out, however, that broadcasters who had been on the air for years had a very strong interest in preserving their favored status and would fight lengthy court battles to keep their "rights." As a result the FRC was largely unsuccessful in its attempts to solve radio's problems on an individual hearing basis.

Throughout its short history the Radio Commission was subjected to great congressional pressure. Not really accepting the independent status of this "independent regulatory commission," Congress continually tinkered with the 1927 act. Since the Radio Commission was originally established for a period of only one year, Congress had to renew the legislation annually (or let the FRC's activities be absorbed by the Department of Commerce). This annual review gave Congress a convenient opportunity to conduct hearings and add further legislative restrictions.

One of the most limiting congressional mandates was the so called Davis Amendment to the 1928 renewal act, requiring the FRC to allocate licenses, frequencies, times of operation, and power equally among five geographic zones and among the states therein. This amendment had been drafted in response to congressional concern that the commission favored high-power stations in the North and East and discriminated against stations in the South and West. The Davis Amendment prevented the FRC from functioning effectively as a harmonious group and seriously impeded the development of radio policy. In his annual message to the Congress on December 2, 1929, President Hoover criticized the Davis Amendment, warning that "there is a danger that the system will degenerate from a national system into five regional agencies with varying practices, varying policies, competitive tendencies, and consequent failure to attain its utmost capacity for service to the people as a whole."[8] Hoover also recommended that the commission be reorganized on a permanent instead of a temporary basis. This recommendation, however, was ignored by Congress.

In 1933 President Roosevelt requested Secretary of Commerce Daniel C. Roper to direct a study of the organization of radio regulation. In January 1934 the Roper Committee issued a report recommending the consolidation of the communications regulatory activities of the FRC, the Interstate Commerce Commission, the postmaster general, and the President into "a new or single regulatory body, to which would be committed any further control of two-way communications and broadcasting."[9] Although it strongly supported the centralization of regulatory activities, the report did not take a stand on whether the organization should be of the independent commission type.

The Birth of the FCC. Spurred by the Roper Committee recommendations and by general dissatisfaction with the existing structure of governmental regulation, Congress proceeded to enact the Communications Act of 1934, which established a new Federal Communications Commission. The Communications Act made various organizational changes in the commission (it called for seven commissioners instead of five, for example, and stipulated the appointment of all chairmen by the President) and gave the new agency a broader scope of activity over all communications, including telephone and telegraph. Title III of the 1934 act, which dealt with radio, was almost identical with the Radio Act of 1927.

Most importantly, the "public interest" criterion in the 1927 legislation was also retained.

An innovation in the 1934 law was congressional emphasis on the long-range planning of broad social goals. Section 303(g) specifically called upon the FCC to "study new uses for radio, provide for experimental uses of frequencies, and generally encourage the larger and more effective use of radio in the public interest." (This provision later led the commission to study such unearthly subjects as communications satellites for broadcasting to local receivers and the use of laser beams as relay mechanisms.) Congress also required the FCC to make studies of, and to report on, possible new legislation necessary for effective long-range goals. Throughout the commission's history, however, the Congress has never provided the agency with sufficient funds to make long-range studies. Former Commissioner Nicholas Johnson put the FCC budget in graphic perspective by pointing out that "the Federal Aviation Administration spends as much on *communications research* as the FCC's total annual budget; the Navy spends five times the FCC's annual budget doing cost-effectiveness studies of the communications system on one ship type; [and] Bell Labs has a budget over 15 times that of the FCC."[10]

Several factors in the commission's early history deserve emphasis because of their relevance to the regulatory process today. The first is the failure of early attempts at industry self-regulation. In an unprecedented and never-repeated phenomenon the infant broadcasting industry itself requested governmental controls to eliminate the audio chaos caused by unregulated radio operations. This factor partly explains how the radio industry gained its powerful influential position with respect to the FCC. Another historical factor which should be noted is the deep and early involvement of Congress. With Secretary of Commerce Hoover's regulatory activities blocked by the courts, the salvation of American broadcasting lay with Congress. When Congress *did* act to establish a regulatory agency, its existence and financing were subjected to yearly congressional consideration.[11] By giving the FRC limited financial and technical resources, Congress effectively ensured the commission's dependence upon congressional good will and kept a firm grip on the control of this "independent" regulatory agency. A third distinctive feature of the federal government's early regulation of broadcast stations is the focus on licensing as the primary regulatory tool. Although regulatory agencies such as the Federal Power Commission and the Interstate Commerce Commission exert control over entry by requiring proof of usefulness, the certificates of authority that are issued are for indefinite terms and are secondary to the regulation of profits and prices. The emphasis on the FCC's licensing role results in part from the fact that the Congress specifically denied the commission the power to regulate the rates or profits of broadcasting stations.[12]

The "Public Interest"— Broadcasting Battleground

Taylor Branch has divided government agencies into two categories: "deliver the mail" and "Holy Grail."[13] "Deliver the mail" agencies perform neutral, mechanical, logistical functions; they send out Social Security checks, procure supplies—or deliver the mail. "Holy Grail" agencies, on the other hand, have the more controversial and difficult role of achieving some grand, moral, civilizing goal. The Federal Radio Commission came into being primarily to "deliver the mail"—to act as a traffic cop of the airwaves. But both the FRC and the FCC had a vague Holy Grail clause written into their charters: the requirement that they uphold the "public interest, convenience and necessity." The vagueness of this congressional mandate is a key factor in understanding today's conflicts over broadcast regulation.

The concept of a public interest in radio communications was first expressed officially by Secretary Hoover in a speech before the Third Annual Radio Conference in 1924. One commentator wrote shortly after the passage of the Radio Act of 1927 that the inclusion of the phrase "public interest, convenience and necessity" was of enormous consequence since it meant that "licenses are no longer for the asking. The applicant must pass the test of public interest. His wish is not the deciding factor."[14]

Conflicts over the meaning of the "public interest" have been recurrent in broadcasting history. Besides lending itself to various interpretations, this vague statutory mandate has also hampered the development of coherent public policy since Congress (or influential congressmen) can always declare, "that is not what *we* mean by the public interest."[15] Few independent regulatory commissions have had to operate under such a broad grant of power with so few substantive guidelines. Rather than encouraging greater freedom of action, vagueness in delegated power may serve to limit an agency's independence and freedom to act as it sees fit. As Pendleton Herring put it, "administrators cannot be given the responsibilities of statesmen without incurring likewise the tribulations of politicians."[16]

Judge Henry Friendly, in his classic work *The Federal Administrative Agencies*, made the following comment on how the origin of the "public interest, convenience and necessity" standard serves to confuse, not enlighten:

> The only guideline supplied by Congress in the Communications Act of 1934 was "public convenience, interest, or necessity." The standard of public convenience and necessity, introduced into the federal statute book by [the] Transportation Act, 1920, conveyed a fair degree of meaning when the issue was whether new or duplicating railroad construction should be authorized or an existing line abandoned. It was to convey less when, as under the Motor Carrier Act of 1935, or the Civil Aeronautics Act of 1938, there would be the added issue of selecting the applicant to render a service found to be needed; but under those statutes there would usually be some demonstrable factors, such as, in air route cases, ability to render superior one-plane or one-carrier service because of junction of the new route with existing ones, lower costs due to other operations, or historical connection with the traffic, that ought to have enabled the agency to develop intelligible criteria for selection. The standard was almost drained of meaning under section 307 of the Communications Act, where the issue was almost never the need for broadcasting service but rather who should render it.[17]

Newton Minow has commented that, starting with the Radio Act of 1927, the phrase "public interest, convenience and necessity" has provided "the battleground for broadcasting's regulatory debate."[18] The meaning of this term is extremely elusive. Although many scholars have attempted to define the "public interest" in normative or empirical terms, these definitions have added little to an understanding of the real relevance of this concept to the regulatory process. A pragmatic but somewhat limited view is that offered by Avery Leiserson, who suggests that "a satisfactory criterion of the public interest is the preponderant acceptance of administrative action by politically influential groups." Such acceptance is expressed, in Leiserson's opinion, through groups which, when affected by administrative requirements, regulations, and decisions, comply without seeking legislative revision, amendment, or repeal.[19] Thus in order for a policy to be accepted by politically influential groups, it must be relevant to and must not conflict unacceptably with their expectations and desires. Defining the interest of the entire general public is considerably more difficult.

The concept of the public interest is important to the regulation of broadcasting in another sense. A generalized public belief even in an undefined "public interest" increases the likelihood that policies will be accepted as authoritative. The acceptance of "the public interest" may thus become an important support for the regulation of broadcasting and for the making of authoritative rules and policies toward this end. For this reason the courts have traditionally given the FCC wide latitude in determining what constitutes the "public interest." This view was expressed by Judge E. Barrett Prettyman in a decision denying the appeal by an unsuccessful applicant for a television station:

> It is also true that the Commission's view of what is best in the public interest may change from time to time. Commissions themselves change, underlying philosophies differ, and experience often dictates change. Two diametrically opposite schools of thought in respect to the public welfare may both be rational; e.g., both free trade and protective tariff are rational positions. All such matters are for the Congress and the executive and their agencies. They are political in the high sense of that abused term. They are not for the judiciary.[20]

On the other hand, ambiguity as to the meaning and lack of consensus over the requirements of the public interest has heightened conflict among participants in the regulatory process. Since Congress has found it inadvisable to define specifically for future situations exactly what constitutes the "public interest," the political problem of achieving consent to the application of this standard has been passed on to the FCC. Thus, the objectively unverifiable and elusive concept of the public interest can be enormously significant to the FCC—both as an undefined general support and, because of its unclarified nature, as a potential source of controversy.

Unresolved Regulatory Problems

The regulation of American broadcasting is no less controversial today than it was in the turbulent twenties and thirties. Many unresolved problems remain. Some of these difficulties stem from specific economic and technical characteristics of the broadcast industry. Others are the direct legacy of the historical development of regulation; certain legal prescriptions and requirements still on the books are interpreted differently by different participants at different times in the regulatory continuum. Still other problems may be traced to generalized public attitudes toward governmental regulation. Seldom can the FCC attempt to frame regulations without becoming entangled in this political thicket.

Statutory Ambiguities and Recurring Controversies. Disputes concerning legal prescriptions imposed by the Communications Act have centered on certain recurring value conflicts—assumptions about what ought or ought not to be done. One such question is the extent to which broadcasting should be related to social as well as economic and technical goals. The emphasis upon the social responsibilities of licensees rests on the view that "the air belongs to the public, not to the industry" since Congress provided in Section 301 of the Communications Act that "[no] license should be construed to create any right, beyond the terms, conditions, and period of the license." During the 1970s, for example, the FCC has adopted rules and policies designed to make broadcasters meet their social responsibilities by requiring them to implement equal employment opportunity programs for women and minorities, schedule television programs for children, and make their facilities available during prime time to federal political candidates.

"Program censorship" versus "free broadcasting" is another value conflict arising from legal prescriptions and requirements. Section 326 of the Communications Act states:

> Nothing in this Act shall be understood or construed to give the Commission the power of censorship over the radio communications or signals transmitted by any radio station, and no regulation or condition shall be promulgated or fixed by the Commission which shall interfere with the right of free speech by means of radio communication.

In the same act, however, Congress also directs the commission to regulate "in the public interest, convenience and necessity."[21] Using that standard as the basis, the commission has promulgated many rules and policies governing broadcast programing that would be regarded by the courts as unlawful censorship in the print media. To the degree that such regulation entails review and evaluation of program content, it can be considered a form of censorship. The ambiguity in the statute leads to divergent views of the desirable balance between freedom and censorship.

Another recurring controversy is whether the First Amendment guarantees the right of broadcasters to be free of government control over the content of broadcast programing or is designed to assure the public's right to hear diverse ideas and viewpoints. J. Skelly Wright, a U.S. court of appeals judge, has commented: "[In] some areas of the law it is easy to tell the good guys from the bad guys. . . . In the current debate over the broadcast media and the First Amendment . . . each debater claims to be the real protector of the First Amendment, and the analytical problems are much more difficult than in ordinary constitutional adjudication. . . . The answers are not easy."[22]

These colliding statutory ground rules governing the freedom and obligations of broadcasters have been melded into one of the law's most elastic conceptions—the notion of a "public trustee."[23] The FCC views a broadcast license as a "trust," with the public as "beneficiary" and the broadcaster as "public trustee." The public trustee concept is a natural consequence of the conflicting statutory goals of private use and nonmarket allocation of spectrum space. Congress gave the FCC the right to choose among various candidates for commercial broadcasting licenses and left it up to the commission to find a justification for providing a fortunate few with the use of a valuable scarce resource at no cost. Legal scholar Benno Schmidt, Jr., regards the public trustee concept as designed to dull the horns of the FCC's dilemma: To give away valuable spectrum space, with no strings attached, would pose stubborn problems of justification.

Technical Factors Influencing Regulation. There are two complementary and determinative features of American broadcasting: spectrum space scarcity and technological innovation. Scarcity, of course, has always been the underlying *raison d'être* for broadcast regulation. Because one man's transmission is another man's interference, Congress concluded that the federal government has the duty both to select who may and who may not broadcast and to regulate the use of the electromagnetic spectrum so that the public interest will be served.

Scarcity has been a special problem in the case of television. Whereas an FM broadcast needs a section of the spectrum twenty times wider than an AM broadcast, a TV broadcast requires a channel 600 times as wide as an AM broadcast station's signal.[24] During the early 1950s the FCC's allocation policy was confined to television within a twelve-channel Very High Frequency (VHF) system incapable of offering even two or three stations in many cities. Broadcasters with the only television station (or with one of the two) in a market at that time were in an awkward position to be complaining about governmental regulation. The All-Channel Receiver Bill of 1962[25] aimed to make additional television service available in many areas, with the expectation that eventually greater diversity in programing would result.

It can be argued that scarcity of service implies close governmental control approaching that of a public utility, while diversity and choice of services implies more relaxed governmental demands.[26] And because scarcity inflates economic potential enormously, it likewise intensifies the conflict over policy alternatives. The FCC's decisions on spectrum allocations have a multibillion dollar impact on the nation's gross national product. As a result of the relative scarcity of broadcast facilities, the FCC serves, in effect, as a substitute mechanism for the free market allocation of resources.

Conversely, as some broadcast services proliferate—such as AM and FM radio—pressures build for a looser rein on broadcast licensees. Broadcasters argue that there is little justification for rigid governmental regulation of ten or twenty competing radio stations in a market while a monopoly newspaper in the same market is free of such restrictions. As scarcity decreases, they argue, so should regulation.[27]

The scarcity of frequency space for commercial broadcasting and citizens band radio is partly a man-made problem with its dimensions defined by the Executive Branch. The FCC's jurisdiction over the radio spectrum is limited by Section 305 of the Communications Act, which exempts from the commission's power all "radio stations belonging to and operated by the United States." The federal government, through its various agencies, offices, and departments, operates a host of radio services occupying approximately one-half of the total available frequency space. With the government's total investment in telecommunications in excess of $100 billion and its annual expenditure for equipment, research, and development over $7 billion, the White House is not anxious to turn these frequencies over to the FCC.[28]

The classic pattern of limited broadcast facilities, which has led on the one hand to a cry for government regulation, also has encouraged technological innovations to expand programing possibilities. Throughout its history the FCC has had to wrestle with new problems brought about by such technical developments as network broadcasting, the possibility of higher transmitting power for AM stations, as well as the emergence of FM broadcasting, VHF and UHF telecasting, color television, cable television, communications satellites, and citizens band radio. The making of public policy in each of these areas goes far beyond resolving technical issues. Frequently technical issues disguise what are actually economic interests vying for control of some segment of the broadcasting market. The politics of broadcasting is thus present in technical as well as clearly social controversies.

Three of those technological innovations—the development of FM broadcasting, the opening up of Ultra High Frequencies to television, and the explosive growth of citizens band radio—together with the FCC's policies regarding them will be examined in more detail in subsequent chapters. It is sufficient here to note that the commission has been subjected to considerable criticism concerning its inability to cope with change—the most common charge being that it is concerned mainly with preserving the status quo and with favoring the well-established broadcast services. From a technological standpoint, for example, it has been said that the television stations constructed in 1952 might have been operating as early as 1937 had the commission actively supported the development of this new medium.[29]

An agency's ability to respond to and foster technological change is largely a matter of how dependent the agency is upon dominant industry factions—the "haves" as opposed to the "have nots." Throughout its history the FCC has lacked sufficient skilled personnel and funds to weigh the merits of new technology and has been forced to rely on outside advice and technical opinion. When faced with complex technical questions, the commission has often taken the easy road of finding in favor of the "haves" over the "have nots." A 1975 study of commission policy concerning the development of FM radio, UHF, cable, and subscription television found that each of these technical innovations developed a status that is ancillary to the dominant commercial system and concluded that rather than use innovations as correctives to obvious problems, the commission sought to control their growth.[30]

The ability of a regulatory commission to protect or to promote a technical innovation that challenges the regulated (and sometimes sheltered) industry is a measure of the vitality and strength of that agency. As will be seen in chapters five, six, and nine, the FCC has failed miserably in a number of attempts to help give birth to new broadcast services and, in fact, has at times almost destroyed innovations. It must be noted that these failures resulted at least in part from the highly political environment in which the FCC must regulate.

Forging a Consensus for Cable Television

The maneuverings with respect to cable television during the period from 1968 to 1972 provide a classic illustration of this political environment. In 1968, after the Supreme Court had affirmed the FCC's authority to regulate cable systems, the commission took the textbook action: It issued a voluminous set of its own cable policy proposals and invited comments from broadcasters, cable operators, citizen groups, members of the general public, and other interested parties. Three years and several thousand pages of dialogue later, FCC Chairman Dean Burch sent the House and Senate Communications Subcommittees a fifty-five-page summary of the kinds of rules the commission tentatively had concluded were necessary for the healthy development of the cable industry. Burch assured Congress that the new rules would not be made effective until several months later—March 31, 1972—in order to allow time for congressional review.

The consideration of cable rules, however, was not to be left to the discretion of the FCC and the Congress. President Nixon became involved in July 1971 by appointing a cabinet-level advisory committee on cable, headed by Dr. Clay T. Whitehead, director of the White House Office of Telecommunications Policy.[31] During the fall of 1971, Chairman Burch and Dr. Whitehead met privately with representatives of cable, broadcast, and copyright interests in an effort to effect a compromise agreement. Meanwhile, the Supreme Court was considering an appeal of a lower court ruling that the FCC had no authority to require cable systems to originate programs—a central element in the commission's regulatory strategy.

All branches of government—legislative, executive, and judicial—were independently considering the future of cable when the FCC, in a 136-page decision in February 1972, adopted new cable rules which were based on a private agreement entered into by cable operators, broadcasters, and a group of copyright owners under the prodding of the White House. In a biting dissenting opinion, former Commissioner Nicholas Johnson, a liberal Democrat, said that "in future years, when students of law or government wish to study the decision making process at its worst, when they look for examples of industry domination of government, when they look for Presidential interference in the operation of an agency responsible to Congress, they will look to the FCC handling of the never-ending saga of cable television as a classic case study." Chairman Burch, a former head of the Republican National Committee, accused Johnson in a special concurring opinion of using a "scorched earth" technique to distort an act of creation into a public obscenity. Burch said that there was no conspiracy, no arm twisting, no secret deals. The cable decision, he said, was the result of months of painstaking study and measured deliberation, culminating in regulatory craftmanship of a high order. Then-Commissioner Richard E. Wiley, quoting Edmund Burke on the need for compromise, defended the decision on the ground that the "choice realistically confronting the Commission, after all, was this particular program—or none at all."[32]

From the foregoing example, it is clear that the regulatory process as applied to broadcasting is laced with an ample dose of political maneuverings. We turn now to a closer look at the people and the institutions comprising this political environment.

Notes

[1] Lee Loevinger, "The Sociology of Bureaucracy," *The Business Lawyer*, 24 (November 1968), 9.

[2] William H. Boyer, *Bureaucracy on Trial: Policy Making by Government Agencies* (Indianapolis: Bobbs-Merrill, 1964), p. 68. Two recent useful surveys of the problems of administrative agencies are: Richard Stewart, "The Reformation of American Administrative Law," *Harvard Law Review*, 88 (1975), 1667; and James Freeman, "Crises and Legitimacy in the Administrative Process," *Stanford Law Review*, 27 (1975), 1041. Another study which views the politics of broadcast regulation in terms of the "ecology of regulation" is Robert J. Williams, "Politics and the Ecology of Regulation," *Public Administration*, 54 (Autumn 1976), 219–331.

[3] *Hoover* v. *Intercity Radio*, 286 F. 1003 (C.A.D.C., 1923).

[4] Quoted in Sydney W. Head, *Broadcasting in America: A Survey of Television and Radio*, 3rd ed. (Boston: Houghton Mifflin, 1976), p. 126.

[5] U.S. Senate, Senate Report No. 772, 69th Congress, 1st Session, 2 (1926).

[6] *A New Regulatory Framework, Report on Selected Independent Regulatory Agencies* (Washington, D.C.: U.S. Government Printing Office, 1971), pp. 117–118.

[7] Llewellyn White, *The American Radio: A Report on the Broadcasting Industry in the United States from the Commission on Freedom of the Press* (Chicago: University of Chicago Press, 1947), p. 200.

[8] Quoted in Robert S. McMahon, *The Regulation of Broadcasting*, Study made for the Committee on Interstate and Foreign Commerce, House of Representatives, 85th Congress, 2nd Session (1958), p. 19.

[9] Senate Committee Print, S. Doc. 144, *Study of Communications by an Interdepartmental Committee*, 73rd Congress, 2nd Session (1934).

[10] Speech before the Federal Communications Bar Association, Washington, D.C., May 10, 1968, p. 9.

[11] Congress has followed a similar approach with the Corporation for Public Broadcasting, which initially received funding and authorization on an annual basis.

[12] Roger G. Noll, Merton J. Peck, and John J. McGowan, *Economic Aspects of Television Regulation* (Washington, D.C.: Brookings Institution, 1973), p. 98. Section 153(h) of the Communications Act provides that "a person engaged in radio broadcasting shall not, insofar as such a person is so engaged, be deemed a common carrier."

[13] Taylor Branch, "We're All Working for the Penn Central," *Washington Monthly*, November 1970, p. 8.

[14] Steven Davis, *The Law of Radio Communications* (New York: McGraw-Hill, 1927), p. 61.

[15] For example, see the discussion in chapter seven of a commission initiative to control advertising "in the public interest," which led to a stern rebuke from the House of Representatives.

[16] Pendleton Herring, *Public Administration and the Public Interest* (New York: McGraw-Hill, 1936), p. 138. Vagueness, however, may also serve to protect the agency when its decisions are challenged in the courts, since the judiciary may be loath to overturn actions protected by a broad statutory mandate.

[17] Henry Friendly, *The Federal Administrative Agencies* (Cambridge, Mass.: Harvard University Press, 1962), pp. 54–55.

[18] Newton Minow, *Equal Time: The Private Broadcaster and the Public Interest* (New York: Atheneum, 1964), p. 8.

[19] Avery Leiserson, *Administrative Regulation: A Study in Representation of Interests* (Chicago: University of Chicago Press, 1942), p. 16.

[20] *Pinellas Broadcasting Co.* v. *F.C.C.*, 230 F. 2d 204, 206 (C.A.D.C., 1956), writ of certiorari denied, 76 S. Ct. 650 (1956).

[21] Congress did not uniformly use the phrase "public interest" in the Communications Act. For example, the standard of "public interest" is specified in Sections 201(b), 215(a), 221(a), 222(c) (1), 415(a) (4), 319(i), and 315; "public convenience and necessity," Section 314(f); "interest of public convenience and necessity," Section 214(a); "public interest, convenience

and necessity," Sections 307(d), 309(a), 316(a), and 319(a); and "public interest, convenience or necessity," Sections 307(d), 311(b), and 311(c) (3).

[22] Quoted in Fred W. Friendly, *The Good Guys, the Bad Guys and the First Amendment: Free Speech vs. Fairness in Broadcasting* (New York: Random House, 1975), p. ix.

[23] This discussion is based on a theme developed by Benno C. Schmidt, Jr., *Freedom of the Press vs. Public Access* (New York: Praeger, 1976), pp. 157–158. The phrase "public trustee" does not appear in the Communications Act.

[24] Richard W. Taylor, "Government and Business," in J. W. Peltason and James M. Burns (eds.), *Functions and Policies of American Government* (Englewood Cliffs, N.J.: Prentice-Hall, 1962), p. 243.

[25] See chapter six, "UHF Television: The Fading Signal Is Revived After Only Ten Years."

[26] Some scholars argue that scarcity is primarily the product of, rather than the justification for, regulation. See Bruce M. Owen, *Economics and Freedom of Expression: Media Structure and the First Amendment* (Cambridge, Mass.: Ballinger, 1975).

[27] A similar argument on scarcity was made by the U.S. Court of Appeals for the District of Columbia Circuit in overturning FCC rules designed to protect broadcasters from siphoning off popular entertainment and sports programs from free commercial broadcasting to pay cable:

> Currently cable systems have the capacity to convey over 35 channels of programming. Technology is now available that would increase capacity to 80 channels, and in the future channel capacity may become unlimited. . . . And even though there is some evidence that local distribution of cable signals is a natural economic monopoly, which may raise the spectre of private censorship by the system owner, there is no readily apparent barrier of physical or electrical interference to operation of a number of cable systems in a given locality. In any case, scarcity which is the result solely of economic conditions is apparently insufficient to justify even limited government intrusion into the First Amendment rights of the conventional press, *see Miami Herald Publishing Co. v. Tornillo*, 418 U.S. 241, 247–256 (1974), and there is nothing in the record before us to suggest a constitutional distinction between cable television and newspapers on this point.

Home Box Office Inc. v. *F.C.C.*, No. 75–1280 et al. (C.A.D.C., March 25, 1977), p. 72; certiorari denied, 46 U.S.L.W. 3216 (U.S., October 3, 1977).

[28] Research and Policy Committee of the Committee on Economic Development, *Broadcasting and Cable Television, Policies for Diversity and Change* (New York: Committee for Economic Development, 1975), p. 87.

[29] See Don R. LeDuc, "The *FCC* v. *CATV, et al.*: A Theory of Regulatory Reflex Action," *Federal Communications Bar Journal*, 23 (1969), 93; and Robert H. Stern, "Regulatory Influences upon Television Development," *American Journal of Economics and Sociology*, 22 (1963), 347.

[30]Vincent Mosco, *The Regulation of Broadcasting in the United States: A Comparative Analysis* (Cambridge, Mass.: Harvard Program on Information Technologies and Public Policy, 1975), p. 102. For support of Mosco's thesis, see chapter nine. See also Don R. LeDuc, *Cable Television and the FCC: A Crisis in Media Control* (Philadelphia: Temple University Press, 1973); and Martin H. Seiden, *Cable Television U.S.A.: An Analysis of Government Policy* (New York: Praeger, 1972).

[31]The Office of Telecommunications Policy (OTP) was created on September 4, 1970, when President Nixon signed an executive order implementing Reorganization Plan No. 1 in 1970, as approved by Congress (see chapter three). Located in the Executive Office of the President, the OTP was headed by a director who reported, at least on paper, directly to the President and who was responsible for formulating and implementing the administration's policy on virtually all telecommunications matters. From the outset, OTP and the FCC were at odds over which agency was to have primacy in the communications area. The hostility would last throughout OTP's brief but stormy existence.

[32]*Cable Television Report and Order*, 36 F.C.C. 2d 141 (1972), pp. 1580, 1589. The FCC's policy on the development of cable television has been subject to considerable criticism. See Clair Wilcox and William G. Shepherd, *Public Policies Toward Business*, 5th ed. (Homewood, Ill.: Irwin, 1975); *Cable Television: Promise Versus Regulatory Performance*, Staff Report of the Subcommittee on Communications, House Interstate and Foreign Commerce Committee, 94th Congress, 2nd Session (January 1976); *Federal Regulation and Regulatory Reform*, Report by the Subcommittee on Oversight and Investigations, House Interstate and Foreign Commerce Committee, 94th Congress, 2nd Session (October 1976), pp. 257–258; LeDuc, *Cable Television and the FCC*; Seiden, *Cable Television U.S.A.*; Richard Olin Berner, *Constraints on the Regulatory Process: A Case Study of Regulation of Cable Television* (Cambridge, Mass.: Harvard Program on Information Technologies and Public Policy, 1975); and Monroe E. Price, "Requiem for the Wired Nation: Cable Rulemaking at the FCC," *Virginia Law Review*, 61 (April 1975), 541–578.

2

Five Determiners
of Regulatory Policy

From its establishment the FCC has enjoyed a broad congressional mandate—at least in theory—to frame responsible public policy regarding broadcasting. Certainly the FCC does play a central role in the regulation of broadcasting, but often the crucial decisions in policy making come about through the action, interaction, or, indeed, the inaction of persons or institutions other than the FCC. This chapter examines five of the six major participants in the regulatory policy-making process: the FCC, the broadcasting industry, citizen groups, the courts, and the White House. The sixth determiner of regulatory policy—the Congress—interacts with the other five at so many levels that it will be studied separately in chapter three. Additional participants such as the Corporation for Public Broadcasting and the Federal Trade Commission could be added, but these six stand out because of their continued and repeated involvement.

The FCC

Former Chairman Newton Minow once described the FCC as "a vast and sometimes dark forest, where FCC hunters are often required to spend weeks of our time shooting down mosquitoes with elephant guns."[1] Over the course of its history, the commission has been bombarded with criticism from various quarters. A good summary of many of the sweeping charges leveled against the FCC was included in the Landis Report on Regulatory Agencies to President-elect John F. Kennedy in December 1960:

> The Federal Communications Commission presents a somewhat extraordinary spectacle. Despite considerable technical excellence on the

part of its staff, the Commission has drifted, vacillated and stalled in almost every major area. It seems incapable of policy planning, of disposing within a reasonable period of time the business before it, of fashioning procedures that are effective to deal with its problems. The available evidence indicates that it, more than any other agency, has been susceptible to ex parte presentations, and that it has been subservient, far too subservient, to the subcommittees on communications of the Congress and their members. A strong suspicion also exists that far too great an influence is exercised over the Commission by the networks.[2]

The Landis Report pinpointed one of the FCC's major problems—its lack of real independence. A regulatory agency may be established by law as independent from the Executive, but this does not by any means imply independence from congressional or industry pressures. Nor does statutory separation from the Executive Branch assure an agency's independence from politics. Indeed, an essential characteristic of independent regulatory commissions is their need of political support and leadership for successful regulation in the public interest. Samuel P. Huntington, in his study of the Interstate Commerce Commission, explains this seeming paradox:

> If an agency is to be viable, it must adapt itself to the pressures from [outside] sources so as to maintain a net preponderance of political support over political opposition. It must have sufficient support to maintain and, if necessary, expand its statutory authority, to protect it against attempts to abolish it or subordinate it to other agencies, and to secure for it necessary appropriations. Consequently, to remain viable over a period of time, an agency must adjust its sources of support so as to correspond with changes in the strength of their political pressures. If the agency fails to make this adjustment, its political support decreases relative to its political opposition and it may be said to suffer from administrative marasmus.[3]

The FCC as a Bureaucracy.   The FCC, however, is more than just an independent regulatory commission wrestling with the problem of its political nonindependence; it is also a bureaucracy. As such it exhibits all the classic symptoms of bureaucracies—massive hierarchy, institutional conservatism, professed rationality, and entrenched self-interest.[4]

Lee Loevinger, a former FCC commissioner, has likened the FCC and other administrative agencies to a pyramid. At the apex of the pyramid (the part most visible from a distance) are the commissioners. The professional and middle staff members of the agency form the base of the pyramid, which supports the structure and determines whether it stands straight upright or leans in any direction.[5] Loevinger maintains that no one can understand the agencies and their operation without "some inquiry into the motivating forces that drive agency members and staff, and into the internal relationships by which work information and agency power are divided among and transmitted between persons comprising the institution."[6]

The attitudes of the FCC's middle staff are a significant factor in the development of its regulatory policy. First, unlike the commissioners and their personal staff aides who are political appointees and therefore subject to periodic change, the FCC's middle staff are government career employees, many of whom have spent their entire working lives at the commission. Second, the commission's middle staff exercises considerable influence through its control of the channels of communications to FCC commissioners. In choosing among various policy alternatives, FCC commissioners usually must base their decisions on information selected by staff personnel as relevant and significant. So common is this practice that former Commissioner Nicholas Johnson perceived the FCC's decision-making process as dominated by entrenched bureau chiefs and agency coordinators who are reluctant to present alternatives to the commissioners for their consideration.[7] Third, since hundreds of decisions must be made daily by the FCC, the formulation as well as the implementation of policy is frequently delegated to the commission's middle staff. When this happens, another bureaucratic symptom is evident—the struggle for power within the hierarchy.

Loevinger contends that the first step toward a realistic understanding of bureaucratic decision making is a recognition that the power motive is to bureaucracy what the profit motive is to business. Government officials and staff generally try to maximize the power of their positions. No exception to this generalization, the FCC commissioners and staff seek almost daily to perpetuate and extend their own power. Newly created bureaus and those hired to staff them attempt to justify and prolong their existence, frequently long after their usefulness has ended. Sometimes the power motive is expressed through the assertion of jurisdiction over new industries (such as cable TV), which are not specifically mentioned in the Communications Act and the creation of new bureaus (such as the Cable Television Bureau), which have been likened to independent "fiefdoms" within the agency.

Another characteristic of bureaucracy, related to its concern for its own institutional survival and power, is a tendency to be inflexible, static, and conservative rather than adaptive, innovative, or creative. As a bureaucracy the FCC is often reluctant to embrace innovative proposals, especially when such actions might mean the abandonment of familiar assumptions and standards. Incremental change—which can be bureaucratically digested in small bits—is often favored over sweeping change. Moreover, a policy that is "rational" in terms of accepted evaluative procedures is to be favored over a risky but potentially high-gain policy that demands different criteria for evaluation. Generally, the FCC has nothing to gain for pushing a successful technological innovation and everything to lose if it fails. Above all, the agency finds that it is best, when in doubt, to demand documentation rather than to make policy. As a result of such bureaucratic tendencies the commission spent nearly a decade searching for a means to encourage development of UHF television, has spent many more years worrying about programing evaluation standards for license renewals, and has fretted about cable television endlessly. In short, what "the FCC as a bureaucracy" means is that the commission often substitutes the act of evaluating and studying a problem or policy for the act of actually dealing with a problem or making policy.

Background Patterns Among the Commissioners. This huge bureaucracy—the FCC—is directed at the top by seven commissioners with varied social and political backgrounds who interact among themselves in a variety of aggregate and individual roles. The diverse roles of commissioners as well as commission staff are shaped to a significant extent by the formal structure of decision making. Bradley Canon has provided an illuminating description of this process:

> Commission meetings are held weekly and last three or four hours. The agenda is usually lengthy; often 50 to 100 items of business (not all of them cases) are considered in a single meeting. Although it varies among individuals, the general level of interaction between Commissioners on policy questions seems low. Thus, only those items considered really important receive any pre-meeting discussion or in-meeting debate. In other cases, the Commissioners vote on the basis of prior judgments and attitudes or follow the recommendations of staff members in whom they have confidence. Commissioners are free to switch their vote between the meeting and the writing of the opinion disposing of the case, but this occurs only occasionally. Opinions are almost

always written by staff members and adopted by the Commission, usually with a minimum of supervision and attention. Dissenting opinions, of course, are the responsibility of the dissident, although staff help is not unknown here. About one-fifth of such votes are not accompanied by an opinion.[8]

The formal political affiliation of commission appointees who are not members of the same party as the President is usually of little significance. Although Section 4(b) of the Communications Act provides that no more than four of the seven commissioners shall be members of the same political party, a study of fifty-one appointments to the FCC and FTC found that the selections from the President's own party typically have been partisan political choices; the others have been "friendly Indians" who are in sympathy with administration objectives rather than "bona fide, honest to God" members of the other party.[9] President Truman, for example, placed Republicans on the staff of the commission, where they were barred by the Hatch Act from all partisan activities.

The seven commissioners invariably come from distinctive and sometimes divergent social and political backgrounds. The characteristics of the forty-four individuals who served as FCC or FRC commissioners between 1927 and 1961 have been analyzed in detail by Lawrence Lichty.[10] Lichty found that individual commissioners held office for periods varying from six months to nineteen years, with the average length of service approximately four and one-half years. Of the forty-four commissioners twenty-three had studied law, twenty-four had some prior experience with broadcasting, and all but four had previously held government office on either the federal or state level. In short, the typical commissioner was trained in law, generally familiar with broadcasting, and quite likely to have had prior government administrative responsibilities.

Wenmouth Williams, Jr., updated the Lichty study by analyzing the backgrounds of twenty-two commissioners who served between 1962 and 1975 and found that the typical commissioner during this period had (1) some government affiliations, (2) strong political affiliations, and (3) some law experience.[11] Williams also found that the political philosophies of the commissioners had an important impact on regulatory philosophies during the 1962–1975 period. He noted a strong correlation between "presidential commissions" and basic regulatory trends: The Kennedy Commission, concerned with stricter regulation of programing and competition, was typified by Newton Minow's "vast wasteland" speech. Conversely, the commission of President Johnson (a President who had conspicuous broadcast interests) preferred to minimize government regulation as evidenced by the former President's appointment of Rosel Hyde, a "hands off" commissioner, as chairman.[12]

One particularly important result of this common legal and administrative background shared by many of the commissioners is the FCC's tendency to see regulatory activities in legal and administrative terms rather than in social and economic terms. Traditionally the FCC has preferred the administratively and legally sound policy over the controversial or more inclusive alternative. Moreover, the background of commissioners is not as diverse as suggested by Lichty and Williams. The FCC, like other regulatory agencies, has been stocked by white males. Over the half century of appointments to the FRC and FCC there have been only two black and three female appointees, with four of these five appointments occurring in the 1970s. A closer examination of the backgrounds of commissioners shows that they have tended to be neutral, generalist types, knowing little about the regulatory task when first appointed. Also, whatever their educational and occupational backgrounds, "consensus" types have predominated over commissioners with strong personalities and philosophies.

While describing the FCC in general terms, it is important to remember that it is not a static institution but one which changes as its personnel change. Critics frequently attack "the commission" as if it were a single, fixed, and unalterable body. In reality, there have been a number of "commissions" at different times with divergent opinions as to how broadcasting should be regulated. As Lichty concluded:

> Changes in the direction and emphasis of the Commission's regulation of broadcasting are a function of the members serving on the Commission at . . . specific times. Further, the personal experience, education, occupational background, and governmental philosophy of the members of the Federal Radio Commission and the Federal Communications Commission directly influence the direction and emphasis of the agency's policy.[13]

In an attempt to show variation within the commission at different historical periods, Lichty and Williams also analyzed distinctive patterns of commissioners' backgrounds during various periods of the FRC and the FCC. Their findings, which we have summarized and updated in Table 1, show a definite correlation

**Table 1.   Patterns of FRC and FCC Commissioners'
Backgrounds: 1927–1977***

Commission Periods	Background Patterns of Commissioners
1. Establishing Technical Standards, 1927–1930	Technical Experts
2. Important Legal Actions, 1930–1934	Legal Background
3. Cleaning-up and Vigorous Application of the Law, 1934–1938	Legal Background Prior Experience in Government
4. Trustbusting of Broadcast Ownership, 1939–1945	Prior Experience in Government, Especially Public Utility and New Deal Agency Background
5. Public Service, New Radio Facilities, and TV Engineering Problems, 1946–1952	FCC Staff Backgrounds as Engineers and Chief Counsels
6. Moderate Regulation, 1953–1960	Prior Experience on State Regulatory Commissions and FCC Staff Background
7. Increased Emphasis on Programing and Competition, 1960–1965	Legal Background Prior Experience in Government
8. Moderate Regulation, 1966–1969	Legal Background Prior Experience in Government
9. Cleaning-up, Clarification of Existing Law, 1970–1977	Prior Experience in Government and Politics

*Adapted and updated from Lawrence Lichty, "The Impact of FRC and FCC Commissioners' Backgrounds on the Regulation of Broadcasting," *Journal of Broadcasting*, 6 (Spring 1962), 97–110; and Wenmouth Williams, Jr., "Impact of Commissioner Background on FCC Decisions: 1962–1975," *Journal of Broadcasting*, 20 (Spring 1976), 244–256.

between commissioner background patterns and predominant commission activities. Both found that the regulation of broadcasting has been influenced to a measurable degree by the occupational backgrounds and political philosophies of these commissioners. For example, the "technical" period was dominated by members who had engineering background and the "trustbusting" era was characterized by attorneys experienced in governmental regulation.[14]

The Influence of Individual Commissioners.   Two other important points about the commissioners should also be mentioned: (1) Commissioners may exhibit factional behavior, and (2) individual commissioners often play pivotal roles in decision making. That groups or factions are important in a collegial voting body such as the FCC is certainly not a particularly new or striking idea; the literature on legislative committees and judicial institutions is replete with findings stressing the importance of internal groups and factions. In a study of the FCC as a decision-making body political scientist Bradley Canon used techniques familiar in judicial behavioral analysis, including bloc analysis and Gutman cumulative scaling. Canon concluded that various voting blocs *are* important in commission decisions and are especially present in dissents. He further found that partisan affiliations of commissioners seem to be related to voting behavior on some issues connected with broad social and economic problems, that appointees of different Presidents seem to vote somewhat differently, that the solo dissenter is not an uncommon occurrence, and that there is some consistency among commissioners in their voting patterns.[15]

Canon's conclusion concerning the individual dissenter should be stressed, for throughout the history of the FCC the role of the individual commissioner has been particularly significant. Lichty has observed that "the problems tackled and solutions proposed were due in part to the individual interests of commissioners and that many important decisions or changes were the result of a crusade by one Commissioner."[16] It cannot be denied that James Lawrence Fly, Nicholas Johnson, Newton Minow, Kenneth Cox, Dean Burch, and Richard Wiley had significant impact on the commission beyond the power of their individual votes.

Unlike the heads of most regulatory commissions, however, the chairman of the FCC has little formal power. For example, Congress has refused to provide the chairman of the FCC with general responsibility for staff and management.[17] Still, the chairman's power is greater than that of the other commissioners; his role as spokesman for the commission, the availability to him of a larger staff, and his visibility as the President's "choice" account for this. Former Commissioner Kenneth Cox has pointed out that the chairman of the FCC can have a significant influence on the planning of the commission's work since he is responsible for the preparation of the agenda at commission meetings and "has a much more direct relationship with the bureau chiefs as to scheduling, the allocation of priorities and so on." According to Cox a chairman "definitely has some edge in influence" since "there is some inclination on the part of some individual commissioners, if they don't feel strongly about a matter, to go along with the Chairman if he wants to say something is a matter of importance to him."[18] Frequently, an FCC chairman can be instrumental in the selection and reappointment of commissioners, especially if he has been working with the White House in furtherance of administration goals. A study of appointments to the FCC and the FTC from 1949 to 1974 revealed that twelve of the fifty-one commissioners appointed were selected largely because of the support of the commission chairman, and very few of those would have been nominated without such an endorsement.[19]

The extent of the power of a chairman, however, depends primarily on ability, determination, and on the willingness of his colleagues to give him the latitude he needs. Richard E. Wiley is regarded by many observers as the most powerful chairman in recent FCC history. Wiley, having served also as general counsel and a commissioner, played an important role in hiring and promoting commission staff members.[20] Les Brown of the *The New York Times* observed that "the Wiley years have been among the most productive in the agency's history for the handling and disposition of cases and the bureaucratic flow of paper."[21] Wiley made the commission a more efficient agency by using various changes in procedure, including a three-month calendar for items which he prepared personally in order to give each issue a priority and a deadline. He moved issues onto the voting agenda when he perceived a consensus among the other commissioners. Compromises in language or modifications in rules were customarily hammered out in his office before the commission meetings. Thus, while the commission produced approximately four times the number of decisions under Chairman Wiley's leadership than under any other previous administration in a comparable period, it probably also produced the fewest dissents.[22] Wiley attributes his success to the fact that the other six commissioners were "compatible [and] of similar philosophy." During most of his tenure as chairman the commission consisted entirely of Nixon appointees, the first time a President had named all seven members of the FCC since its formation in 1934.[23]

Wiley's impressive record of obtaining support from his colleagues was not matched, however, by his record with the courts. In an article entitled "Wiley's FCC: In Danger of Disappearing," *Broadcasting* magazine commented that decisions of the courts in 1976 and 1977 were stripping the Wiley administration of its major milestones.[24] Characterizing the record as "grim," the article referred to the following court actions: (1) the finding by a U.S. district court judge that Chairman Wiley's role in the National Association of Broadcasters' adoption of the family viewing concept for television infringed broadcasters' First Amendment rights; (2) the overturning by the court of appeals of media-crossownership rules permitting the retention of most local newspaper-broadcast combinations (a practice known as "grandfathering"); (3) the reversal on grounds of censorship of the commission's declaratory ruling that a George Carlin comedy record broadcast by a New York City radio station was "indecent"; (4) the overturning, based on statutory and First Amendment grounds, of FCC rules designed to guard against pay cable's siphoning off of movie and sports programing from regular commercial broadcasting; and (5) the expression of dissatisfaction by the court of appeals with the FCC's policy of allowing broadcasters and marketplace forces to determine the formats of radio stations.

Throughout the commission's history, individual commissioners, who expressed continuing interest in certain issues (e.g., ex-Commissioner Freida Hennock on educational broadcasting and Commissioner Robert E. Lee on UHF television), have had a considerable impact on the shaping of FCC policy on these matters. A fascinating example of the role of a single commissioner in forging a majority in favor of a policy is provided by the events surrounding the FCC's issuance of proposed rules, early in 1966, to regulate cable systems. The following passages from a report in *Broadcasting* magazine indicate the importance both of groups within the FCC and of individual commissioners in the formulation of a commission consensus:

> None of the tough new proposals was adopted for rule-making by more than a bare majority of the commission. Thus, a single defection,

even the wavering of a formerly committed commissioner, can kill a proposal or strip it of meaning. Representatives of groups directly affected know this, and are lobbying accordingly, on Capitol Hill as well as at the commission.

The commissioners themselves are uncertain and divided in their guesses as to what kind of rules, if any, will emerge. They talk of "shifting coalitions" among their number, of differing weights various commissioners ascribe to the arguments of different industry figures.

The commission statement on the CATV [cable TV] issue last week is a case in point representing as it does a number of compromises on some extremely controversial questions. . . .

Chairman Henry is credited by his colleagues for the degree of unanimity that was achieved. "It was very close," said one commissioner in commenting on the commission's decision. "It could have failed by an eyelash." "The chairman," he said, "did a very constructive job."

The chairman moderated his own previously hard line and abandoned the even harder line advocated by the staff. This cost him the support of Commissioner Cox, who favored stricter regulation. But it won the support of Commissioner Loevinger and held the vote of the other commissioners.[25]

The potential influence of one commissioner—particularly a chairman working outside the FCC structure—is shown in Newton Minow's attempts to change what he perceived as a "hostile environment" partially paralyzing the commission. He sought to overcome this handicap by appeals to public opinion: "Very early I decided that of all the routes I might take to the best performance of my job, the most effective and the wisest road in the long run was to speak out in the hope of influencing public opinion about television . . . and so I went to the people with public speeches."[26] By seeking to draw upon and to encourage active public involvement in American broadcasting, Minow was, in effect, attempting to strengthen his role as chairman by creating public support for certain types of policies. His characterization of television as "a vast wasteland" electrified a convention of the National Association of Broadcasters shortly after he became chairman and resulted in wide publicity in magazines and newspapers. Minow challenged broadcast executives to sit down in front of their television sets for a full day, assuring them that they would observe a "vast wasteland" of game shows, violence, formula comedies, sadism, commercials, and boredom.[27]

The adjustment that the FCC makes to the demands and actions of interested parties in any case is often a rough balance of

the forces which affect its political environment, its internal operations, and prevailing attitudes of the American public toward
regulatory issues. The problem for a regulatory commission is how
to respond to these pressures while maintaining some integrity of
purpose and freedom of decision. The dilemma is sharp: If a
regulatory commission is content to respond to dominant interests, it
may lose its meaning, whereas if it defies major forces in its
environment, it may lose its existence.

Industry

Introducing the broadcasting industry as a second participant in the
regulatory process raises the threshold issue of the purpose of a
regulatory commission and its relationship to the regulated industry
it was created to regulate. Recognizing the tensions and pressures
routinely applied by industry, Marver H. Bernstein has characterized regulation as "a two-way process in which the regulatory
agency and the regulated interest attempt to control each other."[28]

   Early federal regulatory legislation was designed to curb specific abuses involving concentrated economic power.[29] The Interstate Commerce Act of 1887, the Sherman Act, the Federal Trade
Commission Act, and the Clayton Act all reflect this trend. With the
passage of the Transportation Act of 1920 and subsequently the
Radio Act of 1927 and the Communications Act of 1934, Congress
shifted the mandate of regulatory commissions to the broader but
less well-defined charge of regulating in the "public interest." As
noted in chapter two this ambiguous mandate is made even more
indefinite to an administrator who must consider his responsibilities
to meet ill-formed public expectations of the "public interest" as
well as more often clearly stated congressional and industry desires.
At least to some degree the administrator can legitimately see his
charge as including the preservation and encouragement of the
regulated industry. The crux of his problem, then, is determining to
what degree this goal should be subservient to other considerations,
in particular to a larger conception of the public interest.

Industry-Commission Relationships—a Complex Web.   On a day-
to-day basis, commissioners are forced to immerse themselves in the
field they propose to regulate; however, the line between gaining a
familiarity with an industry's problems and becoming biased
thereby in favor of that industry is perilously thin. It is difficult for

commissioners and their staff to operate closely with an industry without coming to see its problems in industry terms. As Professor Landis reported to President Kennedy, "It is the daily machine-gunlike impact on both agency and its staff of industry representatives that makes for industry orientation on the part of many honest and capable agency members, as well as agency staffs." Landis also observed, however, that direct contacts by industry representatives "of necessity . . . are frequently productive of intelligent ideas," whereas contacts with the general public "are rare and generally unproductive of anything except complaint."[30]

The opinions and demands of the broadcast industry are expressed through consultative groups (such as joint industry-government committees), interchange of personnel, publication of views in the trade press, liaison committees of the Federal Communications Bar Association, social contacts and visits to offices of the commissioners, informal discussions at state broadcaster and trade association meetings, and the formal submission of pleadings and oral argument. The commission is largely dependent for much of its information about proposed policies on industry trade associations and broadcast licensees, especially about the impact of or potential for new technological developments.

Given such numerous opportunities to influence each other, it is hardly surprising that the pattern of industry-commission relationships is dynamic, ever changing, with shifting degrees of industry control. Since a regulatory agency must make enough alliances with effective power centers to retain its vitality, it must necessarily "come to terms" with powerful elements in its environment by knowing which elements are powerful and which participants offer the best hope for continued vitality if an alliance is formed. Former FCC Chairman John Doerfer once offered what is probably an effective justification of extensive consultation with the regulated industry: "It is naive to think that it is possible to legislate without conversations and conferences, without people who know problems of the particular industry."[31]

In the intricate and dynamic relationship between the FCC and the industry, the Washington communications lawyer plays a special role—not only in interpreting FCC policies for broadcast licensees but also in shaping the policy direction of the commission. In a study of Washington lawyers Joseph Goulden noted that while the lawyer's historic role has been to advise clients on how to comply with the law, the Washington lawyer's present role is to advise clients on how to make laws and to make the most of them. Goulden described how the Washington lawyer serves as the interface that holds together the economic partnership of business and government:

> Relations between some Washington lawyers and officials of the regulatory agencies can be so intimate they embarrass an onlooker. The lawyers and the regulators work together in a tight, impenetrable community where an outsider can't understand the language, much less why things are done the way they are. The lawyers and the regulators play together, at trade association meetings, over lunch, on the golf courses around Washington. They frequently swap jobs, the regulator moving to the private bar, the Washington Lawyer moving into the Commission on a "public service" leave of absence from his firm.[32]

The networks also play a special role in lobbying on behalf of industry positions before the FCC, the Congress, and the White House. All three television networks maintain offices in Washington, D.C., consisting of several lobbyists.[33] A 1977 decision of the U.S. Court of Appeals for the District of Columbia Circuit, in discussing the impact of what it regarded as *ex parte*, or unlawful, contacts in the FCC pay cable proceedings, singled out visits by ABC Chairman Leonard Goldenson and President Elton Rule with key members of Congress, who in turn successfully pressured the commission to put a halter on relaxation of pay cable rules. The court also cited the remarks of Everett Erlich, ABC's senior vice-president and general counsel, before the ABC Television Network affiliates on May 10, 1974:

> As most of you know, the FCC just prior to Chairman Burch's sudden departure was on the verge of modifying Pay-TV rules applicable to movies by loosening the 2 and 10-year limitations. They were also considering a so-called "wild card" exception for 12 to 18 pictures a year which would have exempted entirely the most popular features from the application of any rule. We took the leadership in opposing these proposals with the result that key members of Congress made it known in no uncertain terms that they did not expect the Commission to act on such a far-reaching policy matter without guidance. The Commission got the message and has postponed for several months reconsideration of this particular issue.[34]

Former Commissioner Nicholas Johnson characterized as the "subgovernment phenomenon" the domination of an agency's policy making by a coalescence of lobbyists, specialty lawyers, trade associations, trade press, congressional subcommittee staff members, and commission personnel who cluster around each of the regulated industries—and the bar of the Broadcasters Club. This subgovernment, Johnson maintained, grows around any specialized private interest–government relationship that exists over a long period of time, is self-perpetuating, and endures unaffected by tides of public opinion and efforts for reform. Johnson described the broadcasting industry subgovernment as including

> the networks and multiple station owners, the Federal Communications Bar Association, *Broadcasting* magazine, the National Association of Broadcasters, the communication law firms, and the industry-hired public relations and management consultant firms. It also includes the permanent government staff—regulatory, executive and congressional—which is concerned with day-to-day activities of the broadcasting industry. People in this subgovernment typically spend their lives moving from one organization to another within it. Those who pursue the course of protecting the public interest are rarely admitted.[35]

The NAB and Other Broadcasting Lobbies. The leading voice—or trumpet, depending on the occasion—for the broadcasting industry is the National Association of Broadcasters, a trade organization with more than 4,900 member radio and television stations, a $5 million annual budget and a staff of over 100 based in a $2.6 million building situated only a few blocks from the FCC. Over the several decades of its existence the NAB has been remarkably effective in thwarting any efforts to place onerous regulatory burdens on broadcasters. One conspicuous instance was the NAB's success in persuading the House of Representatives to block the FCC's proposed adoption of rules on commercial advertising. (This case study is discussed in chapter seven.) The lobbying prowess of the broadcasting industry—especially during the years before 1947—has been described by Murray Edelman as follows:

> At a public hearing it is the "regulated" who appear and offer argument—regularly, forcefully, and with a show of massed strength. The industrial giants in this field have, moreover, shown marked ability and determination to organize pressure on Capitol Hill, on the Commission, in the press, and over the radio whenever it has appeared to them that a proposed or promulgated Commission policy would affect their interests adversely. Groups that represent listeners are rare, and those that do arise have become impotent with impressive regularity.[36]

In recent years, however, the NAB has encountered increasing difficulty in its efforts to fend off congressional and FCC regulation of the broadcasting industry. The climate in which broadcast regulation takes place has changed markedly in the past decade.[37] Three trends have been primarily responsible for this change, and all have made the NAB's job more difficult.

First, the organizations represented by the NAB have grown in number and diversity, ranging from the smallest "mom and pop" AM radio stations to the largest television networks and conglomerate owners of multiple communications media. Because the NAB's membership is so diverse, smaller, more specialized trade organizations have sprung up over the years to protect the interests of television stations (Association of Maximum Service Telecasters), television translator stations (National Translator Association), UHF television stations (Council for UHF Broadcasting), clear channel AM radio stations (Clear Channel Broadcasting Service), daytime AM stations (Daytime Broadcasters Association), stations owned by blacks (National Association of Black-Owned Stations), religious stations (National Religious Broadcasters), and AM and FM stations (National Radio Broadcasters Association). Moreover, a separate and perhaps more potent lobbying group is made up of the three national networks whose Washington representatives work in a loose kind of alliance. Thus the broadcasting lobby is not truly monolithic but is comprised of multiple associations supporting many different specific interests. These associations have tended to weaken the NAB's lobbying power, since it cannot present a united front on many regulatory policy questions. Nevertheless, it is still a force to be reckoned with. An example of the formidable strength of the broadcasting lobby, when acting as a unified force, is the defeat in June 1977 of a legislative proposal by Senator Ernest Hollings to apply the Fairness Doctrine (a requirement that broadcasters air contrasting viewpoints on controversial issues of public importance) to the broadcast advertising of products containing saccharin. Hollings, who is chairman of the Senate Communications Subcommittee, ascribed the defeat of his proposal by the Senate Commerce Committee to the power of broadcasters over their elected representatives, who will "vote anything that the local broadcasters want." Hollings said that "rather than a chairman of a subcommittee, I felt like a foreman of a fixed grand jury."[38]

Second, the broadcasting lobby must also contend with the potent lobbying efforts of other industries regulated by the FCC.

The American Telephone & Telegraph Company (AT&T), for example, traditionally has had a significant impact on the selection of FCC commissioners. Three of President Dwight D. Eisenhower's first four appointments to the FCC were state public utility commissioners, and those appointments have been traced to the efforts of officers of AT&T.[39] During the 1970s the cable industry, represented by the National Cable Television Association and the Community Antenna Television Association, opposed broadcasters on the cable regulatory issues before the FCC, the courts, and Congress. A powerful adversary of broadcasters on frequency allocation issues is the land mobile industry (whose interests are represented by the manufacturers of two-way radios and various trade associations).

Third, the broadcasting industry no longer enjoys the same position that it did in the early decades of broadcast regulation. Then the regulatory process was dominated by (and largely restricted to) three major participants—Congress, the FCC, and the industry itself. These were the three focal points of a closely knit triangle of pressure, cooperation, and shifting alliances. The lines of influence and power were clear, and the industry knew how to work for what it wanted, as Murray Edelman pointed out. But this balance of forces which prevailed for so long has been altered in the past decade by the increased involvement of three participants in broadcast regulatory policy making: the public, in the form of citizens groups; the White House, by means of special advisory bodies and governmental bureaus; and the courts, in the form of judicial opinions prescribing and precluding FCC policy initiatives. Together, the development of these three activist participants in broadcast regulation has modified the commission's role from one of making peace with Congress and a dominant industry to one of attempting to placate several often antagonistic interests.

Citizens Groups

Former Commissioner Nicholas Johnson has denied the charge that the commission responds only to pressure from the broadcasting industry: "It responds to pressure from anybody."[40] However, until 1966, only those with a demonstrable economic stake in the outcome of a case were permitted to intervene in radio and television licensing proceedings.[41] In a landmark decision adopted in March 1966 the U.S. Court of Appeals for the District of Columbia Circuit forced the FCC to allow the Office of Communication of the United

Church of Christ to challenge the license renewal of WLBT-TV, Jackson, Mississippi, on the ground that the station discriminated against its Negro viewers who constituted 45 percent of the city of Jackson. The court held that responsible community organizations such as "civic associations, professional societies, unions, churches, and educational institutions or associations" have the right to contest license renewal applications. In a unanimous opinion written by Judge Warren Burger (now the chief justice of the United States), the court of appeals ruled that providing legal standing to those with such an obvious and acute concern with licensing proceedings as the listening audience is essential in order "that the holders of broadcasting licenses be responsive to the needs of the audience without which the broadcaster could not now exist."[42]

The challenge by the United Church of Christ appeared to be unsuccessful when the FCC concluded its hearings by granting the license renewal to the owners of WLBT. But the court of appeals again encouraged citizen participation in 1969 by overruling the commission's decision and ordering that the FCC consider new applications for the WLBT license.[43] Because of the court's action the FCC assigned an interim license for this station to a new licensee, pending the outcome of the application hearings.

The long-term significance of the WLBT case was well summarized by *Broadcasting* magazine:

> The case did more than establish the right of the public to participate in a station's license-renewal hearing. It did even more than encourage minority groups around the country to assert themselves in broadcast matters at a time when unrest was growing and blacks were becoming more activist. It provided practical lessons in how pressure could be brought, in how the broadcast establishment could be challenged.[44]

The WLBT case proved not to be a one-time aberration. On January 8, 1975, the FCC refused to renew the licenses of eight stations of the Alabama Educational Television Commission (AETC) and stalled the issuance of a construction permit for a ninth station.[45] This marked the first time the FCC had stripped an educational broadcaster of its license. The action came as a result of petitions filed by a citizens group charging racial discrimination in programing and employment practices at the stations. The commission, after examining the hearing record, found that blacks rarely appeared on AETC programs, that no black instructors were hired in connection with locally produced in-school lessons, and that almost all black-oriented network programing had been preempted from the stations. The commission, however, decided against disqualifying AETC as a licensee, and the state of Alabama has been allowed to operate the stations pending action on new applications which it has filed.

The United Church of Christ, spurred by the WLBT decision and supported by grants by various foundations, has helped hundreds of groups throughout the United States in monitoring programing and assessing the employment practices of broadcast stations, negotiating grievances with local broadcasters, and preparing petitions to deny renewal applications. To encourage broader citizen participation, the United Church of Christ, through its Office of Communication, has conducted regional workshops and published pamphlets to instruct leaders of community groups on their legal rights in FCC proceedings. Following the lead of the United Church of Christ, other citizens groups have focused their efforts on representing the public before the FCC, Congress, and the courts and, in the process, have attracted foundation money and talented young staffs. *Citizen's Media Directory*, a publication issued in April 1977 by the National Citizens Committee for Broadcasting, listed about sixty national media reform groups. Among the most active groups are the following:

Accuracy in Media, Washington, D.C.—AIM strives to correct what it perceives to be serious errors or omissions of fact in national news coverage by both print and electronic media. If news media sources do not correct those errors, AIM publicizes its position through letters to the editor, paid advertisements, or Fairness Doctrine complaints with the FCC. Membership is by contribution.

Action for Children's Television, Newtonville, Mass.—ACT's efforts are directed toward the improvement of children's television programing by a reduction of commercial content during those programs and the elimination of the advertising of potentially dangerous products to children. ACT's message is heard in several arenas including the FCC, the Federal Trade Commission, Congress, the networks, local stations, and advertising agencies. It maintains a reference library, distributes a wide range of print and audio-visual materials, and sponsors an annual symposium on children and television. ACT sponsors research into children's television and has developed a number of study kits designed to help parents and children learn about television. There are local ACT chapters throughout the country and local contacts are available in 100 cities for information on children's television.

Citizens Communications Center, Washington, D.C.—Citizens is a non-profit public interest law firm specializing in communications issues. It brings cases before the FCC and the courts. It assists groups in litigation and negotiations with broadcasters and cable operators. On behalf of its clients, Citizens files comments in FCC proceedings and provides advice on legal matters. Its services are limited to citizen groups that have no direct economic interest in the outcome of the litigation and that cannot otherwise obtain expert legal counsel.

Media Access Project, Washington, D.C.—MAP is a nonprofit public interest law firm specializing in public access, Fairness Doctrine, and other First Amendment issues in communications. MAP represents diverse local and national organizations and individuals before the courts, the FCC, and the Federal Trade Commission. MAP charges no attorney's fees and is reimbursed by its clients for a fraction of expenses incurred.

National Association for Better Broadcasting, Los Angeles, Calif.—NABB was the first national consumer group solely concerned with promoting the public interest in broadcasting. Its major goal is the development of public awareness of its rights and responsibilities in broadcasting. NABB works to reduce violence on television by conducting surveys and monitoring studies and by participating in hearings before Congress and the FCC. In addition to its other printed materials, it produces and distributes an annual evaluation of network and syndicated programs according to their levels of violence.

National Black Media Coalition, Washington, D.C.—NBMC is a coalition of over seventy black media reform groups throughout the country. It was formed to represent local minority needs in programing and employment at the national level. It seeks the means for black people to have access to all facets of the communications industry and encourage unbiased reportage of issues of concern to blacks. NBMC has conducted a number of research studies examining black concerns in media as well as training projects designed to educate local members as to methods for change. It has met with FCC commissioners and network representatives and filed numerous petitions with the FCC.

National Citizens Committee for Broadcasting, Washington, D.C.—NCCB's goal is to make media diverse and responsive to the public interest rather than to governmental, advertiser, or corporate dominance. NCCB facilitates public participation in policy-making and programing decisions by conducting research and analysis, and by aiding communication between citizen groups and media activists around the country through its publications and projects. NCCB publishes *access* magazine, which covers public policy issues and focuses on media reform activities throughout the country. NCCB's projects include a survey of television violence and advertiser support of that violence, a ranking of television station performance in individual states, and a proposal for requiring television stations to air one hour of prime-time public affairs programing weekly. NCCB participates in litigation and FCC rule makings and proceedings. Membership is by donation.

National Citizens Communications Lobby, Washington, D.C.—NCCL is a service organization that acts as a liaison between citizen groups and Congress. It distributes informative reports on legislative issues and testifies before congressional committees on pending bills, FCC appointments, and other communications policy matters. NCCL is wholly dependent upon individual members for its financial and political support.

National Latino Media Coalition, Jamaica Plains, Mass.—NLMC helps Latinos gain access to the media and to have input into the decision-making processes that affect the quality, type, and amount of programing and services to Latinos. It is involved in negotiations with the Corporation for Public Broadcasting in an effort to secure more funding for Latino programing and equal employment opportunity for Latinos. Plans are underway to establish a Washington headquarters.

National Organization for Women, Washington, D.C.—NOW is a national civil rights organization composed of women and men working to bring women into full participation in the American political and economic system. NOW has approximately 800 chapters throughout the country. The Media Task Force was established to give technical assistance and advice to chapters who are promoting the employment and the positive image of women in the broadcast media and also to monitor the FCC. NOW has projects dealing with advertising, newspapers, films, and the arts and humanities. NOW participates in rule-making procedures, testifies before Congress, files petitions to deny license renewals, and participates in informal objections before the FCC. Local chapters have negotiated agreements with broadcasters in numerous cities.[46]

The foregoing listing indicates that despite the description of these groups by some commentators as guardians of the overall public interest, many of the organizations tend to espouse the cause of a single special interest (e.g., blacks, Chicanos, and children). Also, the public is now no longer limited to being represented by citizens groups specifically formed to bring about changes in FCC policies. During the mid-1970s many national organizations with major interests other than broadcasting began to become more actively involved. Both the National Parent-Teachers Association and the American Medical Association have expressed concern about the amount of violence on television, and various religious groups have been vocal on the manner in which sex is depicted on television.

In 1969, for the first time, citizens groups entered into agreements with broadcast stations concerning programing and employment practices. In that year a number of black groups in Texarkana, Texas, aided by the United Church of Christ, negotiated an agreement with KTAL-TV, a local television station, under which a petition to deny the renewal application was withdrawn in exchange for a thirteen-point statement of policy by the station covering employment of blacks, minority programing, news coverage, and programs dealing with controversial issues. The FCC endorsed the KTAL-TV negotiations and agreement as a preferred means by which a station could fulfill its obligation to provide service to meet community needs and interests. In 1970 Capital Cities Broadcasting Corporation signed an agreement with the Citizens Communications Center to commit $1 million over a three-year period to minority programing over the Philadelphia, New Haven, and Fresno television stations which Capital Cities was acquiring from Triangle Publications, Inc. In September 1971 *Broadcasting* magazine commented, "It is hard to find a community of any size without its organizations of blacks, Chicanos, Latinos, liberated women, activist mothers or other concerned types negotiating for stronger representation in broadcasting." [47]

Broadcasters continued to enter into agreements with citizens groups that challenged their renewal or transfer applications during the early 1970s. In return for withdrawal of the challenge broadcasters typically agreed to make certain changes in station programing and employment practices. An important test case involved an agreement between television station KTTV and a citizens group: In return for withdrawal of a petition to deny, KTTV had agreed not to televise forty-two cartoons judged to be "unsuitable for young children," to precede eighty-one other programs with a warning to parents that program content may be harmful to children, and to televise a series of special programs designed to encourage local performers. The FCC refused to give force to the agreement on the ground that it infringed on the licensee's responsibility to serve the public interest. [48] The commission's concern that licensees had been making promises to citizens groups which abdicated their responsibility led to its adoption in 1975 of standards for determining the validity of broadcaster-citizen settlement agreements. [49] The standards generally allow broadcasters to enter into agreements with citizens groups if the former maintain responsibility at all times for determining how best to serve the public interest.

The public attention accorded the WLBT case (mentioned earlier) also prompted individuals and groups in communities throughout the nation to protest station practices that they considered to be unfair and violative of the Fairness Doctrine. Public interest law firms, such as the Citizens Communications Center and the Stern Community Law Firm, began to bring "test" cases before the commission and the courts. The Office of Communication of the United Church of Christ, together with several other religious groups and the National Citizens Committee for Broadcasting, filed amicus briefs with the court of appeals and the Supreme Court in the Red Lion case, in which the Supreme Court in a landmark decision upheld the Fairness Doctrine, stating, "It is the right of the viewers and listeners, not the right of broadcasters, which is paramount."[50]

A rash of other cases were similarly successful. A university law professor, John F. Banzhaf, III, successfully invoked the Fairness Doctrine to obtain free time for the American Cancer Society's anticigarette spot announcements.[51] An environmentalist group, the Friends of the Earth, successfully argued that commercials promoting the sale of automobiles and leaded gasolines raise a controversial issue of public importance (namely, air pollution) and therefore require the broadcast station to provide program balance.[52] The U.S. Court of Appeals for the District of Columbia Circuit has ruled in favor of citizens groups in several important matters: It overturned an FCC decision denying that attorneys' fees were payable to a citizens group as part of a written settlement between the group and the broadcaster; it ordered the FCC to hold hearings on plans of the new owners of a radio station to change program format; it rejected the FCC's new rules permitting the retention of most local newspaper-broadcast combinations; and it ruled that the *ex parte* rules concerning "off the record" contacts extended to all rule-making proceedings.

However, citizens groups have not always been successful in the courts. In 1971 a group called the Business Executives' Move for Vietnam Peace persuaded the U.S. Court of Appeals for the District of Columbia Circuit to rule that members of the public have a First Amendment right to hear diverse viewpoints and that, accordingly, a broadcaster who accepts paid commercial advertising cannot exclude those who want to buy time to present opinion on a controversial issue.[53] Major victory turned to major defeat in 1973, however, when the Supreme Court reversed the court of appeals, basing its decision on the First Amendment rights of broadcasters.[54] This proceeding is the only major communications case involving a citizens group to be decided by the Supreme Court to date. Another significant defeat is the court of appeals' rejection of an attempt by Action for Children's Television to overrule the FCC's decision on children's programming and commercial practices on the ground that the commission's policy statement was too restrictive.[55]

Primarily because of the indirect impact and complex nature of broadcast regulatory issues, the general public has been apathetic and uninformed about them. Until the late 1960s the FCC had done little to promote greater participation by the public in its proceedings or to encourage a better understanding of the role citizens might play in broadcast regulation. In the late 1960s, however, former Commissioner Nicholas Johnson began to use his considerable persuasive powers toward this end. Through various media Johnson took directly to the public the issues on which he had been defeated by his colleagues on the commission. At the same time he acted as a gadfly in prompting other commissioners to take up the cause of greater public participation in broadcast regulation. Johnson "campaigned, through speeches, magazine articles, and a book, *How to Talk Back to Your Television Set*, to alert the citizenry to their rights to challenge a broadcast licensee at license renewal time—as it were, to 'vote' against or for his continuance as a station operator—which was, within the trade, the most unorthodox and unpopular thing an FCC commissioner had ever done."[56]

Such efforts to involve the public to a greater degree have been increasingly successful. After meeting with a group of Boston housewives from Action for Children's Television, Chairman Burch persuaded his colleagues to initiate a rule-making proceeding on proposals to require television stations to carry fourteen hours of children's programing each week and to prohibit the broadcasting of commercials on such programs. More than 100,000 letters were filed in this proceeding by concerned members of the public. The FCC refused to adopt these specific proposals but issued policies and guidelines, rather than rules, on children's programing and commercial policies.[57] The commission, reacting to pressure from Congress and the public, has also taken a number of steps to encourage greater citizen participation. It has published an informational booklet on how to file complaints and intervene in renewal and transfer proceedings. It has also adopted rules requiring broadcast stations to make certain program logs, reports, and applications available locally for public inspection and to broadcast announcements on the first and sixteenth day of each month soliciting criticism of their operations from the public. In 1976 the FCC created a Consumer Assistance Office to provide informational services to the public. The office distributes a weekly publication, *Actions Alert*, which summarizes pending rule makings and announces new commission inquiries.

As will be shown in chapters three and eight, citizens groups, in response to such encouragement to participate, have been taking an increasingly active role in congressional hearings affecting the FCC. In the early 1970s citizens groups began influencing the selection of commissioners, as shown in the appointment of the first black (Benjamin Hooks) as an FCC commissioner. Former Chairman Dean Burch has predicted that "henceforth at the FCC, there will be a woman commissioner and a black commissioner at the least."[58] In 1976 representatives of citizens groups, for the first time, testified at the House Appropriations Subcommittee's hearings on the FCC budget, urging the funding of various consumer group activities. Citizens group representatives also played a prominent role in the 1977 hearings of the House Communications Subcommittee on the proposed revision of the Communications Act.

Recently, the citizens group movement has begun to change its method of operation. Foundations (such as the Ford and Markle Foundations and the Rockefeller Family Fund) and "think tanks" (such as the Aspen Institute on Communications and Policy) are now taking an increasingly active role.[59] Also former activist outsiders are attempting to become activist insiders by operating within the political structure of broadcast regulation. In 1977 former staff members of the Citizen Communications Center, the National Citizens Committee for Broadcasting, and the Stern Community Law Firm were hired as staff members or consultants to the FCC, the Office of Telecommunications Policy, the Federal Trade Commission, and the House Communications Subcommittee. Still another significant change is that former FCC commissioners and staff members have joined forces with citizens groups: Nicholas Johnson heads the National Citizens Committee for Broadcasting; Henry Geller, previously FCC general counsel, chaired the board of the Citizens Communications Center prior to being recommended by the secretary of commerce as assistant secretary of commerce for communications and information; and Benjamin Hooks, the first black appointee and now an ex-commissioner, is executive director of the National Association for the Advancement of Colored People, for which he has created an Office of Communications.

The impact of citizens group activity was summarized tersely by Dr. Clay Whitehead, former director of the White House Office of Telecommunications Policy, who made the following comment in a speech to broadcasters:

> You've always had criticism from your audience but it never *really* mattered—you never had to *satisfy* them; you only had to *deliver* them. Then the Rev. Everett Parker read the Communications Act. You all know the outcome of the *WLBT-United Church of Christ* case. Once the public discovered its opportunity to participate in the Commission's processes, it became inevitable that the rusty tools of program content control—license renewal and the Fairness Doctrine—would be taken from the FCC's hands and used by the public and the courts to make *you* perform to *their* idea of the public interest.[60]

Dr. Whitehead aptly emphasized the combination of "the public and the courts" as the key to effecting change. We now turn to a dicsussion of the unique role played by the courts as a participant in the FCC policy-making process.

The Courts

Even though only a very small proportion of the FCC's actions are reviewed by the courts, the significance of judicial review in the commission's policy-making process cannot be measured by statistical analysis alone. Judicial review, no matter how seldom invoked, hangs as a threatening possibility over each administrative or legislative decision. Thus, potentially every action of the FCC may be reviewed by the courts. Although the courts ordinarily allow other arms of government (such as the FCC and the Congress) to make policy, the judiciary possesses a crucial veto power. Consequently, the FCC must always keep one eye on the courts to make sure that the policies it adopts can successfully run the judicial gauntlet. The continual threat of judicial review thus tends to have an impact on the policies of the FCC even when these policies are not formally adjudicated.

Much of the influence of the judiciary on broadcast regulatory policy comes through the power of statutory interpretation. The vague public interest standard embodied in the Communications Act has given the courts a significant role in overseeing the FCC. As the Supreme Court observed:

> Congress has charged the courts with the responsibility of saying whether the Commission has fairly exercised its discretion within the vaguish, penumbral bounds expressed by the standard of "public interest." It is our responsibility to say whether the Commission has been guided by proper considerations in bringing the deposit of its experience, the disciplined feel of the expert, to bear . . . in the public interest.[61]

Judge Harold Leventhal of the U.S. Court of Appeals for the District of Columbia Circuit has noted that the courts are normally more concerned with how a decision was reached than with the decision itself:

> Its supervisory function calls on the court to intervene not merely in case of procedural inadequacies, or bypassing of the mandate in the legislative charter, but more broadly if the court becomes aware, especially from a combination of danger signals, that the agency has not taken a "hard look" at the salient problems, and has not genuinely engaged in reasoned decision-making. If the agency has not shirked this fundamental task, however, the court exercises restraint even though the court would on its own account have made different findings or adopted different standards.[62]

The restraint that Leventhal speaks of did indeed characterize the policy of the courts of appeals and the Supreme Court in the past. This judicial attitude has been changing in the 1970s,[63] however, giving way to articulation of judicial doubts about the desirability of narrow review of the exercise of administrative authority. Indeed, David Bazelon, chief judge of the court of appeals in the District of Columbia, has declared: "We stand on the threshold of a new era in the history of the long and fruitful collaboration of administrative agencies and reviewing courts."[64] It is, he said, no longer enough for the courts to uphold agency action, "with a nod in the direction of the substantial evidence test and a bow to the mysteries of administrative expertise." Bazelon believes a more positive or activist judicial role is demanded by the changing character of administrative litigation. "Courts are increasingly asked to review administrative litigation that touches on fundamental personal interests in life, health and liberty [and to] protect these interests from administrative arbitrariness, it is necessary to insist on strict judicial scrutiny of administrative action."[65] A textbook example of activist judicial review of commission policy making is the March 1977 decision of the Court of Appeals for the District of Columbia Circuit setting aside the commission's pay cable programing restrictions.[66] The court conducted its own extensive review of the evidence in the record, going so far as to analyze—and criticize—the methodology of mathematical models contained in broadcaster comments as well as the meaning of the results. The court also lived up to its activist role by expanding the scope of prior judicial prohibitions against so called *ex parte*, or off-the-record, contacts between FCC decision-making personnel and parties interested in the outcome of informal rule-making proceedings.

Since the courts play an important role in the FCC policy-making process, it follows that other participants in this process will attempt to influence court action. Obviously, the various interest groups cannot approach the courts through the same methods that would be appropriate in approaching Congress: There are no campaign funds, no ballot boxes, and no lavish lunches with which to influence federal judges.[67] Generally, there are only two methods by which pressure may be exerted on the courts. The first is through the appointment of judges. Here, influence must proceed indirectly through the President and the Senate. The other and more direct means of pressuring the courts is through the regular procedure of litigation. Filing an appeal with the courts is largely a defensive maneuver, since by the time a group is forced to resort to judicial review the policy has already been made by the FCC. But whereas the FCC and the Congress are most often influenced by politically powerful and wealthy groups, the courts may be influenced almost as easily by a single individual or very small groups as by a large and powerful interest. Even in cases where the outside groups are not parties to the case, a court may allow them to participate in the role of *amici curiae* ("friends of the court"). In litigation the decisions of the court are frequently influenced by factors such as the strategic timing of a bona fide test case, the submission of a well-written brief, the rendition of persuasive oral argument, or the publication of a thoughtful law review article or book on the specific issue.

Under Section 402(b) of the Communications Act, appeals from FCC decisions in broadcast licensing matters must be filed with the United States Court of Appeals for the District of Columbia Circuit. (Appeals involving compliance with FCC rules and orders must be filed with the federal district courts under Section 402(a) of the Communications Act, whereas appeals of FCC rule changes may be filed in any of the ten circuit courts of appeals.) The Communications Act also provides that the decisions of the court of appeals shall be final, subject only to review by the Supreme Court of the United States upon issuance of a writ of certiorari. Congress established the writ of certiorari in 1925 to enable the Supreme Court to cut down the volume of its work. As a result most cases are now finally decided by the court of appeals.

The court of appeals is comprised of nine judges, appointed for life by the President with the advice and consent of the Senate. With few exceptions the decisions of the court of appeals are made by panels of three judges. Since the late 1960s, as we have seen, the Court of Appeals for the District of Columbia Circuit has played an increasingly important role as a participant in the making of broadcast regulatory policy. The court of appeals has decided a large number of cases involving broadcast regulatory issues *only* because citizens groups began raising questions that had never been subjected to the crucible of judicial review. Since the Anglo-American judicial system limits judicial review to properly presented cases and controversies involving real legal disputes, the courts are basically passive: They cannot reach out to solve problems but must wait until the problems are brought to them. Issues are now being raised before the court of appeals which previously went unnoticed by the FCC and other parties. No one, for example, thought to file a Fairness Doctrine complaint against a nationally broadcast speech by President Eisenhower, whereas a Fairness Doctrine complaint was filed with the commission and the courts virtually every time President Nixon's words were carried by the broadcast media.

Whether the FCC has reached "right" or "wrong" policy decisions is not the kind of issue that has brought the courts to their present activist role in broadcast regulation. As Steve Millard noted in a perceptive article entitled "Broadcasting's Pre-emptive Court":

> The problem has been, in case after case, that the commission simply has not grappled to the court's satisfaction with the issues raised by those who demand to be heard, whether at the commission itself or on the air. Whatever ambiguities may reside within the court's opinions, this much is clear: The court has installed the citizen—almost any citizen—as a party of primary interest in any case that may be before the FCC.[68]

The White House

Professor William Cary, a former chairman of the Securities and Exchange Commission, has pointed out what should be apparent to any serious observer but is often overlooked or ignored: that the President is a person but the White House is a collection of people.[69] The FCC, like most other government departments and agencies, does not deal with the President (except on matters of the greatest national or international importance) but with the White House staff. For example, during the Kennedy, Johnson, and Nixon administrations the FCC and other regulatory agencies sent detailed monthly summaries of their principal activities and pending projects to a key presidential aide. Different Presidents, moreover, have varied in their level of interest in the FCC. Franklin D. Roosevelt had been very interested in FCC policy decisions (especially the question of ownership of radio stations by newspapers), but his successor, Harry Truman, showed little or no concern about commission policies. Again, Presidents Kennedy and Nixon were actively interested in broadcast matters, whereas Presidents Johnson and Ford played a relatively passive role on issues of concern to broadcasters.

The Power of Appointment. The White House influences the FCC in a wide variety of ways. The most important of its formal controls is the power of the President to choose commissioners as their terms expire and to appoint a chairman. The appointment power enables the President to set the tone for the agency during his administration. Although the Communications Act specifies that only four commissioners may have the same party affiliation, the President has wide latitude in appointing those whom he thinks will reflect his own political and administrative ideas. As noted earlier virtually every President has tried to select persons as commissioners who agree with his administration's philosophy, regardless of party identification.[70]

In making appointments to the FCC, the President is subject to diverse types of pressures from Congress, the industry, the press, and the public. According to the Hoover Report the senatorial power of confirming commission appointments has often caused the President to consider not so much his appointees' abilities or qualifications for the job as the probability of their acceptance by the Senate.[71] Furthermore, since appointments to the FCC are closely watched by the regulated industries, the President rarely appoints a commissioner if the regulated industries are politically aligned against him. As Roger Noll points out, "While the appointment process does not necessarily produce commissioners who are consciously controlled by the industry they regulate, it nearly always succeeds in excluding persons who are regarded as opposed to the interests of the regulated."[72] Trade publications such as *Broadcasting, Television Digest,* and *Variety* play an important role in influencing industry opinion on various candidates and in letting broadcasters know who is opposed to their interests. A recent study of the manner in which the FCC and FTC commissioners are appointed noted that *Broadcasting* magazine probably monitors FCC vacancies with greater care than the White House: "There are very few trade journals which are more politically potent than *Broadcasting* magazine: the number of FCC aspirants who have had their ambitions either assisted or quashed as a result of this magazine's coverage defies estimation."[73] Since the early 1970s, however, minority groups have begun to influence the selection of commissioners, as shown in the appointment of two black FCC commissioners.

The Communications Act authorizes the President to designate one of the seven commissioners as chairman. Since the chairman holds that position subject to the will of the President, it is to be expected that the conduct of individuals serving as chairman might be influenced by the expectations and viewpoints which radiate from the White House. Moreover, both with respect to the chairman and other commissioners,[74] a sense of loyalty and considerations of reappointment (or appointment to other governmental posts) may have a subtle influence on the thinking and behavior of those appointed.

The White House also exercises some informal control over major personnel selections at the FCC, including such positions as general counsel, executive director, and chief of the Broadcast Bureau. Prior to making high-level staff appointments, the chairmen of the FCC have usually checked with the White House to secure a "political clearance."

The Office of Management and Budget. Another form of White House pressure is exerted through the Office of Management and Budget (formerly the Bureau of the Budget). This office, one of the President's staff agencies, reviews and revises all departmental and agency budget estimates before they are presented to the Appropriations Committees of the House and Senate. In addition,

agencies such as the FCC must submit their legislative recommendations to OMB before asking for congressional consideration; further action depends upon word from the director of
OMB that a proposal is consistent with the President's program.
OMB also has the power to authorize agencies such as the FCC to
add "supergrade" (high-salaried) staff positions. In this connection
Professor Cary points out that a regulatory agency is paralyzed
unless it is allowed to recruit able staff and fill vacancies at the top.[75]
Other Forms of Executive Influence. The White House also
exercises its authority by supporting substantive legislation.
Professor Cary believes that "despite the jealousy that Congress may
exhibit over White House participation in an agency's functioning, it
is unlikely to enact constructive legislation on behalf of a regulatory
agency unless it has some backing from the President."[76] A less
tangible form of control is the mood set by the President and the
White House for the regulatory agency. Especially at the beginning
of an administration, the White House may be able to create a more
hospitable political climate for the agency. President Kennedy's
"New Frontier" theme, for example, set a favorable mood for a
more active regulatory role by Newton Minow. Similarly, President
Gerald Ford exercised a leadership role, complementary to
Chairman Wiley's "deregulation" program of eliminating archaic
and duplicative FCC regulations, by conducting White House
"summit conferences" and submitting legislation urging regulatory
agencies to eliminate rules and paperwork requirements un-
necessarily burdensome to businesses.

For purposes of this chapter we have included the Department
of Justice in the White House since it is the President's legal arm. As
the agency generally responsible for the enforcement of federal
laws and with the specific responsibility of deciding what FCC
broadcast licensing cases should be pursued in the courts, the Justice
Department exerts a strong influence on the FCC. The Solicitor
General's Office in the Justice Department has authority to decide
which cases the federal government should ask the Supreme Court
to review and what position the government should take in cases
before the courts. At times the Justice Department has even challenged FCC decisions by appealing them to the courts. When the
Justice Department protested the commission's approval of the
proposed ABC-ITT merger, the case caption read: *United States* v.
Federal Communications Commission. The Justice Department's
appeal was one of the factors that prompted ABC and ITT to

abandon their plans for merger. In another court of appeals proceeding the Justice Department intervened on the side of community groups who eventually won the right to be voluntarily reimbursed for legal fees incurred by groups who challenged a station's renewal application.

The Justice Department's Antitrust Division has taken an activist role in FCC proceedings and was successful in breaking up common ownership of a daily newspaper, cable system, and television station in Cheyenne, Wyoming. In Beaumont, Texas, the Antitrust Division asked the FCC to deny an application to transfer the license of KFDM-TV to the publisher of the only daily newspaper in Beaumont. Faced with such opposition, the parties withdrew the application. The Antitrust Division also played a key role in FCC proceedings which resulted in a ban on crossownership of local television stations and cable systems and the prohibition on a prospective basis of local crossownership of both AM radio and television stations and daily newspapers and broadcast stations. In addition, the Justice Department has participated in FCC proceedings involving pay cable, network-affiliate relationships, the proposed "drop in" or opening up of VHF channels, and the prime-time access rule (which forbids television stations in the top fifty markets to program more than three hours of network offerings during the 7:00–11:00 P.M. period). The Antitrust Division has filed suit against the three commercial television networks charging them with the unlawful monopoly over prime-time programing.

The White House has also been able to create leverage in the past by the formation of advisory commissions. During his administration President Johnson created a Task Force on Communications Policy. The report of this task force, issued in December 1968 and released to the public in May 1969, contained a sixteen-month study of telecommunications problems which was the work of fifteen departments and agencies of the federal government and a large number of consultants. The creation of the task force had the effect of delaying for several years FCC action on the controversial subject of communications satellites. President Nixon, in 1971, created a cabinet-level Committee on Cable Television. The possibility of support for cable television served as a weapon in the Nixon administration in its feud against the networks.

The Office of Telecommunications Policy.   The most recent type of White House control, however, has been the transition from the use of ad hoc advisory commissions to the establishment of a permanent office in the Executive Branch designed to coordinate operations of the federal government's communications system and formulate the nation's telecommunications policy. In February 1970 President Nixon submitted to Congress Reorganization Plan No. 1 to create within the Executive Office of the President a new Office of Telecommunications Policy.[77] This new office was to become the President's principal adviser on domestic and international telecommunictions policy. According to the President the OTP would not acquire any prerogatives or functions of the FCC but would take over the functions of the director of Telecommunications Management in the Office of Emergency Preparedness. In March 1970 FCC Chairman Dean Burch (a Nixon appointee who left the FCC in 1974 to serve in the White House during the Watergate crisis) told the House Reorganization Subcommittee that the commission favored "a strong, centralized entity to deal with telecommunications issues within the executive."[78] When neither the Senate nor the House voted to disapprove the Reorganization Plan within sixty days after its submission to Congress, the Office of Telecommunications Policy became effective April 20, 1970.

At hearings in the House, Congressmen expressed concern that the new office might dominate the FCC. A legal assistant to Commissioner H. Rex Lee viewed the OTP as a threatening and improper political encroachment upon the independence of the commission. The FCC, he said, "is easily overwhelmed by the power, prestige and influence of the President."[79] The *Wall Street Journal*, in a front-page article on July 11, 1970, charged that OTP's tactics with respect to the FCC's decision on domestic satellites show that "the Nixon Administration is boldly trying to influence regulatory policy more than any previous Administration did."[80] Chairman Burch, however, assured members of the House Subcommittee on Executive and Legislative Reorganization that he had "absolutely no fear of either an actual or possible undue influence by the White House on the Commission by virtue of this Office."[81]

OTP, especially in its first three years, made a significant impact on broadcast regulatory policy. In the fall of 1971 OTP played a broker's role in bringing together representatives of the broadcasting, cable, and copyright industries and acted as a mediator in getting the parties to accept a compromise agreement on cable rules. OTP was successful in forging a compromise because of the. vacuum created by prior FCC indecisiveness in developing an overall cable policy and the willingness of OTP to exert pressure in private sessions on groups representing broadcasters, cable system owners, and copyright holders. In response to a proposal by OTP the FCC initiated an inquiry in 1972 looking toward the deregulation of radio, thus anticipating the lessening of regulatory controls on radio programing and commercial practices. OTP also took stands and thereby stimulated debate on a wide number of substantive issues, including standards on license renewals, the substitution of a limited right of paid access in place of the Fairness Doctrine, the role of the Corporation for Public Broadcasting in financing network programing of the Public Broadcasting Service, and spectrum allocation policy. Based on a study prepared by OTP, the FCC made extensive changes in the Emergency Broadcast System.

Throughout its life, but particularly as a result of two policies it articulated in 1972, OTP has been the focus of intense criticism by many who saw in the Nixon administration a shift of power from the Congress and toward the Presidency. In February of that year, Dr. Clay T. Whitehead, OTP's first director, told the House Subcommittee on Communications and Power that the administration opposed, at that time, any permanent financing for the Corporation for Public Broadcasting unless local public stations were given greater power to control programing. In December he suggested that television station owners be held strictly responsible at license renewal time for the content of network-originated programing, particularly news; he then linked increased affiliate pressure on the networks to reduce "ideological plugola" and "elitist gossip" with an extended five-year license term long sought by the broadcast industry. Post-Watergate research on the Nixon administration shows that Dr. Whitehead's attacks on the networks, public broadcasting, and the affiliates were elements of a deliberate assault on the centralized, national media from a White House that had viewed the media as a tormentor.[82]

In July 1977 President Carter sent to Congress a plan to reorganize the Executive Office. It would eliminate the Office of Telecommunications Policy, shift most of its policy advisory functions to the Commerce Department, lodge other duties with the Office of Management and Budget, and retain a small policy staff in the White House to advise the President.[83] The Carter reorganization plan became law on October 20, 1977, when neither the House nor the Senate voted to oppose it. The President's Domestic Policy Staff is now responsible for providing advice on telecommunications and information policy, especially on national security, emergency preparedness, and privacy issues. OMB is responsible for federal telecommunications procurement and management and for arbitrating interagency disputes regarding frequency allocations. All other OTP functions have been transferred to the Commerce Department headed by a new assistant secretary for communications and information, appointed by the President and subject to Senate confirmation.

Notes

[1] Newton Minow, *Equal Time: The Private Broadcaster and the Public Interest* (New York: Atheneum, 1964), pp. 258–259.

[2] James M. Landis, *Report on Regulatory Agencies to the President-Elect*, published as a committee print by the Subcommittee on Administrative Practice and Procedure of the Senate Committee on the Judiciary, 86th Congress, 2nd Session (1960), p. 53. Seventeen years later a major congressional study of the FCC offered an assessment of the commission very similar to that in the Landis report:

> The Commission's principal handicaps have been (1) insufficient public representation to offset the assiduous attention paid by commercial interests, (2) failure to anticipate or keep pace with technical and commercial developments in communications, (3) a deficiency of technical expertise for analysis of complex issues resulting in failure to develop facts basic to regulation of the broadcasting and telephone industries, and (4) inertial acceptance of prevailing patterns.

Federal Regulation and Regulatory Reform, Report by the Subcommittee on Oversight and Investigations of the House Interstate and Foreign Commerce Committee, 94th Congress, 2nd Session (October 1976), p. 246.

[3] Samuel P. Huntington, "The Marasmus of the I.C.C.: The Commissions, the Railroads, and the Public Interest," *Yale Law Journal*, 61 (April 1962), 470. The demise of the OTP discussed on pages 60–61 is an apt illustration of the disease Huntington characterizes as "administrative marasmus."

[4] See Anthony Downs, *Inside Bureaucracy* (Boston: Little, Brown, 1967). The work, especially the chapters on "Internal Characteristics Common to All Bureaus," "Officials' Milieu, Motives, and Goals," and "Bureaucratic Ideologies," is an excellent starting piece for any assessment of bureaucratic behavior.

[5] The analysis which follows is based primarily on articles by Lee Loevinger entitled "The Sociology of Bureaucracy," *The Business Lawyer*, 24 (November 1968), 7–18, and "The Administrative Agency as a Paradigm of Government—A Survey of the Administrative Process," *Indiana Law Journal*, 40 (Spring 1965), 1.

[6]Lee Loevinger, Review of William L. Cary, *Politics and the Regulatory Agencies*, in *Columbia Law Review*, 68 (1968), 382.

[7]"Lack of Direction Is Handcuffing the FCC," *Television/Radio Age*, April 3, 1972, p. 61. See also Richard Berner, *Constraints on the Regulatory Process: A Case Study of Regulation of Cable Television* (Cambridge, Mass.: Harvard Program on Information Technology and Public Policy, 1975), pp. 75–76.

[8]Bradley C. Canon, "Voting Behavior on the FCC," *Midwest Journal of Political Science*, 13 (November 1969), 593–594. Until the early 1970s the FCC usually met only once each week. Former Chairman Dean Burch increased the number to three times, and during the administration of Chairman Richard E. Wiley the commission meetings were held four and sometimes five times each week. In 1977 the FCC opened most of its meetings to the public as a result of the Government in Sunshine Law (Public Law No. 94-9409). (Exceptions to the open meeting requirement include discussions of agency personnel practices and financial information obtained under a pledge of confidentiality.) For a detailed description of an FCC agenda meeting, see Nicholas Johnson and John Dystel, "A Day in the Life: The Federal Communications Commission," *Yale Law Journal*, 82 (1973), 1575–1634.

[9]James M. Graham and Victor H. Kramer, *Appointments to the Regulatory Agencies, the Federal Communications Commission and the Federal Trade Commission (1949–1974)*, printed for the use of the Committee on Commerce, U.S. Senate, 94th Congress, 2nd Session (April 1976), pp. 385–386.

[10]Lawrence Lichty, "Members of the Federal Radio Commission and Federal Communications Commission: 1927–1961," *Journal of Broadcasting*, 6 (Winter 1961–1962), 23–34.

[11]Wenmouth Williams, Jr., "Impact of Commissioner Background on FCC Decisions: 1962–1975," *Journal of Broadcasting*, 20 (Spring 1976), 239, 244.

[12]Ibid., p. 256. Williams's claims that there was a Minow Commission is perhaps overstated. Newton Minow rarely could command a majority of his fellow commissioners and was a frequent dissenter in the commission he chaired. Whatever regulatory philosophy Minow inspired did not really appear until the term of E. William Henry as chairman.

[13]Lawrence W. Lichty, "The Impact of FRC and FCC Commissioners' Backgrounds on the Regulation of Broadcasting," *Journal of Broadcasting*, 6 (Spring 1962), 97, 109.

[14]Ibid., 108.

[15]Canon, "Voting Behavior on the FCC," 609–611.

[16]Lichty, "The Impact of FRC and FCC Commissioners' Backgrounds on the Regulation of Broadcasting," 108–109. However, Roger Noll contends: "Policies of multiheaded bodies such as regulatory commissions tend to be at the median position within the group. The middle-of-the-road individual can always lead a majority against any proposal that he opposes." Roger G. Noll, *Reforming Regulation* (Washington, D.C.: Brookings Institution, 1971), p. 43.

[17]In 1961 President Kennedy submitted Reorganization Plan No. 2,

which would have allowed the chairman of the FCC a greater degree of power to delegate commission responsibility to individual commissioners, commission panels, and staff members. The House of Representatives defeated the FCC reorganization plan by a resounding vote of 323 to 77. The unpopularity of the President's proposal was a direct result of Newton Minow's "vast wasteland" speech, which was delivered five weeks before the House vote. See "Did Minow Scuttle FCC Reorganization?" *Broadcasting*, May 22, 1961, pp. 56–57.

[18] Kenneth A. Cox, "What It's Like Inside the FCC," *Telephony*, September 5, 1970, pp. 56, 57.

[19] Graham and Kramer, *Appointments to the Regulatory Agencies*, p. 382. For example, Newton Minow, while serving as chairman of the FCC, played an important role in blocking the reappointment of John Cross as an FCC commissioner and in selecting Kenneth Cox as Cross's successor. Graham and Kramer, pp. 185–195.

[20] See Scott H. Robb, "Wiley's Impact on FCC Staff Will Still Be Felt as Power Shifts to Carter Administration," *Television/Radio Age*, March 28, 1977, p. 93.

[21] Les Brown, "Broadcasting Industry Is Wary over Carter's Choice as Chairman of the F.C.C., Succeeding Wiley," *New York Times*, December 7, 1976, p. 82C.

[22] During fiscal year 1975 Wiley's vote was with the majority 98.9 percent of the time. The commissioner with the most dissents, Benjamin Hooks, voted with the majority 96.3 percent of the time. See "In Search of Dissent at the FCC: The Commission that Sails Together Fails Together," *access 16* (August 11, 1975), 7.

[23] Brown, "Broadcasting Industry Is Wary over Carter's Choice."

[24] *Broadcasting*, April 11, 1977, p. 27. In an editorial entitled "Who's in Charge Here?," *Broadcasting* magazine said that "the FCC has suffered one humiliating defeat after another in the U.S. Court of Appeals for the District of Columbia Circuit." *Broadcasting*, April 4, 1977, p. 106.

[25] "How the FCC Takes Control," *Broadcasting*, February 21, 1966, p. 31, and "Heavy Hands on Government Controls," *Broadcasting*, February 21, 1966, p. 50.

[26] Minow, *Equal Time*, pp. ix–x.

[27] "Minow Observes a 'Vast Wasteland,'" *Broadcasting*, May 15, 1960, pp. 58, 59.

[28] Marver H. Bernstein, *Regulating Business by Independent Commission* (Princeton, N.J.: Princeton University Press, 1955), p. 279.

[29] Noll, *Reforming Regulation*, pp. 37–38.

[30] Landis, *Report on Regulatory Agencies*, p. 71.

[31] Quoted in Victor G. Rosenblum, "How to Get into TV: The Federal Communications Commission and Miami Channel 10," *The Uses of Power: 7 Cases in American Politics*, Alan F. Westin, ed. (New York: Harcourt Brace Jovanovich, 1962), p. 196. There are legal restrictions on the manner in which interested parties may make known their views to the FCC. These restrictions are known as the *ex parte* rules.

[32] Joseph C. Goulden, *The Superlawyers: The Small and Powerful World of the Great Washington Law Firms* (New York: Weybright and

Talley, 1972), p. 6. President Carter has taken steps designed to curb what is known as the "revolving door" phenomenon by requiring all policy-making officials (top staff aides as well as commissioners) to agree to a two-year ban on paid representation of any party before any officer or employee of the agency for which the individual has worked. Also, to guard against a rapid turnover of personnel (a problem which over the years has plagued the commission), every prospective appointee is now required to state his intention to serve for the entire term for which he is named or, if the term is indefinite, to remain in government as long as the President wishes. See "Carter Shuts Revolving Doors," *Broadcasting*, January 10, 1977, pp. 26–27.

[33] For a description of the manner in which the network lobbyists function, see "Moving Muscle to Washington," *Broadcasting*, February 21, 1972, pp. 38–42.

[34] *Home Box Office, Inc.*, v. *F.C.C.*, No. 75–1280 et al. (C.A.D.C., March 25, 1977), pp. 86–87, fn. 112; certiorari denied, 46 U.S.L.W. 3216 (U.S., October 3, 1977).

[35] Nicholas Johnson, "A New Fidelity to the Regulatory Ideal," *Georgetown Law Journal*, 59 (March 1971), 883, 884.

[36] Murray Edelman, *The Licensing of Radio Services in the United States, 1927 to 1947: A Study in Administrative Formulation of Policy* (Urbana: University of Illinois Press, 1950), pp. 220–221.

[37] Bruce Thorp, "Washington Pressures—Radio-TV Lobby Fights Losing Battle Against Rising Federal Control," *National Journal*, August 22, 1970, p. 1807.

[38] "Whistling Dixie," *Broadcasting*, August 15, 1977, p. 66.

[39] Graham and Kramer, *Appointments to the Regulatory Agencies*, p. 373. Graham and Kramer state that from April 1953 until March 1960 the chairmen of the FCC were men who were fully acceptable to AT&T.

[40] Nicholas Johnson, *How to Talk Back to Your Television Set* (New York: Bantam, 1970), p. 163.

[41] A 1977 report of the Senate Committee on Governmental Affairs agreed with Johnson's statement when it commented that regulatory agencies, rather than being "captured" by industry interests, simply are responding to the input they receive; the committee recognized, however, that until the recent past, the regulated industries were the source of almost all input to the agencies. *Study on Federal Regulation, Public Participation in Agency Proceedings*, vol. 3, Committee on Governmental Affairs, 95th Congress, 1st Session (July 1977), p. 2.

[42] *Office of Communication of the United Church of Christ* v. *F.C.C.*, 359 F. 2d 994, 1002 (C.A.D.C., 1966).

[43] *Office of Communication of the United Church of Christ* v. *F.C.C.*, 425 F. 2d 543 (C.A.D.C., 1969).

[44] "The Pool of Experts on Access," *Broadcasting*, September 20, 1971, p. 36.

[45] *Alabama Educational Television Commission*, 50 F.C.C. 2d 461 (1975).

[46] Pamela Draves (ed.), *Citizens Media Directory* (Washington, D.C.: National Citizens Committee for Broadcasting, 1977). See also Donald L. Guimary, *Citizen's Groups and Broadcasting* (New York: Praeger, 1975),

which traces the development and impact of citizen groups and contains case studies on Action for Children's Television, the Greater Cleveland Radio-Television Council, and the Citizens Communications Center.

[47] Leonard Zeidenberg, "The Struggle over Broadcast Access II," *Broadcasting*, September 27, 1971, p. 24.

[48] *Citizens Communications Center*, 55 F.C.C. 2d 800 (1975); rehearing denied, 58 F.C.C. 2d 966 (1976).

[49] *Broadcaster-Citizen Agreements*, 57 F.C.C. 2d 42 (1975).

[50] *Red Lion Broadcasting Co.* v. *F.C.C.*, 395 U.S. 372, 390 (1969).

[51] *Banzhaf* v. *F.C.C.*, 405 F. 2d 1082 (C.A.D.C., 1968).

[52] *Friends of the Earth* v. *F.C.C.*, 449 F. 2d 1164 (C.A.D.C., 1971). The commission, however, in essence overturned the Banzhaf cigarette doctrine and the Friends of the Earth holding in its 1974 *Fairness Doctrine Report*:

> We do not believe that the underlying purposes of the Fairness Doctrine would be well served by permitting the cigarette case to stand as a Fairness Doctrine precedent. . . . We do not believe that the usual product commercial can realistically be said to inform the public on any side of a controversial issue of public importance. . . . Accordingly, in the future, we will apply the Fairness Doctrine only to those commercials which are devoted in an obvious and meaningful way to the discussion of public issues.

The Handling of Public Issues Under the Fairness Doctrine and the Public Interest Standards of the Communications Act, 48 F.C.C. 2d 1, 26 (1974). The commission's *Fairness Doctrine Report* was appealed to the U.S. Court of Appeals for the District of Columbia Circuit by the Friends of the Earth and the National Citizens Committee for Broadcasting. The court affirmed the commission's decision not to apply the fairness doctrine to standard product commercials and advertisements making product efficacy claims about which there is a dispute.

[53] *Business Executives' Move for Vietnam Peace* v. *F.C.C.*, 450 F. 2d 642 (C.A.D.C., 1971).

[54] *CBS* v. *Democratic National Committee*, 412 U.S. 94 (1973).

[55] *Action for Children's Television* v. *F.C.C.*, No. 74-2006 (C.A.D.C., July 1, 1977).

[56] Les Brown, *Television: The Business Behind the Box* (New York: Harcourt Brace Jovanovich, 1971), pp. 256, 257.

[57] *Children's Television Report and Policy Statement*, 50 F.C.C. 2d 1 (1974). This FCC policy statement provides general guidelines urging television stations to reduce the level of commercialization on programs designed for children and to devote a reasonable amount of time to children's programs, a significant portion of which should be educational or informative in nature. As noted earlier, the U.S. Court of Appeals for the District of Columbia Circuit affirmed the commission's decision.

[58] *Study on Federal Regulations, The Regulatory Appointments Process*, vol. 1, Senate Committee on Government Affairs, 95th Congress, 1st Session (January 1977), p. 254.

[59] Albert H. Kramer, "The Elephant that Squeaked, Foundations and Media Change," *access* 35 (May 31, 1976), 6-9.

[60]Speech by Clay T. Whitehead before the International Radio and Television Society, October 6, 1971.

[61]*F.C.C.* v. *RCA Communications, Inc.*, 346 U.S. 86, 91 (1953).

[62]*Greater Boston Television Corp.* v. *F.C.C.*, 444 F. 2d 841, 851 (C.A.D.C., 1971); certiorari denied, 403 U.S. 923 (1971).

[63]Bernard Schwartz, "Administrative Law: The Third Century," *Administrative Law Review*, 29 (Summer 1977), 3. Perhaps an explanation for such judicial restraint can be found in the views of Chief Justice William Howard Taft, who served on the Supreme Court during broadcasting's early years. When asked to explain his reluctance to review cases involving radio law, Taft is reported to have said, ". . . interpreting the law on this subject is something like trying to interpret the law of the occult. It seems like dealing with something supernatural. I want to put it off as long as possible in the hope that it becomes more understandable before the court passes on the questions involved." Cited in Ronald Coase, "The Federal Communications Commission," *Journal of Law & Economics*, 2 (1959), 40.

[64]*Environmental Defense Fund* v. *Ruckelshaus*, 439 F. 2d 584, 597 (C.A.D.C., 1971).

[65]Ibid., p. 598.

[66]*Home Box Office, Inc.* v. *F.C.C.*, No. 75-1280 et al. (C.A.D.C., March 25, 1977); certiorari denied, 46 U.S.L.W. 3216 (U.S., October 3, 1977).

[67]The following discussion is based on Loren P. Beth, *Politics, The Constitution and the Supreme Court* (New York: Harper & Row, 1962), chap. four.

[68]*Broadcasting*, August 30, 1971, p. 23.

[69]William Cary, *Politics and the Regulatory Agencies* (New York: McGraw-Hill, 1967), pp. 6-7.

[70]The fact that the FCC has seven commissioners, unlike most other regulatory agencies which have five, serves to diffuse power on the commission and to limit the influence of any President in gaining early "control" of the agency. The ability of the President to influence FCC decisions on broadcast issues is also limited by the sensitive nature of the commission's regulatory mission, touching as it does on First Amendment matters.

[71]See Graham and Kramer, *Appointments to the Regulatory Agencies*.

[72]Noll, *Reforming Regulation*, p. 43.

[73]Graham and Kramer, *Appointments to the Regulatory Agencies*, pp. 200 and 378. For insight into the role played by the trade press in FCC broadcast matters, see Barry G. Cole and Mal Oettinger (once a reporter for *Broadcasting* magazine), *The Reluctant Regulators, the FCC and the Broadcast Audience* (Reading, Mass.: Addison-Wesley, 1978).

[74]Although the Communications Act does not deal with the issue of removal of commissioners for "cause," the President may remove a commissioner only upon a showing of extreme inefficiency, neglect of duty, or malfeasance in office. See *Humphrey's Executor* v. *United States*, 295 U.S. 602 (1935); and *Wiener* v. *United States*, 357 U.S. 249 (1958). Although it has never been done, Congress has the power to remove a regulatory commissioner through the formal process of impeachment. During the Eisenhower administration Richard Mack in 1958 and John Doerfer in 1960 resigned from the FCC at the request of the Eisenhower White House. Neither

resisted the request, obviating the need for further action. See Graham and Kramer, *Appointments to the Regulatory Agencies*, p. 41.

[75] Cary, *Politics and the Regulatory Agencies*, p. 12.

[76] Ibid.

[77] Reorganization Plan No. 1, H.R. Doc. No. 71-222, 91st Congress, 2nd Session (1970).

[78] Hearings before the Subcommittee on Executive and Legislative Reorganization of the House Government Operations Committee, *Reorganization Plan No. 1 of 1970*, 91st Congress, 2nd Session, p. 50.

[79] Edwin B. Spievack, "Presidential Assault on Communications," *Federal Communications Bar Journal*, 23 (1969), 157.

[80] *Wall Street Journal*, July 11, 1970, p. 1.

[81] Bruce Thorp, "Agency Report: Office of Telecommunications Policy Speaks for the President and Hears Some Static," *National Journal*, February 13, 1970, p. 343.

[82] See William E. Porter, *Assault on the Media: The Nixon Years* (Ann Arbor: The University of Michigan Press, 1976), which contains the text of Whitehead's infamous Sigma Delta Chi speech, Vice President Spiro Agnew's Des Moines and Montgomery speeches attacking the media, and White House memoranda between H. R. Haldeman, Jeb Stuart Magruder, Lawrence Higby, and Charles Colson.

[83] "Answers Begin to Emerge on How OTP's Functions Are to Be Absorbed," *Broadcasting*, August 1, 1977, p. 28.

3

Congress: Powerful Determiner of Regulatory Policy

The United States Congress is noteworthy for the enthusiasm with which it has historically embraced the job of directing and overseeing broadcast regulatory policy. There has been a tradition of almost daily congressional oversight of, or intervention in, activities involving the FCC. "When I was Chairman," Newton Minow has written, "I heard from Congress about as frequently as television commercials flash across the screen."[1] Despite the enthusiasm of some members of Congress in making their views known to the FCC, Congress has been subject to recurring criticism for "its failure to provide guides and standards for the Commission to follow, and for its frequent and often premature interference in the Commission's rare attempts to formulate policy on its own."[2] In this chapter we will pose three questions about Congress as a determiner of regulatory policies: Who do we mean when we speak of Congress? What form does this congressional involvement take? What impact does the Congress have on the FCC's formulation and implementation of broadcast policy?

Congress and the FCC

When we refer to Congress's role in the regulation of broadcasting we are not talking only about Congress as a whole, for power is distributed quite unevenly in Congress, especially in a specialized area such as broadcast regulation. The vital groups in Congress relevant to broadcast regulatory policy are the House and Senate Commerce Committees, their respective Communications Subcommittees, and, specifically, in many cases, their chairmen. A "highly placed" FCC staff member has said privately that the word of Senator Warren Magnuson, chairman of the Senate Commerce

Committee, is practically law to the FCC. "They bow and scrape for him. He doesn't have to ask for anything. The commission does what it thinks he wants it to do." The same was true of Oren Harris, former chairman of the House Interstate and Foreign Commerce Committee. "He cracked the whip lots of times down here." [3] Other committees, especially the Appropriations Committees, take occasional interest in broadcasting and regulatory issues, but the two Commerce Committees undoubtedly are the center of congressional interest and activity in the field of broadcasting.

Sometimes the Senate Commerce Committee takes particular interest in a policy (as it did in the FCC's license renewal procedures in 1970); at other times, congressional activity comes mainly from the House Commerce Committee (such as the bill to block the FCC's consideration of commercial time limits). [4] In addition, individual congressmen or committee chairmen may be principal actors involved in a particular policy. Congressional interest may actually be limited to only a few congressmen who gain their impact in the FCC policy-making process because of their seniority or their influential standing in a committee. As a result, in William Boyer's words, "an administrator must . . . sensitize his decision-making to the wishes and predilections of committee chairmen primarily and legislators generally." [5]

A main reason why Congress has involved itself so closely in broadcast regulatory policy is that it feels it has special obligations in this area. The FCC was established both as an independent regulatory commission and as "an arm of the Congress." Consequently, many legislators consider review of this agency's performance an integral part of Congress's mission. To Congress the independence of regulatory commissions such as the FCC means independence from White House domination, not independence from its congressional parent.

The power of the Congress over the commission is both pervasive and multifaceted. Since the FCC has neither the political protection of the President or a cabinet official, nor an effective means of appealing for popular support, congressmen have little fear of political reprisal when dealing with the commission or any of the other independent agencies. [6] Newton Minow tells a trenchant story about the day, shortly after his appointment to the commission, when he called upon House Speaker Sam Rayburn. "Mr. Sam" put his arm around the new FCC chairman and said, "Just remember one thing, son. Your agency is an arm of the Congress; you belong to us. Remember that and you'll be all right."[7] The Speaker went on to warn him to expect a lot of trouble and pressure, but, as Minow recalls, "what he did not tell me was that most of the pressure would come from the Congress itself."[8]

This pervasive atmosphere of congressional concern with commission activities makes the FCC extremely wary about possible reactions from Congress—a phenomenon which political scientists call the process of "anticipated reactions," "feedback," or "strategic sensitivity." In this connection Boyer has commented:

> What matters here is not that an administrator is forced by a vote or an overt instruction of any legislative committee to initiate a particular policy, for seldom does this happen. More important is an administrator's assessment of the given ecology within which he must make his policy decisions. For efficacious policy initiation, he must attempt to perceive and anticipate the behavior of legislative committees and the environment reflected by them.[9]

Congress and the Broadcasting Industry

Congressional involvement in regulatory policy and its close supervision of the FCC may also be traced to the fact that many congressmen are sympathetic to the broadcasting industry. Thus they may transmit their ideas and views to the FCC and mediate between the commission and the industry. This community of views is sometimes attributed in part to the financial interests of congressmen in broadcasting. However, direct or family-related investments of congressmen in broadcasting are not as extensive as often thought. In the 94th Congress, nine senators and twelve representatives had either a direct or a family-related interest in broadcast stations; in the 95th Congress, only six senators and ten representatives had broadcast interests.[10] Congressional support for industry is more accurately viewed, in part, as attempts by legislators to satisfy the demands of important, prestigious, and useful constituents. That the industry regards these efforts as important has been indicated by Paul B. Comstock, former vice president and general counsel of the National Association of Broadcasters, who remarked: "Most of our work is done with congressional committees. We concentrate on Congress. We firmly believe that the FCC will do whatever Congress tells it to do, and will not do anything Congress tells it not to do."[11]

This relationship between the broadcasting industry and Congress has been pithily described as a two-way umbilical cord.[12] Broadcasters control the very lifeline of most politicians—media exposure. An estimated 70 percent of United States senators and 60 percent of representatives regularly use free time offered by broadcast stations back home.[13] Such free time assists politicians in their efforts to get reelected, and broadcasters benefit from carrying "public affairs" programing when they apply to the FCC for license renewal. Robert MacNeil's analogy describing the "tense mutual interdependence" of the Congress and the broadcasting industry is apt:

> Imagine the situation of a street peddler who sells old-fashioned patent medicines. He needs a license to stay in business, and the city official who issues them is dubious about most of the peddler's wares. Yet it just happens that one product, a magic elixir, is the only thing that will cure the official's rheumatism and keep him in health. So the two coexist in a tense mutual interdependence, the peddler getting his license, the official his magic elixir.[14]

Since media exposure over the airwaves is practically essential for election to Congress, usually the only politicians who criticize the media with relative impunity are national leaders, who are too prominent for the media to ignore them[15] or elected officials who come from one-party or "safe" districts. By contrast, a congressman may be reluctant to criticize local broadcasters if his reelection depends in great measure on the amount and tone of the exposure obtained from them. Nevertheless, most members of Congress have an intrinsic fascination with communications issues, reflecting the concerns of their constituents with the impact of broadcasting on society, and are not hesitant to criticize the broadcasting industry on such matters as sex and violence on television and the quality of children's programing.

Congressional Strategies for Overseeing Broadcast Regulation

Congressional influence on FCC policy making assumes many forms, including control by statute, the power of the purse, the spur of investigations, the power of advice and consent, the continuing watchfulness of standing committees, supervision by multiple committees, pressures of individual congressmen and staff, and congressional control by legislative inaction.[16] Each of these forms of influence on broadcast policy making will be examined in turn and then documented at the end of the chapter by a detailed review of eight years of congressional-commission activities (1970–1977) illustrating these various types of influence.

Control by Statute. This most obvious and public congressional activity is noteworthy for its relative unimportance in broadcast regulation. In fact, the Congress has infrequently chosen to influence the administration or formulation of policy by the FCC by enacting specific legislation.[17] We have already seen that the Radio Act of 1927 and the Communications Act of 1934 provide the commission with little more guidance as to its goals, duties, or policies than a vague reference to the "public interest, convenience and necessity." Congress was willing to grant such a broad mandate to the FCC by means of vague legislative language because the legislature neither possessed the desire nor the expertise to grapple with the complex problem of regulating a new technology. They left this task to the new agency. The absence of substantive guidelines for FCC policy making makes the commission all the more vulnerable to other forms of congressional influence. As Professor Louis Jaffe observes, the continuing threat of congressional investigation is virtually inevitable where the regulatory area is a "jungle without statutory directives."[18] Thus, *nonstatutory* controls—frequently in the form of overseeing by raised eyebrow—are of key importance in the FCC's relationship with the Congress.

The Power of the Purse. Legislative appropriations take on special importance for the FCC, which is governed by the Communications Act, a statute that Congress was unable or unwilling to write in detail. Through its hold on the purse strings, Congress has absolute discretion not only over the amount of money allocated to the commission but also over the purposes for which such funds are to be used. Appropriations Committees have determined the direction of the FCC by limiting the use of funds for personnel. In 1942, for example, the House Appropriations Committee adopted an amendment denying funds for the payment of salary to an FCC foreign broadcasting agent whose appointment had been criticized.[19]

The "power of the purse" resides primarily at the subcommittee level of the Appropriations Committee of each house of Congress. Both the Senate and House Appropriations Subcommittees hold hearings each year for the purpose of examining the FCC's budget requests and questioning FCC commissioners and top-level staff. Many opportunities arise, both at the hearings and on other occasions, for the subcommittees to scrutinize commission behavior and to communicate legislative desires to the officials involved.

Another effective technique of legislative review involves the suggestions, admonitions, and directions conveyed to the FCC by means of committee reports accompanying appropriations bills. Although the reports are not law, the Appropriations Committees expect that they will be regarded almost as seriously as if they were—an expectation the commission usually fulfills.

Perhaps more vividly than any other form of influence, the appropriations process underscores the myth of the FCC's "independent" status. Professor William Cary has aptly described the FCC and other "independent" agencies as "stepchildren whose custody is contested by both Congress and the Executive, but without very much affection from either one."[20] These so-called independent stepchildren often suffer from malnutrition, subsisting on crumbs from the federal budget. As a result the FCC finds itself beholden to the source of its bread—which essentially means Congress.

The Spur of Investigations. Perhaps no other federal agency has been the object of as much vilification and prolonged investigation by Congress as the FCC. From its inception the commission has almost always been under congressional investigation or the threat of one; it is frequently "viewed by its progenitors on Capitol Hill as a delinquent creature, not to be trusted, and requiring frequent discipline."[21] The "punitive and often inquisitional character [of these investigations] over a long period of time has created in the public mind an image of depravity with respect to the FCC that severely handicaps the agency in the exercise of its function."[22] Often, the entire operation of the FCC has been dissected under klieg lights in hearings by hostile committees. One such investigation which received much public attention was initiated and conducted in the early 1940s by Representative Eugene Cox of Georgia, one-time supporter but then a bitter critic of the FCC. Cox was the author of a resolution calling for the establishment of a select committee to scrutinize the organization, personnel, and activities of the commission.

Although some investigations (especially those marked by antagonism on the part of members of the congressional committee) have had a debilitating impact on the commission, other congressional investigations have helped to keep the FCC viable by focusing attention on problems posed by new technologies, by eliciting constructive approaches to deficient areas of regulation, or by uncovering areas where new legislation is necessary. One of the best-known investigations was conducted in 1959–1960 by the Special Subcommittee on Legislative Oversight of the House Interstate and Foreign Commerce Committee, chaired by Representative Oren Harris of Arkansas, which uncovered "payola" in the recording and broadcasting industries and rigged television quiz shows. Whether they are harmful or salutary, however, one inevitable result of congressional investigative activities is to further attune the commission to the wishes and expectations of Congress.

The Power of Advice and Consent. The statutory limitation of the tenure of commissioners and the requirement that the Senate confirm all appointments to the commission provide Congress with a further means of controlling the FCC. The late Senator Edwin C. Johnson, former chairman of the Senate Commerce Committee, was of the view that "the existing system of giving the Executive the appointive power to the commissions which are the arms of Congress is basically unsound" since "it is only natural that those who owe their jobs to the Executive would be reluctant to oppose Executive policy and suggestions." He suggested that the appointive power be vested in the Speaker of the House and the confirmation requirement remain with the Senate.[23] Although this suggestion was not adopted, it is indicative of congressional suspicions about Executive appointments. In the first three years of the Federal Radio Commission's existence, from 1927 until 1930, a distrustful Congress limited the tenure of commissioners to one year.

Even with the present seven-year terms (staggered so that the term of only one commissioner expires in any one year), the need for confirmation by the Senate continues to be an important means of congressional control for several reasons. First, before a President makes any nomination requiring senatorial approval, he follows the custom of consulting a senator who is from both the nominee's state and the President's party.[24] Second, if some powerful senator has strong objections to a nomination, he has opportunities to delay or block the appointment.[25] Third, since every presidential appointment and reappointment to the FCC is first passed upon by the Senate Commerce Committee, the opinions on communications matters expressed by individual senators at confirmation hearings are likely to receive careful consideration by new commissioners. Frequently, in fact, the confirmation process is used by members of Congress as a means of influencing the nominee's position on various policy matters. Especially at hearings involving reappointment, senators have tried to extract promises as to the formulation of particular policies or the submission of future reports on specific projects. For example, during the confirmation hearings on the nomination of Glen Robinson, former Senator John Pastore, a staunch defender of the Fairness Doctrine, expressed concern with a law review article that Robinson had written questioning the doctrine's constitutionality. In response to close questioning by Pastore, Robinson promised not to lead a "crusade" to eliminate the doctrine.[26]

A fascinating study, published in 1976 by the Senate Commerce Committee, reviewed the circumstances of appointment of fifty-one members of the FCC and Federal Trade Commission over a twenty-five year period (1949–1974). The authors, lawyers James Graham and Victor Kramer, provide an interesting account of the important role played by members of both houses in the appointment process. They found that about one-half of the appointments to the FCC and FTC involved a significant degree of active congressional sponsorship and that fourteen of the commissioners were appointed—and some subsequently reappointed—almost entirely due to the efforts of a single congressman.[27] They concluded that most commission appointments are the result of "well-stoked campaigns conducted at the right time with the right sponsors, and many selections can be explained in terms of powerful political connections and little else."[28]

Continuing Watchfulness of Standing Committees. Under the Legislative Reorganization Acts of 1946 and 1970, each standing committee of the Senate and the House is directed to exercise continuous watchfulness over the execution by administrative agencies of any law within its jurisdiction.[29] The House Committee on Interstate and Foreign Commerce and the Senate Committee on Commerce are charged with making continuing studies of problems in the communications industry, and these committees have prime responsibility for the initiation and consideration of legislation affecting the FCC. One of the potential advantages of such continuous contact between an agency and a standing committee is that the members and staff of the congressional committee acquire the substantive knowledge necessary to meet the agency's officials in a battle of the experts. As a result of such a continuing relationship there develops in some cases "a healthy, mutual respect between the committee and administrator, both of whom have a common objective and, in substantial measure, a common fund of information."[30] Too often, however, the contact between congressmen and administrators is instead sporadic, ill tempered, basically uninformed, and mutually aggravating.

Standing committees are frequently able to have a major impact on agency decisions merely by holding hearings. During these sessions, committee members have an opportunity to communicate their views to a captive audience of FCC commissioners, who usually try to portray themselves as flexible, hard-working members of a public-spirited agency.[31] The history of congressional supervision of the FCC is replete with examples where policies of the commission were shaped by a single committee or its chairman, often without even an official policy directive.

Supervision by Multiple Committees.   Professor Cary, who served four years as chairman of the Securities and Exchange Commission, has commented that congressional supervision of agency policies "is sometimes wearing, almost unendurable, but is an integral part of the system."[32] During the past decade, the number of congressional committees which have assumed an oversight function has increased significantly. Such supervision by multiple committees allows more members of Congress, representing a greater range of interests, to have a voice in agency policies, but it often leads to duplication and overlapping legislative review. In recent Congresses commission oversight functions have been performed by the Senate and House Government Operations Committees (with respect to "regulatory reform"), the Science and Astronautics Committees (in connection with satellite broadcasting), the Judiciary Committees (with respect to cable, broadcast copyright laws, newsmen's rights, and antitrust aspects of the communications industries), the Senate Foreign Relations Committee (concerning the ratification of broadcasting treaties), the Select Committee on Small Business (on such matters as spectrum allocation, TV advertising practices, and all-channel radio receivers), and the Joint Economic Committee (with respect to the efficiency of the FCC and other regulatory agencies)—all in addition to the normal review of commission activities by the House and Senate Commerce Committees and the appropriate House and Senate Appropriations Subcommittees.

In one case alone (when the Communications Satellite Act of

1962 was under consideration) the FCC commissioners testified before the following nine committees and subcommittees: House Committee on Science and Astronautics, House Committee on Interstate and Foreign Commerce, Communications Subcommittee of the Senate Committee on Commerce, Senate Committee on Aeronautical and Space Science, Senate Committee on Commerce, Senate Committee on Foreign Relations, Antitrust Subcommittee of the House Judiciary Committee, Subcommittee on Monopoly of the Senate Select Committee on Small Business, and Subcommittee on Antitrust and Monopoly of the Senate Judiciary Committee.

Pressures of Individual Congressmen and Staff. Although it is difficult to measure their impact, the actions of individual members of Congress are frequently influential in shaping the course and direction of FCC policy. Newton Minow pointed out that "it is easy—very easy—to confuse the voice of one congressman, or one congressional committee, with the voice of Congress."[33] Professor Kenneth Culp Davis contends that day-to-day influences of members of Congress may be even more important to agencies than committee hearings and that these individual influences seldom come to public attention. He cites as an example private meetings between the chairman of the House Commerce Committee and the chairman of the FCC for the purpose of "working over" cable regulations prior to their being issued by the commission.[34]

The influence of congressional staff members in this process should not be overlooked. The staff members of the relevant congressional committees maintain a close liaison with the FCC and impart the views and expectations of committee members to the commissioners, personnel of the FCC's Legislation Division, and other commission staff members. A 1975 Senate study found that staff communication with agency personnel was the technique most frequently used by Congress in overseeing the operation of regulatory agencies.[35] Although they usually have low visibility (with Nicholas Zapple, former counsel to the Senate Communications Subcommittee, and Harry Shooshan, III, counsel to the House Communications Subcommittee, being notable exceptions), committee staff members, especially lawyers, play a crucial role both in shaping the body of laws and in overseeing the activities of regulatory agencies.

Control by Legislative Inaction. Inaction by the Congress may in many instances have as great an impact on the commission and its making of policy as has the enactment of legislation. Professor Louis

Jaffe contends that where Congress is unable to determine a policy on issues which demand congressional expression, the failure to act should be viewed as an abdication of its legislative authority and a delegation of power to the agency. Jaffe points out that it is not unusual for a problem to be left to administrative determination "because the issue is politically so acute, so much a matter of conflict that Congress is unable to formulate a policy."[36] Such irresolution, however, has not prevented Congress from later responding to a commission interpretation with hostility. Even when Congress has been willing to delegate important decisions to the commission, it has reserved the right to criticize and oppose these decisions. One of the tasks of the FCC, then, is to make crucial decisions when the *wishes* of Congress are quite unclear, but its *presence* is very real.

Congressional Activity Related to Broadcasting, 1970–1977

In the course of examining the multiple roles of Congress, we have identified eight different types of congressional control or influence on broadcast regulation. We now turn to the record of the 91st through the 95th Congresses to review in some detail congressional activities concerning broadcast regulation during the eight-year span from 1970 to 1977.

Control by Statute. The only major new amendment to the Communications Act enacted during the 1970–1977 period continued the congressional pattern of enacting amendments designed to direct the policies of the commission without clear guidelines. The Federal Election Campaign Act of 1971 states that willful or repeated failure by a broadcast licensee to provide "reasonable access" to a candidate for federal office may result in a loss of license. Neither the law nor the legislative history clarify what the Congress had in mind by the phrase "reasonable access." This determination has been left to the discretion of the FCC.

There was only one other measure of significance enacted during this period which has had an impact on the FCC's regulation of the broadcasting and cable industries. In 1976, following fifteen years of debate, Congress passed a new copyright revision act which replaced the Copyright Act of 1909. It requires that in exchange for a compulsory license, cable systems pay copyright royalties in accordance with the number of distant (as opposed to local) broadcast signals carried and a fee schedule based on a decreasing percentage of revenues. The politically sensitive issue of copyright fees by cable television systems was one of the reasons why Congress had been unwilling to act earlier on copyright revision measures. Former Chairman Dean Burch, in a concurring opinion to the FCC's 1972 *Cable Television Report and Order*, observed that "the obstacle to legislation has long been the ability of any or all of the contending industries—cable, broadcasting, copyright—to block any particular legislative approach with which they might take issue."[37]

Despite the enactment of the new copyright law, differences among program copyright owners, cable operators, and broadcasters have not been resolved. Many cable operators still harbor considerable distaste for paying any copyright fees, and virtually all segments of that industry regard the commission's reporting and accounting requirements as needlessly onerous. The prospect of broadcaster-initiated infringement suits arising from violations of the FCC's signal carriage rules is also anything but pleasant for cable operators. The copyright owners, on the other hand, contend that the fees paid by cable operators are inadequate and remain concerned about the loss of control over distribution of their product. Broadcasters were upset at being left out of an agreement on cable royalties entered into between the Motion Picture Association of America and the National Cable Television Association that cleared the way for congressional passage of copyright revision legislation. They still contend that a cable industry paying low royalty fees competes with them on an unfair basis.

The House Communications Subcommittee is in the midst of a review of the entire Communications Act, and the results of this effort may change the fundamental manner in which the broadcasting, cable, and common carrier industries are regulated. Beginning in 1976 the subcommittee began an extensive study of the act, and in April 1977 the subcommittee staff released a series of option papers suggesting various methods of restructuring the telecommunications industry. At hearings held in the summer of 1977 over fifty witnesses participated in informal round-table discussions with members of the subcommittee on the sections of the act governing the regulation of broadcasters.

The Power of the Purse. The presence of violent and sexually explicit material on television has been a subject of congressional concern throughout the 1970s. In June 1974 this concern came to the fore during hearings before the House Appropriations Committee. The FCC was ordered to "submit a report to the Committee by December 31, 1974, outlining specific positive actions taken or planned by the Commission to protect children from excessive programing of violence and obscenity."[38] Indicating displeasure with what it saw as a dereliction of the commission's duty, the committee also stated: "The Committee is reluctant to take punitive action to require the Commission to heed the views of Congress and to carry out its responsibilities, but if this is what is required to achieve the desired objective such action may be considered."[39]

Responding to instructions contained in the reports of both the House and Senate Appropriations Committees, Chairman Richard Wiley initiated a series of meetings with the top officers of the networks and the National Association of Broadcasters. The meetings continued through the fall, and early the next year, in 1975, the family viewing policy was born. The family viewing standard, inserted in the spring of 1975 into the NAB Television Code, generally provides that the first hour of network prime-time programing and the preceding hour (7 through 9 P.M.) consist of programing suitable for viewing by the entire family. Former Senator Pastore, then chairman of the Communications Subcommittee and the Appropriations Subcommittee on the FCC budget, applauded family viewing as a responsible answer to the problem of televised violence. On October 30, 1975, several individuals and groups that were engaged in the creation and sale of programs to the networks and local television stations filed suit, charging that the code provision and the efforts of Chairman Wiley to effect action violated the First Amendment. On November 4, 1976, U.S. District Court Judge Warren Ferguson issued a decision holding that the FCC, certain members of the commission, the networks, and the NAB had violated the First Amendment.[40]

Senator Ernest Hollings of South Carolina and his predecessor as chairman of the Senate Communications Subcommittee, Senator Pastore, enjoyed the unique position of serving as both chairman of the Appropriations Subcommittee responsible for FCC appropriations requests and the Communications Subcommittee. The dual positions provided a unique opportunity for both individuals to command the attention of the commission. In June 1977 Senator Hollings wrote to Chairman Wiley stating his objection to the FCC's request to reallocate $350,000 from other commission projects to fund a special ten-member staff to work on the network inquiry[41]—a wide-ranging inquiry instituted by the FCC in January 1977 in response to a petition by Westinghouse Broadcasting Company to reexamine network-affiliate relationships. Senator Hollings virtually acknowledged that his refusal to authorize the funds was politically motivated—in his words, "a desire to preserve the options of the soon to be named new chairman of the commission."[42] The FCC, by a vote of 7 to 0, accepted Senator Hollings's letter as decisive.

The manner in which the FCC spends the funds appropriated by Congress is not the exclusive province of the Appropriations Committees. Individual members of Congress often try to influence the commission as to projects and research the agency should fund. In the 92nd Congress, for example, there was pressure applied on the FCC from both sides of Capitol Hill concerning the commission's decision, late in 1971, to discontinue the second phase of hearings with respect to the rates of the American Telephone and Telegraph Company. (The AT&T proceedings are of particular concern to broadcasters insofar as they have an impact on the rates charged to radio and television stations for the use of telephone lines.) The decision was attacked publicly in many quarters, but perhaps most forcefully by Senator Fred Harris of Oklahoma. Senator Harris charged the commission with failing in its responsibility to the public and announced his intention to introduce legislation to compel the FCC to complete its investigation. On January 13, 1972, Chairman Burch sent a lengthy letter to key figures in Congress defending and explaining the commission's action. But on the first day of the new session of Congress Senator Harris held a news conference at which he once again publicly prodded the commission to act. Six days later Harris introduced legislation which would provide the commission additional staff and up to $2 million in increased funding in order to resume the formal inquiry. There was no need for Congress to hold hearings on the Harris bill; later that week the commission announced that it was reinstating the second phase of formal hearings.

The Spur of Investigations.   Many of the investigations conducted by congressional subcommittees during the period from 1970 to 1977 focused on aspects of network operations. For example, in the early 1970s three CBS documentaries were the targets of investigations by the Special Investigations Subcommittee of the House Interstate and Foreign Commerce Committee: a program on pot smoking at Northwestern University, a planned documentary on an invasion of Haiti which never took place, and a documentary entitled "The Selling of the Pentagon." Pressure on the FCC to take a more aggressive role in reviewing the accuracy and fairness of documentaries was increased when Representative Harley Staggers of West Virginia, chairman of the House Commerce Committee and its Investigations Subcommittee, in effect made a personal crusade to obtain out-takes (unused film) from the CBS "Selling of the Pentagon" documentary so that the subcommittee could judge whether the network had distorted the comments of those interviewed in the documentary. The documentary had won the Peabody Award and several other journalistic honors. CBS argued that out-takes were analogous to a reporter's private notes and protected by the First Amendment. The battle over a possible contempt of Congress citation, resulting from CBS President Frank Stanton's refusal to obey a Commerce Committee subpoena, was fought ultimately on the floor of the House largely on the constitutional issue. But a fear also was voiced by some congressmen that the power of television (especially the networks) had gone unchecked for too long. In the end the resolution citing Stanton for contempt was effectively rejected when the House, by a vote of 226 to 181, recommitted it to the Commerce Committee.

A comprehensive investigation of the FCC and eight other regulatory agencies was conducted in the 94th Congress by the House Commerce Committee's Oversight and Investigation Subcommittee. The subcommittee's report, entitled "Federal Regulation of Regulatory Reform," was the product of nearly two years of investigation that included 28 days of public hearings, some 220 witnesses from both government and the private sector, a hearing record of 3,500 pages, and extensive written submissions from individuals and agencies.[43] Indeed, the FCC's answer to the subcommittee's 96-page informational questionnaire required some 18,000 pages.

The study ranked the agencies by measuring various aspects of their performance, including such criteria as fidelity to the public protection mandate as defined by Congress, the quality and quantity of agency activity, the effectiveness of agency enforcement programs, and the quality of public participation. The subcommittee ranked the nine agencies by three grades (top, middle, and bottom) and placed the FCC in the middle grade. Justifying this ranking, the report noted, "The Federal Communications Commission has shown signs only recently of loosening its close relationship with the broadcasting and telephone industries. It has begun to encourage competition in the sale of telephone equipment and has opened most of the television markets to cable television."[44]

The Power of Advice and Consent. In the 1970s the Senate's attitude toward the confirmation process underwent significant changes. Until President Nixon's second term in office, the Senate had usually contented itself with a passive "rubber stamp" role in confirming the President's nominees. The early 1970s, however, were marked by confirmation struggles, the most notorious of which involved two Nixon nominees to the Supreme Court, G. Harold Carswell and Clement Haynsworth. In 1973 Chairman Warren Magnuson and other Commerce Committee members urged Senate rejection of a nominee to the Federal Power Commission, William Morris, on grounds that he had served as counsel to a major oil company subject to the jurisdiction of the FPC for a number of years prior to his nomination. The Senate rejected the Morris nomination by a vote of 49 to 44, the first time in nearly forty years that the Senate had formally voted to reject a nominee to a regulatory agency.

The Senate's increased concern over the quality of regulatory appointments is reflected in Senator Magnuson's remarks to a consumer group in 1973:

> We have always given the President—without regard to party—the benefit of the doubt on [regulatory] appointments—But I must tell you that we have swallowed nominees by [the Nixon] administration who have left a bitter aftertaste, and our tolerance for mediocrity and lack of independence from economic interests is rapidly coming to an end.[45]

On September 21, 1973, only three months after the Senate had rejected the Morris nomination, President Nixon nominated a former broadcaster, James Quello, as an FCC commissioner. As a result of objections from various consumer groups and members of Congress, the Senate held an eight-day hearing on the Quello nomination (the longest hearing ever conducted for an FCC nominee) and delayed confirmation for seven months. In 1974 President Nixon's nominee for the FCC was Luther Holcomb, a former vice-chairman of the Equal Employment Opportunity Commission (EEOC). He had been described as a Democrat, but the discovery of correspondence on EEOC stationery indicating that Holcomb was an active campaigner for Nixon and other Republicans caused the nomination to be withdrawn.

Graham and Kramer, in their study of FCC and FTC appointments, have pointed out that although the Senate's new vigilance with respect to the advice and consent process coincided with and was strengthened by Watergate, murmurings of an evolutionary change in Senate attitude could be heard years before.[46] They have cited Senator Pastore's persistent demands during President Nixon's first term for a black appointee to the FCC as suggesting a new militancy. Pastore, in 1971 and 1972, refused to take action on any Nixon nominee to the FCC until a black appointee (eventually Judge Benjamin Hooks) was announced for the next vacancy.

Continuing Watchfulness of Standing Committees. During the 1970s the Commerce Committees have held general oversight hearings at the beginning of each session. These hearings cover a wide range of topics and usually constitute the major opportunity for committee members to keep abreast of commission activities.

The issues of sex and violence and children's television were frequently discussed at the annual oversight sessions and, on several occasions, were the subject of special hearings and reports. Some members of Congress, especially Senator Pastore, were particularly active in overseeing the FCC's handling of the issue of television violence. Pastore was responsible for the creation of the Surgeon General's Advisory Committee on Television and Social Behavior, which conducted a study on television violence. Since the early 1970s the Advisory Committee's report and other studies on televised violence have been the subject of hearings by both Commerce Committees in each new Congress.

The FCC pays more than passing attention to suggestions made during FCC oversight hearings. At such hearings in 1971 the late Torbert Macdonald (then House Communications Subcommittee chairman) suggested that the commission establish a permanent Children's Television Bureau to deal with programing and advertising aimed at young people. In a letter to then Chairman Dean Burch on May 11, 1971, Representative Macdonald referred to children's television as "a terribly overlooked area" and asked Burch to consider retaining specialists to work on the problem. After several months of private discussion on the matter with Macdonald and his staff, Chairman Burch announced on September 14, 1971, that the commission had decided to establish such an office and planned to staff it with experts in the field who would be prominently involved in advising the commission on children's programing. (However, after Burch left the FCC and Macdonald died, this special office faded into the background. During the last year of the administration of Chairman Wiley the office was staffed by only one professional employee.)

Supervision by Multiple Committees. Over thirty committees and subcommittees of the Congress attempted to review some aspect of the FCC's regulatory practices and policies from 1970 to 1977. In many cases this multiple supervision led to duplication and overlapping efforts. Various aspects of the FCC's regulation of cable television, for example, were studied by the Judiciary, Commerce, and Government Operations Committees of both houses. The adequacy of user fees was pursued not only by the Senate and House Appropriations Committees but also by the Special Studies Subcommittee of the House Government Operations Committee. Hearings on satellite communications were conducted by the Subcommittee on National Security Policy and Scientific Developments of the House Foreign Affairs Committee as well as by the Subcommittee on Space Sciences and Applications of the House Science and Astronautics Committee.

A number of congressional committees, including the Government Operations, Judiciary, and Commerce Committees of both houses, have held hearings, conducted studies, and issued reports on legislation to provide federal assistance for the establishment of independent consumer agencies and legal offices to provide more effective representation of consumer interests. Several of the hearings focused on the extent to which the FCC was representing consumer interests.

Congressional committees used a variety of techniques in attempting to influence FCC action. During hearings in 1976 on the regulation of cable television the House Subcommittee on Communications used a satellite to present the testimony of a cable operator from San Diego (a city represented by Subcommittee Chairman Lionel Van Deerlin). The subcommittee had arranged a satellite hook-up from a California studio to an earth station parked outside the Rayburn House Office Building and then on to monitors in the hearing room. One of the issues then pending before the FCC was the role of satellites in distributing programs to cable systems. Another instance of committee influence on the commission involved the Subcommittee on Administrative Practice and Procedure of the Senate Judiciary Committee. In March 1970 the FCC formed a Procedure Review Committee and published a notice in the

Federal Register soliciting suggestions for reform of its operations. Meanwhile, the Subcommittee on Administrative Practice and Procedure had sent each FCC commissioner a questionnaire inquiring about the extent of citizen involvement. When the notice appeared in the Federal Register, the Subcommittee responded by printing the results of the questionnaire and filing written comments with the FCC.

Pressures of Individual Congressmen and Staff. From time to time, individual congressmen may espouse a particular cause with such vigor that their words alone have an impact on broadcast regulation. In April 1970, for example, Representative Paul Rogers wrote letters to pharmaceutical companies, major television networks, the National Association of Broadcasters, the FTC, and the Food and Drug Administration seeking to restrict television advertisements of mood drugs. Late the following fall Rogers announced that the NAB had adopted guidelines, to become effective February 1, 1971, on advertisements for nonprescription drugs, including stimulants, calmatives, and sleeping aids.

Senator Howard Baker of Tennessee, when serving as ranking minority member of the Communications Subcommittee, played a key role in a controversial proceeding initiated by the United Church of Christ (UCC) proposing the dropping in of ninety-six Very High Frequency (VHF) channels. (UCC had two principal goals in mind: to provide certain communities their first VHF noncommercial stations and to open the door to greater ownership by minorities of television stations.) In March 1977 the FCC, by a vote of 4 to 2, proposed to consider assigning short-spaced VHF drop-ins in Knoxville, Tennessee (as strongly urged by Senator Baker), and three other markets. *Broadcasting*, in an editorial entitled "Nobody's Baby," commented:

It is obvious . . . that nobody on the FCC is enthusiastic about this proceeding. Maybe there is something to those reports that the rule-making was forced upon the FCC by the insistence of Senate Minority Leader Howard H. Baker (R-Tenn.) that a V be dropped into Knoxville, Tenn. The assumption is that the commission had to include some other markets to reduce the visibility of the Knoxville accommodation.

At the end the FCC will have to decide whether the public as well as Senator Baker and the interests he represents would be served by these proposals.[47]

During the 91st Congress (1969–1970) the legal staff of the Special Investigations Subcommittee of the House Committee on Interstate and Foreign Commerce was primarily responsible for instituting major investigations into such controversial subjects as trafficking in broadcast construction permits, deceptive broadcast programing practices, and the processing of license renewal applications.[48]

During the 1970s individual members of Congress have participated actively in FCC proceedings involving the enforcement of the Fairness Doctrine and Section 315, the equal opportunities provision of the Communications Act. For example, Representative Patsy Mink of Hawaii, the sponsor of an anti–strip-mining bill, filed a Fairness Doctrine complaint with the FCC in 1974 against a Clarksburg, West Virginia, radio station that refused to broadcast her eleven-minute program supporting her legislation. In 1976 the FCC agreed with the congresswoman and cited the station for not covering the local strip-mining controversy.[49] The decision was the first commission ruling that a station, as part of its obligations under the Fairness Doctrine, had to cover a specific controversial issue of public importance because of its special significance to the station's community.

Another member of Congress was involved in a court decision that paved the way for the League of Women Voters to sponsor and televise a series of presidential and vice-presidential debates. In 1975 the FCC issued a ruling exempting from the equal opportunities requirement the press conferences of candidates and political debates sponsored by third parties.[50] Representative Shirley Chisholm of New York, together with the Democratic National Committee and the National Organization for Women, appealed the FCC decision to the U.S. Court of Appeals for the District of Columbia Circuit, which upheld the commission.[51] Later during the 1976 presidential campaign former Senator Eugene McCarthy of Minnesota was unsuccessful in persuading the courts either to block the Carter-Ford debates or to order him included in them.

The creation of the Congressional Black Caucus has added another dimension to the ways in which individual congressmen can exert pressure on the FCC. The caucus had its genesis in 1970 when black members of the House first began to work together on specific issues. Early in 1972 the caucus created a Task Force on the Media, which has held public hearings, conducted conferences, issued position papers, and participated in FCC rule-making proceedings on issues pertaining to minority ownership, employment, and programing.

Congress has taken several actions during the early 1970s designed to improve the ability of its committees and members to oversee the activities of the FCC and other regulatory agencies. The Congressional Research Service, expanded in function and strengthened by the Legislative Reorganization Act of 1970, provides a staff of 800 employees to assist members of Congress by evaluating legislative proposals, analyzing testimony, and preparing background memoranda. The Budget Office of the Congress, created in 1974, provides congressmen with budgeting and fiscal information. The Office of Technology Assessment (OTA), authorized in 1972, provides information to Congress on scientific and technological issues and is authorized to undertake research projects either on its own initiative or at the request of any congressional committee chairman. For example, Herman Talmadge of Georgia, chairman of the Senate Agriculture Committee, persuaded OTA to hold hearings and issue a report on ways to bring broadband cable facilities to rural communities. OTA has agreed to assist the House and Senate committees and subcommittees assessing the benefits and problems presented by new technologies. In 1974 Congress authorized the General Accounting Office (GAO) to provide additional oversight assistance. GAO currently is conducting a comprehensive study of a wide range of FCC rules and policies and their impact on the broadcasting industry and the public.

Control by Legislative Inaction. Congressional failure to act on the issue of subscription pay television (STV) during the 91st Congress (1969–1970) allowed the FCC to authorize STV on a permanent basis. In the previous Congress the House Committee on Interstate and Foreign Commerce had adopted resolutions requesting that the FCC defer final consideration of rules authorizing STV operations. However, in the 91st Congress the House Commerce Committee was almost evenly divided on this issue. After a dispute between the Communications Subcommittee, which essentially favored the proposed FCC rules, and opponents of STV on the full committee, the Commerce Committee, by a vote of 15 to 13, approved a bill which would allow STV operations under much more restrictive regulations than those favored by the subcommittee and the FCC. No further action was taken on the bill, and in August 1970 the FCC authorized the first technical system for STV by granting advance approval to Zenith Radio Corporation's Phonevision System.

There have been persistent pleas in the 1970s by the courts, the affected industries, and the FCC itself for congressional guidelines on the development of cable television. For example, in a concurring opinion to the Supreme Court's decision in *United States* v. *Midwest Video Corporation*, Chief Justice Warren Burger said congressional action on cable television was imperative. "The almost explosive development of CATV," according to Burger, "suggests the need of a comprehensive reexamination of the statutory scheme as it relates to this new development so that the basic policies are considered by Congress and not left entirely to the Commission and the Courts."[52] Despite such calls for action Congress—by inaction—has allowed the FCC to set the standards for cable development and growth. Similarly, Congress has not responded to repeated FCC requests for legislative guidance on such key regulatory issues as obscenity and license renewal standards.

As noted in chapter two, the Congress, by its failure to act, permitted the creation of an Office of Telecommunications Policy to serve as the President's principal adviser on domestic and international telecommunications policy. Similarly, in 1977 congressional failure to act allowed that office to be abolished. (It is interesting to note that the House Government Operations Committee had issued reports in 1965, 1966, and 1967 urging the President to submit a reorganization plan to the Congress "to reconstitute the functions and responsibilities of the Director of Telecommunications Management in a separate office in the Executive Office of the President.")[53]

In a field such as communications where the interests of powerful industry forces frequently collide with one another as well as with the interests of the general public, nothing is more unsettling to many lawmakers on Capitol Hill than the prospect of making a law! Thus, rather than enact new laws or amend the Communications Act, the Congress has preferred to use a variety of informal techniques in directing and overseeing the activities of the FCC. Such informal controls are not subject to review by the Congress as a whole and enable legislators to advance personal or constituent interests without the need for a full-scale political battle. Hearings, investigations, and studies provide the Congress with an effective means of assuring that the FCC is constantly aware that it is an "arm of the Congress."

Notes

[1] Newton N. Minow, *Equal Time: The Private Broadcaster and the Public Interest* (New York: Atheneum, 1964), p. 36.

[2] Robert S. McMahon, *The Regulation of Broadcasting*, Study made for the Committee on Interstate and Foreign Commerce, House of Representatives, 85th Congress, 2nd Session, 1958, p. viii.

[3] Louis M. Kohlmeier, Jr., *The Regulators: Watchdog Agencies and the Public Interest* (New York: Harper & Row, 1969), p. 67.

[4] These policy controversies are examined in chapters seven and eight.

[5] William W. Boyer, *Bureaucracy on Trial: Policy Making by Government Agencies* (Indianapolis: Bobbs-Merrill, 1964), p. 46.

[6] Roger G. Noll, *Reforming Regulation* (Washington, D.C.: Brookings Institution, 1971), p. 35.

[7] Minow, Book Review of William Cary, *Politics and the Regulatory Agencies, Columbia Law Review*, 68 (1968), 383–384.

[8] Minow, *Equal Time*, p. 35.

[9] Boyer, *Bureaucracy on Trial*, p. 42.

[10] "The Congressmen with Holdings in Broadcasting," *Broadcasting*, November 14, 1977, pp. 26, 32.

[11] Quoted in Bruce Thorp, "Washington Pressures," *National Journal*, August 22, 1970, p. 1809.

[12] Robert MacNeil, *The People Machine: The Influence of Television on American Politics* (New York: Harper & Row, 1968), p. 243, citing Bernard Rubin.

[13] Ibid., p. 246. Since 1971, radio and television stations are required by Section 312(a) of the Communications Act to "allow reasonable access to or to permit purchase of reasonable amounts of time for the use of a broadcasting station by a legally qualified candidate for Federal elective office on behalf of his candidacy."

[14] Ibid., p. 243.

[15] Members of Congress often find that they can exploit the natural differences between affiliates and networks, permitting floor speeches that are critical of national programing or news coverage while simultaneously finding the local broadcaster's efforts praiseworthy. Similarly, former Vice President Spiro Agnew, often critical of TV news coverage of the Nixon administration, primarily criticized the networks rather than individual stations.

[16] For an excellent review of the various forms of congressional review of the FCC and other regulatory agencies, see *Study on Federal Regulation*, vol. 2, *Congressional Oversight of Regulatory Agencies*, Committee on Government Operations, U.S. Senate, 95th Congress, 1st Session (1975).

[17] Exceptions to this generalization will be examined in chapter six, which deals with the All-Channel Receiver Law, and chapters seven and eight, which probe the attempts by Congress to pass bills dealing with commercials and license renewal procedures.

[18] Louis Jaffe, *Judicial Control of Administrative Action* (Boston: Little, Brown, 1965), p. 48.

[19]Carl J. Friedrich and Evelyn Sternberg, "Congress and the Control of Radio-Broadcasting," *American Political Science Review*, 37 (December 1943), 807.

[20]William Cary, *Politics and the Regulatory Agencies* (New York: McGraw-Hill, 1967), p. 4. Roger Noll, Merton Peck, and John McGowan also point out that one of the important characteristics of the environment in which the FCC operates is the fact that its budget is molehillish indeed among the mountains customarily appropriated by Congress:

> In 1971 the FCC budget was $25 million in a $200 billion total. Even for congressmen who are members of the subcommittee with special responsibilities for monitoring the FCC, evaluating its performance is only a tiny fraction of their over-all responsibilities. Furthermore, the low budget means that the FCC does not attract the attention of relatively remote interest groups that, in the competition for federal funds, focus on the major items. Thus, one important constraint on the FCC's operations—its budget—is easily lost in the shuffle of congressional business.

Noll, Peck, and McGowan, *Economic Aspects of Television Regulation* (Washington, D.C.: Brookings Institution, 1973), p. 121.

[21]Walter Emery, *Broadcasting and Government: Responsibilities and Regulations* (East Lansing: Michigan State University Press, 1971), pp. 395–396.

[22]Ibid., p. 400.

[23]Edwin G. Johnson, "Carrying Coals to Newcastle," *Federal Communications Bar Journal*, 10 (1949), 183.

[24]The views of key senators are given great weight in the President's selection of a nominee. In response to a question posed at the confirmation hearing of Judge Benjamin Hooks as to background on the steps leading to the appointment of Hooks, Senator Howard Baker (R.-Tenn.), ranking minority member on the Senate Communications Committee, said that the idea of naming a black originated with Senator Pastore and that the two of them later found a "sympathetic ear" for the proposal at the White House. Baker looked for a candidate in Tennessee, one who was not a Republican (the FCC had its full statutory complement of four Republicans) and who would not be "a special-interest commissioner." He selected Judge Hooks, whom he had known for a long time, and discussed his nomination with Senator Pastore and then the White House. "Road Looks Clear for Hooks, Wiley," *Broadcasting*, May 29, 1972, pp. 28, 29.

[25]Senator Tobey of New Hampshire launched a one-man crusade against a favorable report on the renomination of Colonel Thad Brown in 1940 and used the hearings to condemn Brown for his handling of monopoly charges against the networks. Commissioner Brown's renomination was rejected by the Senate. Friedrich and Sternberg, "Congress and the Control of Radio-Broadcasting," 806–807.

[26]"FCC Nominees Breeze Through Senate Hearing," *Broadcasting*, July 1, 1974, pp. 22–23.

[27]James M. Graham and Victor H. Kramer, *Appointments to the*

Regulatory Agencies, printed for the use of the Committee on Commerce, U.S. Senate, 94th Congress, 2nd Session (April 1976), pp. 381–382.

[28] Ibid., p. 391.

[29] Congress thought the phrase "continuous watchfulness" contained in the 1946 Legislative Reorganization Act was too vague and renamed the oversight function in the 1970 act "legislative review."

[30] Nathaniel L. Nathanson, "Some Comments on the Administrative Procedure Act," *Northwestern University Law Review*, 41 (1946), 421, 422.

[31] William L. Morrow, *Congressional Committees* (New York: Scribner's, 1969), p. 162.

[32] Cary, *Politics and the Regulatory Agencies*, p. 137.

[33] Minow, *Equal Time*, p. 35.

[34] Kenneth Culp Davis, *Discretionary Justice* (Baton Rouge: University of Louisiana Press, 1969), p. 148.

[35] *Study on Federal Regulation*, vol. 2, *Congressional Oversight of Regulatory Agencies*, p. 81, Committee on Government Operations, U.S. Senate, 95th Congress, 1st Session (1975).

[36] Jaffe, *Judicial Control of Administrative Action*, pp. 41, 43–44.

[37] 36 F.C.C. 143, 290 (1972).

[38] House Report No. 1139, 93rd Congress, 2nd Session (1974), p. 15; see also Senate Report No. 1056, 93rd Congress, 2nd Session (1974), p. 17.

[39] House Report, ibid.

[40] *Writers Guild of America, West, Inc. et al.* v. *F.C.C. et al.*, 423 F. Supp. 1064 (1976). The decision has been appealed by each of the defendants to the U.S. Court of Appeals for the Ninth Circuit.

[41] A House Appropriations Subcommittee had approved the FCC's request.

[42] "FCC Gives Up on Investigation of TV Networks," *Broadcasting*, July 4, 1977, p. 23.

[43] "Federal Regulation and Regulatory Reform," Report by the Subcommittee on Oversight and Investigations of the House Interstate and Foreign Commerce Committee, 94th Congress, 1st Session (1976), p. iii.

[44] Ibid., pp. 12–13.

[45] *Washington Post*, February 19, 1973, p. 6D.

[46] Graham and Kramer, *Appointments to the Regulatory Agencies*, p. 406.

[47] *Broadcasting*, March 14, 1977, p. 86.

[48] Remarks of Rep. Paul Rogers on the death of Robert W. Lishman, Chief Counsel of the Special Subcommittee, 116 *Congressional Record* 11949 (daily ed., Dec. 17, 1970).

[49] *Rep. Patsy Mink*, 59 F.C.C. 2d 987 (1976).

[50] *Aspen Institute Program on Communications*, 55 F.C.C. 2d 697 (1975).

[51] *Chisholm* v. *F.C.C.*, 538 F. 2d 349 (C.A.D.C., 1976).

[52] 406 U.S. 649, 676 (1972).

[53] House Report No. 91–930, p. 5.

4

Broadcast Regulation:
An Analytic View

It is remarkable that the independent regulatory commissions, and in particular the FCC, have rarely been subjected to rigorous, analytical examination. Rather, the literature on regulatory commissions is replete with formalistic, legalistic, and purely descriptive accounts of how such agencies are structured, what their legal powers and authority are, and what they have or have not done. One looks in vain for studies of the independent regulatory commissions which approach their inquiry with theoretical and conceptual vigor.

Yet theory is both useful and necessary in order to organize the abundance of data, phenomena, and information concerning the regulatory process and to allow for the development of meaningful generalizations rather than the continued accumulation of episodic or anecdotal descriptions. Theory serves to link the specific to the general, to direct attention to politically significant events and relationships, and to integrate such findings by the use of concepts, generalizations, and hypotheses. Former FCC Commissioner Lee Loevinger has commented, "Mere observation will not suffice to establish the relations between institutional structures and functions and social values." Scientific analysis, he maintains, "requires both observations and coherent theories to direct and relate the observations"—"theories without observations are mere illusion; observations without theories are pure confusion." [1]

A Systems Analysis Approach
to Broadcast Regulation

This chapter presents the politics of broadcast regulation in terms of an analytical framework or model termed the "broadcast policy-making system." The purpose of this examination is to demonstrate the usefulness of a "systems approach" to the regulatory process and to suggest to scholars a framework for conceptually oriented research in this area.

As is the case with any model, the one utilized here is an analogy or metaphor—a schematic representation of the way things are conceived to be. As such, it is by definition a simplification of reality. Yet to simplify is to streamline, to strip off surface complexities in order to show the essential elements of a system. Because virtually any economic or political process may be graphically analyzed in terms of this systems approach, it also affords a uniform way to evaluate and compare a variety of complex situations or processes. A model directs attention to, and focuses it on, key relationships and activities, and, by doing so, helps define order in the complex real political world with its many subtleties. An analytic system of this type is, in the words of Robert A. Dahl, "an aspect of things in some degree abstracted from reality for purposes of analysis."[2] Its primary test is not whether it is elegant or neat but whether it fosters an understanding of the political process or processes being studied.

Figure 1 presents a simplified and general version of an input-output systems model. This particular model was created by political scientist David Easton as part of his development of a general systems theory of political processes.[3]

In this basic model, policy making (or in Easton's terms, the authoritative allocation of values for the society as a whole) occurs through the conversion activities of a political system which transforms *inputs* of *demands* and *support* concerning various policy alternatives (including the alternative of no policy) into policy outputs. This conversion occurs by means of a "core" of authoritative decision-making activities or agencies (the middle box in Figure 1) and results in *outputs* of public *policies* and *decisions* which themselves return, by means of a *feedback* link, through the general *environment* to constitute and influence new inputs.

Figure 2 offers an elaboration and adaption of the basic model presented in Figure 1. In this representation of the broadcast policy-making system input-output systems analysis is utilized in a specific policy area. The system here is no longer a general one but is rather a subsystem of a larger political system. Only those participants which regularly and significantly involve themselves in regulatory policy making are included in Figure 2, and it incorporates only those aspects of their activities having to do with broadcast regulation.

Unlike Figure 1, the "core," or middle part, of Figure 2 is

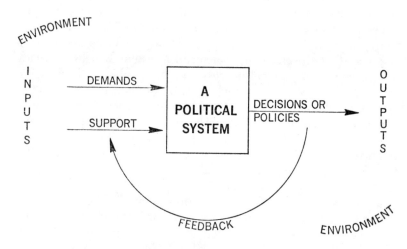

FIGURE 1. THE POLITICAL SYSTEM

opened up and its component elements identified. The six recurring participants in the regulatory process—which are identified and discussed in chapters two and three—are the authoritative decision-making agencies within the "core." In addition, Figure 2 charts the various channels of influence among these six participants. It is significant that there is no one pathway through this core of the broadcast policy-making system, and any one of various different routes necessarily involves multiple participants. The key to the politics of broadcast regulation lies in the interactions among these core participants. As Gary Wamsley and Mayer Zald point out, "Policy is as much or more a product of factors within the interstices of the system's 'black box'—the conversion process—as it is of pressures or inputs from outside."[4] Although these pressures and inputs raise issues and define alternatives, it is the political relationships and interactions among the six key determiners that are key to which policies will be adopted.

The role of three of the principals (the White House, the courts, and citizens groups) is usually less immediate and direct than that of the other three (the FCC, Congress, and industry). Thus the primary

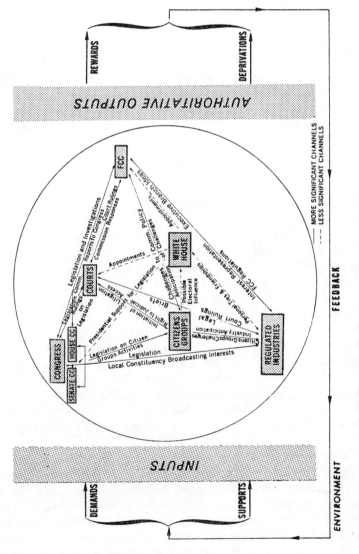

FIGURE 2. THE BROADCAST POLICY-MAKING SYSTEM

channels of influence, information, and contact are traced among these three points of the outer triangle in Figure 2. And, because ultimately it is the FCC which performs the vital task of converting demands into outputs, it must be considered the key participant in the system. Hence its position in Figure 2 at the point adjacent to *authoritative outputs.* One might also say that the FCC is the final recipient of all inputs and appears graphically to be at the spot where they converge.

In addition to suggesting the interplay among the participants in the policy-making process, Figure 2 places this "core activity" in the context of an input-output system essentially similar to Figure 1. This model, then, is a conceptualization of the sequential process through which inputs of policy demands and supports are converted into outputs of authoritative decisions about broadcast regulatory policy. The outputs are FCC rules and decisions, final court decisions, and laws enacted by Congress, which bestow rewards or impose deprivations upon the various affected interests. Reactions to these system outputs are subsequently channeled back through feedback loops to become new input demands and supports relevant to future policies.

This conversion process, of course, does not operate in a political vacuum but rather is carried out in the context of an *environment* shaped by such factors, identified in chapter one, as the historical development of broadcast regulation, the basic characteristics of broadcasting, and legal prescriptions. The environment of broadcast regulation also encompasses other factors such as generalized public attitudes toward broadcasting and governmental regulation and the actions of related systems—the Federal Trade Commission, for example—which may at times inspire and influence the broadcast policy-making system. These various contextual factors together not only constitute constraints upon the conversion process but also determine to a considerable degree the character and substance of many of the input demands and supports themselves.

In the course of the evolution of public policy various *demands* and *supports* concerning policy alternatives are transmitted to the different participants involved in the making of public policy. Some inputs are specific, such as a detailed recommendation for the frequency shift of a broadcast service,[5] whereas others are more general, such as the "mood" cast over independent regulatory commissions by a President or by the current public image of a regulatory agency. It is important to realize, too, that the system does more than merely respond to demands; it also molds both political demands and policy preferences.

Outputs are the authoritative decisions resulting from interaction among those various participants represented in the central core area of the broadcast policy-making system. These may take the form of legislation, such as the statutory requirement that all television sets sold after a certain date have UHF as well as VHF receiving capability.[6] Or they make take the form of agency decisions—for example, that broadcast stations be compelled to follow voluntary industry standards limiting commercial time,[7] or that incumbent licensees should have preferred status in renewal challenges.[8]

Conflict over outputs (either actual or anticipated) is an inevitable feature of a policy-making system which allocates scarce resources. There is a distinction, however, between conflict over policy outputs and severe stress threatening the survival of the system itself. When outputs fail to manage the stress present in the system, output failure results. But, although conflict over policy outputs is unavoidable as long as scarcity of resources continues, output failure is not inevitable. The ability of a system to produce outputs productive of its own survival and the willingness of participants in a system to act to promote systematic survival are important variables in the analysis of a political system.

Policy *outputs*, the immediate policy decisions, should be distinguished from policy *outcomes*, which are the longer-term consequences of such decisions. As Easton puts it, "An output is the stone tossed into the pond and its first splash; the outcomes are the ever widening and vanishing pattern of concentric ripples. The actual decisions and implementing actions are the outputs; the consequences traceable to them, however long the discernible claim of causation, are the outcomes."[9] The "success" of an output, then, is measured by means other than the degree to which it meets an immediate social need; it also includes the effect of the outputs on patterns of present and future inputs.

Where a policy output fails to meet expectations of the affected parties or is seen as an inappropriate or inadequate solution to the problems giving rise to such expectations, the output is likely to be overturned by subsequent actions as frustrated demands rise anew. Indeed, *if the system is perceived as being unresponsive to the expectations of key participants over a substantial period of time, the system itself then may prove vulnerable.* In either case, it is the feedback loop which links policy outputs with inputs, and it is the policy-making system which converts these new inputs into future policy decisions.

An Example of the Input-Output System

During the television freeze of 1948–1952, when no new television stations were being authorized pending a reexamination of the TV frequency allocation table, residents in states which had no television service demanded that the freeze be partly lifted. These demands were transmitted by the Colorado congressional delegation, which made strong representations both on Capitol Hill and to the FCC for interim channel assignments in areas without television. Support for the existing freeze, however, arose from some broadcasting interests (especially those with stations already on the air) desiring a careful study of possible interference prior to the authorization of additional stations.

Colorado's interests were well represented at the time by its senator, Edwin C. Johnson, who held the influential chairmanship of the Senate Commerce Committee. Despite Johnson's pivotal position with its built-in access both to the FCC and to the entire Senate, the commission refused to make interim TV assignments. The resulting policy output deprived Colorado of immediate television and rewarded those who felt that additional TV service had to be based on an allocation table designed to protect (at least from the standpoint of spectrum engineering) existing broadcasters. Interests favoring more TV stations, however, then shifted their efforts from seeking interim television assignments to requesting that the commission bring its study of the TV allocation table to a speedy conclusion. Thus, the feedback process provided new inputs for the FCC as it tried to deal with the development of postwar television.

General Patterns in Policy Making

The operation of the policy-making system in specific instances of regulatory policy making is inherently unique; each policy-making situation is likely to differ in some important respect from all others. However, certain recurring patterns in the politics of broadcast regulation can be identified. Six such patterns in the broadcast policy-making process are proposed: [10]

1. Participants seek conflicting goals from the process. Pluralism and dispersion of power in policy making do not by themselves suggest that the process is typically a struggle for control or influence. Conceivably, the participants in such a process could share common perspectives concerning what is to be done. Such is rarely the case, however, in the broadcast policy-making process. As the case studies in chapters five through nine will show, the gains of one set of participants are usually made at the cost of the interests of another. The policy demands of different groups are seldom compatible, and they must usually compete for scarce rewards.

2. Participants have limited resources insufficient to dominate the process in hierarchical fashion. In a pluralistic complex such as that outlined in Figure 2 policy-making power tends to be somewhat divided and dissipated. Although the FCC frequently initiates policy proposals, it lacks the ability to implement them single-handedly. To prevail, it must have significant support from other participants. Similarly, none of the other five participants has hierarchical control over the policy-making process. In such a system, policy making results from the agreement—or at least the acquiescence—of all participants, not from domination by one.

3. Participants have unequal strengths in the struggle for control or influence. Inequality among participants can arise because one side is inherently stronger, cares more, or develops its potential more effectively. In the 1940s, for example, FM broadcasters had considerably less political strength than established and well-financed AM networks, and their ability to influence the policy-making process was affected correspondingly (see chapter five). Favorable public opinion, legal symbols, congressional allies, and the like are potential sources of strength which participants possess in differing degrees, and which they may use with varying success on different issues.

4. The process follows certain informal rules of procedure, such as policy progression by small or incremental steps rather than by massive changes. One means of minimizing opposition to a policy initiative is to show its close relationship to existing and generally accepted policy. Frequently, earlier actions are cited to prove that the desired change is not an unprecedented step but a logical outgrowth of past concerns and policies. (One of the beauties of administrative law is that precedents can usually be found for almost any initiative!) Such slow and gradual shifts in policy are not only strategic but probably inevitable, given the multiplicity of participants with conflicting goals, unequal strengths, and limited resources. The five case studies which follow indicate that the political resources necessary to accomplish significant policy innovations are greater than those necessary to achieve more clearly incremental changes.

5. *Legal and ideological symbols play a significant role in the process.* Throughout the evolution of policy a recurring theme of various participants is the legal and ideological implications of alternatives. Some policies are seen as threatening (or protecting) the legal rights of licensees; others may be viewed as destructive (or supportive) of free speech or of the right to private property. Often stock phrases such as "localism," "access," or "free broadcasting" become cherished in and of themselves. In the case of the FCC policy statement on license renewals discussed in chapter eight, not one citizens group contesting the statement had actually filed a competing license application, but they were profoundly interested in preserving their "right" to do so. They perceived the FCC's expressed concern for "industry stability" as synonymous with indifference to the rights of the broadcast audience. Thus ideological concepts became symbols which superseded real actions in importance.

6. *The dominant pattern in the process is that of mutual accommodation among participants.* Participants in broadcast policy making do not customarily attempt to destroy one or more of their opponents. Rather, the process is characterized by consensual, majority-seeking activities. This mutual adjustment among participants may occur in a variety of ways, including negotiation, the creation and discharge of obligations, direct manipulation of the immediate circumstances in which events are occurring, the use of third persons or political brokers capable of developing consensual solutions, or partial deferral to others in order to effect a compromise. Only one case study—the advertising controversy—will not show a pattern of mutual adjustment and accommodation. Possible reasons for this exception will be suggested in chapter ten.

In the case studies we will be looking at the politics of broadcast regulation in actual instances involving struggles over policy alternatives. Evaluating each case in terms of the generalizations just presented, we will see the six participants using their varying (perhaps insufficient) financial, political, and social resources to obtain desired goals in the face of probable or actual opposition from other participants. We will see that, if they wish to be successful—even incrementally—the participants must be relatively moderate in their goals, must respect legal and ideological symbols, and must exhibit a willingness to adjust their positions.

Notes

[1] Lee Loevinger, Introduction to Glendon Schubert, *The Political Role of the Courts: Judicial Policy-Making* (Chicago: Scott, Foresman, 1965), pp. iii–iv.

[2] Robert A. Dahl, *Modern Political Analysis*, 2nd ed. (Englewood Cliffs, N.J.: Prentice-Hall, 1970), p. 9.

[3] See David Easton, *The Political System* (New York: Knopf, 1953); see also, by the same author, "An Approach to the Analysis of Political Systems," *World Politics*, 9 (April 1957), 383–400; *A Framework for Political Analysis* (Englewood Cliffs, N.J.: Prentice-Hall, 1965); and *A Systems Analysis of Political Life* (New York: Wiley, 1965), p. 247. Figure 1 was presented for the first time in the 1957 *World Politics* article, and can be found there on page 384.

[4] Wamsley and Zald, *The Political Economy of Public Organizations* (Lexington, Mass.: Heath, 1973), p. 89.

[5] See chapter five, "Smothering FM with Commission Kindness."

[6] See chapter six, "UHF Television: The Fading Signal Is Revived After Only Ten Years."

[7] See chapter seven, "The Commercial Time Fiasco."

[8] See chapter eight, "Comparative License Renewal Policies: The Nonindependence of an Independent Regulatory Agency."

[9] Easton, *A Systems Analysis of Political Life*, p. 352. In Figure 2, some of the "outcomes" can be seen as part of the feedback.

[10] The generalizations which follow are adapted from Charles E. Lindblom, *The Policy-Making Process* (Englewood Cliffs, N.J.: Prentice-Hall, 1968).

PART TWO
FIVE CASE STUDIES

5

Smothering FM with Commission Kindness

The early history of Frequency Modulation (FM) broadcasting in the United States shows how an important technical innovation was delayed and nearly destroyed by an FCC decision based heavily upon unstated social and economic factors as well as stated technical considerations.

When FM broadcasting developed in the latter part of the 1930s, it promised many advantages over existing AM radio, including: (1) a static-free signal; (2) increased frequency range allowing for high-fidelity broadcasting; (3) the ability for one FM station to exist quite close to other FM stations on the same frequency without the mutual interference experienced with AM; (4) the opportunity for a significant increase in broadcast competition through large numbers of new stations in a new frequency band; and (5) the resulting possibility of a challenge to network control of programing through diversification of broadcasting services.

These advantages made FM a potential threat to the dominance of existing AM broadcasting. Moreover, as FM developed, it found itself in direct competition—for frequencies, advertisers, audience, and financial support—with television, a technical innovation heavily backed by traditional broadcasting interests. The inability of FM to develop as a major broadcast service in the immediate postwar period, however, was ensured when the FCC in 1945 decided to uproot this sapling medium from its existing frequencies and to move it into a higher band, thereby making obsolete all existing FM receivers and transmitters. This action, together with the growth of television in the late 1940s, compelled FM radio to wait until the late 1950s and early 1960s to find a secure place in American broadcasting.

Full commercial FM broadcasting was initially authorized by the FCC in May 1940, following a five-year experimental period. The commission allocated thirty-five channels for commercial FM in the 43–50 mc. range and reserved five more channels in the 42–43 mc. band for educational use. The commission at this time gave FM a strong endorsement. It noted that engineers in both the manufacturing and broadcasting industries agreed that FM was highly developed and ready for full commercial development.[1] The commission, however, hedged on the finality of its decision to authorize FM broadcasting in the 44 mc. band by stating that the effect of skywave interference would not be known until additional stations were placed in operation, and that the use of higher frequencies might be reconsidered after evaluating the performance of these new stations.[2]

Starting with the FCC's authorization in 1940, FM began to make some progress, but its development was halted in 1942 following the United States' entry into World War II. No further licenses were granted, and the scarcity of electronic parts kept many stations already authorized from going on the air. FM was frozen at a critical stage of development during the war years. A total of forty-seven stations were on the air and approximately 500,000 sets in operation as of June 30, 1944, but there was no immediate hope of expansion. As the end of the war drew near a massive backlog of over 400 applications for FM stations accumulated and General Electric officials predicted that FM radio sales in the immediate postwar years would be well over 5 million.[3] Great expectations were held for FM broadcasting. It was heralded as providing not only considerable economic gain but also "radio's second chance" for diversity and improvement.

During this time, however, the FCC was beginning to reconsider its 1940 spectrum allocations. As it often does, the commission attempted to determine the sense of the industry about a given problem, and it requested broadcasters to coordinate their views concerning frequency allocations. As a result, the Radio Technical Planning Board (RTPB), an advisory committee of industry engineers, under the chairmanship of W. R. G. Baker of General Electric, was established in late 1943. The task of the RTPB was to recommend an allocation of frequencies, taking into account such problems as the burgeoning demands of television for additional spectrum space. Panels were established for the various broadcast services, and after much consideration Panel Five on FM, under the chairmanship of C. M. Jansky, Jr., a consulting engineer, voted 19 to 4 against recommending a shift in FM allocations to a higher band. The panel concluded that there was no technical proof that skywave interference would be reduced if FM were shifted to a different frequency location.[4] Changes were proposed, however, which would considerably expand the existing band to allow seventy-five commercial FM channels in the 41 to 56 mc. range. This change would have added greatly needed channels to FM while not rendering existing equipment obsolete.

Despite RTPB's recommendations for continued low band FM the commission unanimously issued a report on January 15, 1945, suggesting that FM be reestablished in the frequencies between 84 and 102 mc. In a statement accompanying the report the FCC rejected the conclusions of the RTPB and discounted the efforts of FM broadcasters and the extent of FM set sales up to that time. Using the convenient justification of the "public interest," the commission declared, "Public interest requires that FM be established in a permanent place in the radio spectrum before a considerable investment is made by the listening public in receiving sets and by the broadcasters in transmitting equipment."[5]

The FCC believed that the technical need to move FM into a region free of skywave interference far outweighed the economic readjustments which such a shift would require. However, its expectation that FM would be technically superior in the higher band was not shared by the chief proponents of FM. *Broadcasting* magazine, the day following the commission's January 15 report, commented that "no clairvoyance is needed to deduce that there will be a storm of protest from Major E. H. Armstrong and his disciples for booting FM up the spectrum on grounds of interference."[6]

The technical case against low-frequency FM (on which the commission based its decision) rested largely on the testimony of K. A. Norton of the Signal Corps. Norton believed that "sporadic E" and "F_2 layer" interference would plague FM in the next few years at its present frequency as the sunspot maximum approached. In its *Annual Report for 1945* the commission referred to such factors as "ground wave coverage, skywave interference, transmitting and receiving equipment, present investment, and other matters of a minor character" (p. 20). The exact nature of the "other matters" was not specified. Norton testified under a cloak of military secrecy, making it difficult to rebut his testimony. During Senate Commerce

Committee hearings on the progress of FM radio in 1948, Senator Tobey expressed "a sense of outraged feelings and indignation" about the Norton testimony and later reports based upon it. Indeed, there were serious shortcomings in the 1944 testimony on propagation at various frequencies. In the mid-1930s Marconi had performed experiments demonstrating that signals in the 40–100 mc. band could be picked up at a greater distance than "theory" would predict—even as late as 1944.

The Norton testimony was generally accepted as true. And, since everybody agreed that moving FM in a few years would be much worse than changing the band before expanded postwar service began, it was argued that such a frequency shift should be undertaken at once. Based on its perception of the political and economic costs of a later move, the commission felt compelled to make an immediate decision even though conclusive technical data were not yet available.

It is very difficult to judge the merits of the technical arguments of the antagonists in this battle. FCC and industry engineers stated that they were simply trying to give FM the best possible frequencies for broadcasting,[7] yet Major E. H. Armstrong and others who had fought hardest to see FM develop as a wide-band, high-fidelity, static-free service wanted FM to stay in the "interference-ridden" lower band. The dispute seems to have revolved on the weight to be given projections of *future* interference. On the one hand, FCC engineers expressed great fear about a dramatic increase in low-frequency FM problems in future years; on the other, Major Armstrong held that "we can't predict sunspot interference."[8] This debate was carried out in papers submitted to the 1945 Institute of Radio Engineers Convention by Norton, Armstrong, and E. W. Allen of the FCC's Technical Information Division, and it came to a head in conflicting technical testimony offered at an FCC hearing on February 28 of that year. C. M. Jansky, Jr., chairman of RTPB Panel Five, told the commission they could "believe Norton and the errors he has made" or "Dellinger, Beverage, and Armstrong," three of the leading propagation experts in the country.[9] The errors noted by Jansky were mistakes in Norton's figures which Armstrong pointed out, and ones which Norton admitted as errors in November 1947.[10] At the time, however, the commission was inclined to accept, as the factual basis for its FM decisions, testimony based on classified (and hence unquestioned) propagation data because of Norton's standing as the FCC's former assistant chief engineer on wartime loan to the Signal Corps.

Between January and May 1945 the commission held numerous hearings on frequency allocations for FM and other services. Those testifying or filing briefs for the FM move included manufacturers committed to speedy development of TV (Philco, Crosley, Motorola, and Hallicrafters), the three national radio networks all preparing to enter extensively into TV, the Television Broadcasters Association, and individual television broadcasters. Those opposed to changing the FM frequencies included RTPB Panel Five, Major Armstrong, FM Broadcasters, Inc., an established FM regional network (the Yankee Network), manufacturers with FM interests (Zenith, General Electric, and Stromberg-Carlson), and individual FM broadcasters. Throughout this time, however, the commission continued its official position that it had not made a final decision concerning FM allocations and that its proposed allocations of January 15 were only suggestions for the purpose of eliciting comments from the affected parties.[11] This, of course, is a very useful position for any launcher of a trial balloon.

On May 16, 1945, the FCC made final allocations for all spectrum space being considered *except* the 44–108 mc. band. The commission announced that it was considering three alternatives for FM, all of which would entail a shift from its present assignments: 50–68 mc., 68–86 mc., or 84–102 mc. (the proposal of January 15).[12] Each of these plans would give FM 18 mc. instead of the then existing 8 mc., thereby providing more than double the number of possible stations; however, each proposal also would entail a shift of FM into an entirely new band. In effect, the commission was ruling that FM broadcasting would have to start anew, thereby rendering 500,000 FM radios obsolete.

In its May 16, 1945, announcement the commission indicated that it would defer a final decision until the completion of a summer-long series of propagation studies. Since 90 percent of sporadic E occurs during the summer months, this seemed a favorable time to determine the effect of such interference on FM at various frequencies. The FCC felt it had the time for these tests since the War Production Board had given its assurance that production of AM, FM, and TV transmitters or receivers would not be possible during 1945 and was unlikely during the first quarter of 1946.[13] Subsequently, however, the War Production Board reversed itself and advised the commission that the manufacture of AM, FM, and TV transmitters might begin at a much earlier date than originally indicated. Thus the anticipated ending of the war made it necessary for the commission to come to an immediate decision on FM allocations. The data which had been developed to date suddenly became the basis for decision—without the proposed FM propagation studies.

One significant change in the pattern of forces occurred at this point. The Television Broadcasters Association (TBA) and the FM Broadcasters, Inc. aligned for the first time and, with the chairmen of RTPB Panel Two (allocations), Panel Five (FM), and Panel Six (TV) as well as eleven manufacturers of FM receivers, requested the adoption of the first alternative—the 50-68 mc. band—for FM.[14] Despite the position of the TBA, however, most interests favoring speedy television development continued to support a shift of FM to a higher band and the use of the lower frequencies for television. The late alliance in favor of low-band FM did not succeed, for pressure for a quick resolution of this allocations problem forced the FCC to revert to its earlier stand favoring high-frequency FM. Consequently, in a surprise move on June 27, 1945, the commission, by unanimous vote, allocated 92-106 mc. for commercial FM[15] and rejected the second alternative (68-86 mc.) as "completely unfeasible." The commission based its decision against the widely supported first alternative on the assumption that "the region of the spectrum above 84 megacycles is markedly superior to the region below 68 megacycles with respect to sporadic E." The commission said that it would not propose to provide "an inferior FM service during the decades to come merely because of the transitory advantage which may be urged for an inferior type of service."[16]

By justifying its action on the basis of the long-range technical interests of FM, the commission drew upon general support for long-range planning in broadcast regulation and thereby made opposition to its goal of technical perfection seem shortsighted and greedy. The decision to evict FM from the 44 mc. band on grounds of the undesirability of those frequencies, however, appears contradictory in light of the subsequent assignment of the same frequencies to TV—which is far more susceptible to interference than FM—and later to the land mobile services—such as police and fire department radios, where static-free service is even more crucial.[17]

Major Armstrong's immediate reaction to the decision was one of resignation: "The allocation has been handed down. Now it's up to all of us to do everything we can to have a service ready for the people at the earliest possible moment."[18] Armstrong, nevertheless, continued to seek limited use of the 40 mc. band for a few regional FM stations and FM intercity relay. He was also unsuccessful in this endeavor.

Congress took no meaningful action while the FCC was considering the FM shift.[19] Senator Burton K. Wheeler, chairman of the Senate Commerce Committee, told *Broadcasting* magazine that the allocation of frequencies is generally a technical matter and that Congress gave the commission full authority to allocate frequencies.[20] The technical nature of the dispute, together with the unquestioned authority of the commission to act in this area, made congressional involvement unlikely in the actual decision-making process. Major congressional investigations did occur later, but not until 1947, and their main function was to review what had already occurred. Safety and special broadcasting services had occupied the 40–50 mc. band by that time, and all FM could hope for as a result of congressional activity was the possibility of a few high-powered relay stations somewhere in the lower band.[21]

The FM shift impeded the growth of this new service for several crucial years while TV developed. In many respects, FM's history can be seen as the story of its rivalry with TV; two innovations were competing for public acceptance (as well as frequency allocations).[22] In the postwar years, the result of this struggle became evident—FM station authorizations fell and TV expanded. In its *Annual Report for 1949* (page 2) the commission noted "a sudden surge in TV applications and a leveling off of FM requests." Recognizing a further reduction in authorized FM stations in 1950, the FCC concluded that this decline "was largely due to economic problems and uncertainties occasioned by the rapid growth of television and the limited number of satisfactory FM receivers which have been purchased and placed in use."[23] Instead of the expansion anticipated in the late 1940s there was a gradual reduction in FM service[24] coupled with an extremely small sale of FM sets into the 1950s. Not until the late 1950s and early 1960s, with the high-fidelity boom and the development of FM stereo, did FM broadcasting achieve the stability and growth expected of it fifteen years earlier.

It can be argued that the FCC's policy crippled FM broadcasting at a crucial time. Although the shift provided space for more than twice the number of existing FM stations and thereby permitted the subsequent development of FM some twenty years later, such expansion of FM frequencies was also provided for in virtually all the frequency proposals considered by the FCC in 1945, including the various plans for low-frequency FM. The uprooting of FM from its existing band coupled with its reassignment to a band which was technically less desirable (at least in the eyes of FM's promoters) undercut the new service at a key time in its development. Perhaps the most generous assessment of the FCC's role in this case is that the commission initiated the proposal to shift FM out of genuine concern for the technical future of FM and a desire to provide additional broadcasting channels, but without realizing the destructive impact of such a move upon a developing service. Faced with an imperative to make a decision—any decision that could be legitimized—the commission settled on its initial proposal of high-frequency FM. This was a convenient choice for the FCC, which had been marshaling arguments in favor of this decision for some time, but it was the one least helpful to the future of FM.

The FCC was able to prevail largely because its policies favored powerful, well-established broadcasting interests pushing the development of postwar television. The development of FM broadcasting posed a triple threat—to the dominance of established AM stations and networks, to RCA's hopes for quick postwar development of TV, and to RCA's patents. Thus a delay in the expansion of FM, such as the one that resulted from the FM shift, may have seemed desirable to these interests. Fred W. Albertson, lawyer and broadcast engineer, believes that RCA wanted to suppress FM: "The best way to pull the rug out from under FM was to throw everything out the window and move the system upstairs. . . . There was a definite effort by RCA to oppose FM."[25] As early as the 1930s RCA had forced Armstrong to remove his experimental FM apparatus from the Empire State Building in order to make way for some experimental television equipment.[26]

Although the FCC's policy was suggested and justified on purely technical grounds, the potential economic effects were quite clear to most participants and, in fact, largely defined involvement in the dispute. However, the interests supporting low-band FM, such as the Yankee Network and the FM Broadcasters Association, were far fewer in number and less influential—in terms of their ability to obtain effective access to the FCC—than those well-established interests which stood to gain from the shift, such as RCA, television broadcasters, and television manufacturers. Those groups supporting low-frequency FM were mostly newcomers to broadcasting and as such were powerless to make demands on the FCC policy-making process. Appeals to other participants—such as to Congress or even the public—"to save FM" were unlikely to succeed because of the "purely technical" nature of the dispute. Moreover, none of the participants seriously questioned the legal authority (and functional duty) of the FCC to determine bands of frequencies to be used by various broadcast services. Consequently when the commission—under the pressure of time—unanimously adopted an earlier proposal based on faulty technical data, FM interests had little recourse but to accept the policy as authoritative. In effect, the feedback process was closed to them. The technical nature of the dispute made it impossible for these dissatisfied groups effectively to oppose a decision supposedly made "in the best interest of FM broadcasting."

Notes

[1] Quoted in FCC, *Annual Report for 1940* (Washington, D.C.: U.S. Government Printing Office, 1941), p. 66.

[2] Murray Edelman, *The Licensing of Radio Services in the United States, 1927 to 1947: A Study in Administrative Formulation of Policy* (Urbana: University of Illinois Press, 1950), p. 26.

[3] Lawrence Lessing, *Man of High Fidelity: Edwin Howard Armstrong* (New York: Lippincott, 1956), p. 256. Although a number of these sales would be to replace sets worn out during the war years, the vast majority would represent real expansion for FM.

[4] FCC, "Statement on FM Broadcast Service," in Docket No. 6651, January 15, 1945. Reprinted in *Broadcasting*, January 16, 1945, p. 17.

[5] Ibid., p. 17.

[6] "Allocation Proposals Announced by FCC," *Broadcasting*, January 16, 1945, p. 13.

[7] Washington interview with E. W. Allen, chief engineer of the FCC, October 18, 1965. In the FCC *Annual Report for 1945* the commission expressed the fear of "serious skywave interference nullifying to a great extent the possibilities of interference-free reception expected of FM" (p. 20).

[8] "Military to Confide Secret Data to Radio," *Broadcasting*, March 5, 1945, p. 67. *Broadcasting* observed that Norton's figures "have been attacked as 'theory' not based on fact but on his predictions of what the next sunspot cycle maximum will be." "Shifting of FM Upward in Spectrum Seen," *Broadcasting*, March 19, 1945, p. 18.

[9] *Broadcasting*, March 5, 1945, p. 66.

[10] W. Rupert Maclaurin, *Invention and Innovation in the Radio Industry* (Philadelphia: Macmillan, 1949), p. 231, and "Armstrong of Radio," *Fortune*, February 1949, p. 209. Although admitting the errors in his calculations, Norton has maintained over the years that these mistakes did not meaningfully affect his conclusions. See Kenneth A. Norton, *The Five-Dimensional Electromagnetic Spectrum: A Major Economic and Engineering Research Responsibility (or The Silent Crisis Screams)*, partially completed book manuscript, 1967, vol. II, appendix 21, especially pp. 21.27–21.29.

[11] "FCC Has Open Mind on FM and Television," *Broadcasting*, February 12, 1945, p. 15.

[12] "FM Decision Delayed as FCC Allocates," *Broadcasting*, May 21, 1945, p. 13. Each plan also recognized the "high-fidelity" nature of FM by assigning 100 kc for each station's channel, thus providing for a 15,000 cycles per minute frequency range. A narrower band would have limited FM to a 10,000 cycle range and thus made impossible FM's later development as part of the hi-fi boom. See Major E. H. Armstrong, "Discussion of Postwar Broadcasting," *FM and Television*, October 1944, p. 24.

[13] "FM Decision Delayed as FCC Allocates," p. 13.

[14] "WPB to Lift Construction Bans on V-J Day," *Broadcasting*, June 11, 1945, p. 15. Like the other plans, this alternative would have meant the obsolescence of all existing FM sets and transmitters; however, FM backers preferred the lower band for reasons of greater transmission distance for less cost and the possibilities of direct off-the-air relay for FM networks.

[15] 88–92 mc. were reserved, as they are today, for educational noncommercial broadcasting. 106–108 mc. were added to the FM band on August 24, 1945.

[16] "FCC Report on Allocations from 44 to 108 Megacycles," Docket No. 6651, June 27, 1945, reprinted in *Broadcasting*, July 2, 1945, pp. 64, 68.

[17] Lawrence P. Lessing, "The Television Freeze," *Fortune*, 40 (November 1949), 127. See also Lessing, *Man of High Fidelity*, p. 258.

[18] Quoted in "Industry Supporting Decision on FM Move," *Broadcasting*, July 9, 1945, p. 18.

[19] Neither the White House, preoccupied with the war, nor the courts, due to the apparent lack of ambiguity in the commission's legal authority, involved themselves in these events. The entry of citizens groups into the regulatory process was still a development far in the future.

[20] "FCC Allocates 88–106 Mc. Band to FM," *Broadcasting*, July 2, 1945, p. 13.

[21] Lessing, "The Television Freeze," 157.

[22] Maclaurin, *Invention and Innovation in the Radio Industry*, p. 230. See also Lessing, *Man of High Fidelity*. As early as 1940 Paul Porter, then legal counsel for CBS, who became chairman of the commission in 1944, stated that "if there is a conflict, as there appears to be in the allocation problem with respect to television and frequency modulation, it is the opinion of the Columbia Broadcasting System that preference should be given to the new public service of television rather than an additional system of aural broadcasting."

[23] FCC, *Annual Report for 1950* (Washington, D.C.: U.S. Government Printing Office, 1951), p. 109.

[24] From the 1946–1950 totals of 55, 238, 458, 700, and 733, the number of "on the air" FM stations began to drop in 1951 and 1952 to 676 and 637, hitting a low, in 1957, of 530 stations—the vast majority of which operated at a loss. Most of these stations did not contribute to program diversity since they simulcast the broadcasts of AM stations.

[25] Washington interview with Fred W. Albertson, October 19, 1965.

[26] See Lessing, *Man of High Fidelity*, pp. 219–223.

6

UHF Television: The Fading Signal Is Revived After Only Ten Years

One of the persistent problems plaguing the FCC throughout the 1950s and early 1960s was the midwifing of Ultra High Frequency (UHF) television. Introduced in 1952 on an intermixed basis with VHF stations (Channels 2 to 13) in the same markets, UHF television (Channels 14 and above) was unable to compete with VHF for advertisers or audience. Although the commission repeatedly expressed its concern during this period about the development of UHF television, it failed to implement any reliable plan for strengthening the infant medium. By 1961 the commission was faced with a failing broadcast service.

The roots of UHF's problems go back to 1945 when the commission allocated only thirteen VHF channels (subsequently cut to twelve) to serve all the needs of television. Its action rested on two assumptions: (1) that twelve VHF channels would fill TV's immediate needs and (2) that when UHF broadcasting became technically feasible, this new service could be introduced as either a supplement to, or a replacement for, VHF television. Neither of these assumptions, however, proved to be true. In 1952 the commission issued its *Sixth Report and Order* on television allocations, which rejected "all-UHF" television—either nationally or in selected areas—as economically disastrous for existing broadcasting. As a result, although authorized in the same report as a supplement to VHF television, UHF faced crippling competition from established, economically secure VHF stations.

Throughout the 1950s the FCC spent much time dealing with the consequences of this 1952 decision. UHF broadcasting did not prove economically feasible during this period, and the commission involved itself in a series of controversial, inconclusive, and ultimately unsuccessful moves to remedy this situation. Among these were: (1) the consideration and rejection, in 1954, of proposals for the "deintermixture"[1] of seven markets then assigned both VHF and UHF television—all of these to be made UHF; (2) the reconsideration, in March 1955, of five of these deintermixture proposals; (3) the decision, in November of that year, not to undertake deintermixture in these five cases—or in any of the thirty other proceedings which meanwhile had been initiated; (4) the statement, on January 20, 1956, that deintermixture was, of course, a very real possibility and that the FCC was still considering it; (5) the announcement, on June 25, 1956, of plans to deintermix thirteen markets (including five that were rejected twice before); and (6) the failure, during the period from 1956 to the 1960s, to implement deintermixture in even the majority of these thirteen cases.

Only five of the thirteen deintermixtures proposed in 1956 actually were carried out, and these did little to help the UHF industry generally. It is likely, moreover, that the lengthy debates and disputes over UHF during the 1950s served more to point out its sickness to advertisers and viewers than to relieve its problems.

By 1961 the condition of UHF had deteriorated to such an extent that some new initiative seemed required. The production of all-channel television sets—capable of receiving UHF as well as VHF channels—had fallen to a record low of 5.5 percent of all new sets, thus giving the 83 commercial UHF stations still on the air little hope of increasing their already tiny audiences.[2] Lack of audiences made UHF unattractive to advertisers, and lack of advertising revenue spelled an end to operations for many UHF broadcasters. These conditions greatly concerned the FCC in the Kennedy years, especially the commission's new chairman, Newton N. Minow, who had been outspoken about the need to counter the "vast wasteland" of TV's standardized programing fare through the development of additional channels offering program variety and diversity—channels that could come only through an unprecedented utilization of the UHF band.

Stimulated by these concerns and hopes for the future of UHF television, the commission announced, on July 27, 1961, a package proposal including such varied items as: (1) deintermixture of UHF and VHF in eight markets, (2) a "shoe-horning in" of new VHF assignments at less than the standard mileage separation in eight other cities, and (3) a request for congressional action on legislation authorizing the FCC to require that all new sets be capable of receiving both VHF and UHF signals.[3] The idea of dealing with

UHF problems by attacking the low level of all-channel receiver penetration was not new. Proposals had been made by the House Judiciary Committee during the 1950s for some type of legislative requirement that all new television sets be capable of receiving both VHF and UHF channels, and in 1957 Congressman Emanuel Celler had suggested that the heart of the problem was in the limited sales of TV sets with UHF receiving capabilities.[4]

If the combination package of the FCC's three different plans seems unwieldy and somewhat contradictory, it was because on specific proposals—such as that calling for renewed efforts at deintermixture—the commission was split 4 to 3 and was able to obtain a final unanimous vote on the package only by combining several items.[5] Such a combination of diverse proposals had one advantage which may have been anticipated by some FCC commissioners and staff: One part of the package could be easily jettisoned at a later time to aid the prospects of other parts of the package. Such, is, in fact, what happened. The FCC was, however, unanimous in deciding to request all-channel television legislation.[6]

The two most important elements of the 1961 package were the plans for renewed efforts at deintermixture and the request for all-channel television legislation. This combination created considerable fear that the FCC was moving toward an all-UHF television system. Dr. Frank Stanton of CBS confessed to feeling "nervous when the Commission talks about deintermixture at the same time it talks about all-channel sets."[7] Chairman Minow tried to calm such fears by pointing out that Robert E. Lee was the only commissioner who then favored a shift of all television to UHF—a possibility which Commissioner Lee himself later described as "an exercise in futility."[8]

While the combination of deintermixture and all-channel television made broadcasters nervous, deintermixture by itself distinctly alarmed them. Unlike the 1955 and 1956 proposals which would, in most cases, have eliminated VHF assignments unfilled as of 1956, the new proposals would move existing VHF stations to the UHF band. In an editorial on the new deintermixture proposals, *Broadcasting* magazine warned:

> There was a time—before the new VHF stations were built in single station markets—when deintermixture would have been workable with minimal injury to the public and broadcasters. Any change now may be a major wrench and we have the notion that the public will make itself heard.[9]

All eight members of the congressional delegation for the state of Connecticut, for example, opposed the proposal to shift Hartford's only VHF station to the UHF band.[10] By early 1962 *Broadcasting* reported that almost all senators and congressmen representing markets slated for deintermixture were against the plan.[11] Those industry groups opposed to deintermixture were to make good use of such congressional opposition.

During much of 1961, while controversy developed over deintermixture, little action occurred on all-channel television legislation. In late September 1961, however, Chairman Minow suggested that such a bill might resolve many of the same problems as deintermixture.[12] In January 1962 Minow announced that an all-channel television bill was the FCC's "chief legislative proposal of 1962."[13]

Bills designed to grant the commission the desired all-channel authority were introduced by Senator John Pastore of Rhode Island, chairman of the Senate Communications Subcommittee, and Representative Oren Harris of Arkansas, chairman of the House Interstate and Foreign Commerce Committee. Both bills gave the FCC authority to make rules requiring that television sets shipped in interstate commerce have the capacity to receive all channels—UHF as well as VHF—allotted to television. Hearings on this legislation were held by the Senate Commerce Committee in February 1962 and by the House Committee on Interstate and Foreign Commerce in March.

Much of the testimony at these hearings revolved around the topic of deintermixture rather than all-channel television. Many bills had been introduced to halt deintermixture, and strong sentiment seemed to exist in both Commerce Committees for a rider to any all-channel television bill which would specifically prohibit changes in existing VHF assignments designed to achieve the deintermixture of television markets. As *Broadcasting* concluded, "It was made clear in both the Senate and House Committee proceedings that there will be no all-channel bill without a commitment to forego deintermixture now."[14]

In an attempt to head off such a legislative prohibition Chairman Minow testified against any statutory moratorium on deintermixture proceedings: "Unless Congress wants to go into the frequency allocation business, we should be left free to make such decisions."[15] It soon became clear, however, that unless the commission abandoned its deintermixture plans, any all-channel receiver legislation which might pass would be certain to contain a provision prohibiting further deintermixture proceedings. Consequently, the commission, on March 16, sent Chairman Harris a letter stating:

> If the all-channel receiver television legislation is enacted by this Congress, it is the judgment of the Commission . . . that it would be inappropriate, in the light of this important new development, to proceed with the eight deintermixture proceedings initiated on July 27, 1961, and that, on the contrary, a sufficient period of time should be allowed to indicate whether the all-channel receiver authority would in fact achieve the Commission's overall allocations goals. . . . Before undertaking the implementation of any policy concerning deintermixture, the Commission would advise the Committee of its plans and give it an appropriate period of time to consider the Commission's proposals.[16]

Thus, in the words of Commissioner Robert E. Lee, "Congress in effect made a deal with the Commission—drop deintermixture, and we get the all-channel television bill."[17] Legislative support for the bill quickly increased and included a number of Representative Harris's committee members representing districts threatened by the commission's deintermixture proposal.[18] Thus the linking of deintermixture and all-channel television in the original 1961 package greatly enhanced the prospects of an all-channel television bill in 1962.

With the support of those opposing deintermixture the all-channel bill faced comparatively little opposition. Some congressmen had reservations about the "loss of freedom" involved in requiring people to purchase television sets equipped in a certain way, and vocal but isolated concern was expressed by the Electronic Industries Association about the rise in set costs—variously estimated as from $25 to $40 retail—which would result from having to include a UHF tuner on each set.[19] This opposition, however, was minor compared to the support for the bill by the President, industry groups such as the three networks, major manufacturers such as General Electric and RCA (despite the Electronic Industries Association stand), and several industry trade organizations, including the National Association of Broadcasters.

Favorably reported out of the House Committee on Interstate and Foreign Commerce on April 9, the bill passed the House by a vote of 279 to 90 on May 2. The Senate version was favorably reported by the Senate Commerce Committee on May 24, and was approved by the Senate by a voice vote on June 14. Minor differences between the Senate and House bills were settled in the House by a voice vote on June 29, and on July 10, 1962, President Kennedy signed the legislation into law. As the last stage in this process the FCC availed itself of its newly conferred authority on September 13, 1962, by instituting rule making to require that all television sets shipped in interstate commerce be all-channel television receivers.[20] This rule was adopted on November 23, 1962, to go into effect April 30, 1964.

In one respect the history of UHF is an exact reversal of the FM shift proceeding[21]: No one seemed to realize how *well* the all-channel television law would work.[22] Because of the boom in portable TV sets and the great growth in color TV sales, the percentage of all-channel receivers increased more quickly than anticipated.[23] By 1976, 92 percent of TV homes had UHF-VHF receivers.[24]

The politics of this controversy were rather curious, for, as has been suggested, the threat of deintermixture was the major reason that the All-Channel Receiver Bill passed in 1962. The opposition to deintermixture was particularly strong, since in every area considered for deintermixture in 1961, existing VHF stations would have been affected. This strong resistance to deintermixture was transformed into positive support for an alternative policy—the All-Channel Receiver Bill. Combining a highly unpopular measure with a proposal acceptable to VHF interests, then, ensured sufficient support for passage of the bill by Congress and its implementation by the commission—once the unpopular idea had been publicly dropped. In this controversy the interests of industry converged with those of the FCC. Broadcasters sought to avoid a repugnant policy at almost any cost, while the commission wanted to provide for diversity and additional competition in TV broadcasting. The result was a pattern of forces favoring the All-Channel Receiver Bill sufficient to ensure its adoption as definitive public policy.

The initiation of the request for action on all-channel receiver legislation came from the commission itself—although, as earlier noted, the idea of such legislation derived from a suggestion contained in the 1957 House Judiciary Committee report, "The Television Broadcasting Industry." The FCC, fresh from berating the television industry's "vast wasteland," took a renewed interest in UHF as a means of broadening program choice for viewers. In addition, the commission had been under pressure from the Senate Commerce Committee for more than five years to find some means of alleviating UHF's woes. The result of this commission interest and congressional pressure was the package of proposals on July 27, 1961. The subsequent focus on all-channel legislation as the chief means of UHF development, however, came about largely because it alone, of the various proposals, did not face immediate overwhelming opposition.

To obtain congressional support for all-channel set requirements, the commission gave up only a proposal on deintermixture, which was limited in applicability and backed by a slim majority of commissioners. In return, the FCC received authority to implement a policy which had favorable results beyond all expectations. In this sense those UHF investors and operators who had so long suffered financially "really won," for in the successful FCC initiative to obtain the manufacture and sale of all-channel sets, the means were found for at least the potential realization of long-held hopes for UHF television.

Notes

[1]"Deintermixture" involves the reallocation of television channel assignments so that each community would have either VHF or UHF stations. As a result of "deintermixture" a community would not have both VHF and UHF stations. Hence, viewers wanting to tune in the popular network programs would be forced to buy UHF converters; in "intermixed" markets (where both UHF and VHF channels were allocated), network affiliations invariably were awarded to VHF stations first, and many viewers settled for those signals rather than going to the additional expense of adding a converter.

[2]"Statistical Analysis, 1946–63: The Television Industry," table titled "The UHF Story," *TV Factbook No. 34 for 1964* (Washington, D.C.: Television Factbook, Inc., 1964), p. 38a. It should be noted that this all-channel receiver production figure of 5.5 percent was a national average, and in some areas, such as central Illinois, where major network service was provided largely or entirely by UHF stations, the all-channel set "penetration rate" was much higher—even up to 65 to 70 percent. These areas, however, were outnumbered by markets where network service was supplied by VHF stations, and UHF stations, if they existed at all, had but second-rate programs to broadcast to an audience largely unequipped to receive UHF transmission.

[3]FCC Public Notice: "Comprehensive Actions to Foster Expansion of UHF TV Broadcasting," July 28, 1961 (mimeo). See also *Broadcasting*, August 7, 1961, p. 54. Since the Communications Act did not explicitly

provide the FCC with authority to adopt uniform receiver standards, congressional legislation appeared necessary to require the manufacture of all-channel receivers.

[4] U.S. House, House Judiciary Committee, *Report of the Antitrust Subcommittee Pursuant to House Resolution 107 on the Television Broadcasting Industry*, 85th Congress, 1st Session (March 15, 1957), p. 9.

[5] Washington interviews with Commissioner Robert E. Lee, October 25, 1965, and Phil Cross, legal assistant to Commissioner Robert T. Bartley, October 25, 1965.

[6] U.S. Senate, Senate Commerce Committee, *Hearings on All-Channel Television Receivers*, 87th Congress, 2nd Session (February 20, 21, and 22, 1962), p. 31.

[7] "Is the FCC Ready to Take Half a Loaf?" *Broadcasting*, March 12, 1962, p. 44.

[8] Washington interview with Commissioner Lee, October 25, 1965.

[9] "Too Much Too Late?" *Broadcasting*, August 7, 1961, p. 114.

[10] "Hill Rallies to Save V's," *Broadcasting*, August 21, 1961, p. 50.

[11] "Richards Urges NAB Focus on Hill," *Broadcasting*, February 26, 1962, p. 56.

[12] "Parting Shot," *Broadcasting*, October 2, 1961, p. 4.

[13] This speech to the National Press Club on January 11, 1962, can be found in Newton Minow, *Equal Time: The Private Broadcaster and the Public Interest* (New York: Atheneum, 1964), chapter VI.

[14] "Wedding of the U's and V's," Editorial in *Broadcasting*, March 12, 1962, p. 106.

[15] "FCC's All-Channel Set Bill Falters," *Broadcasting*, February 26, 1962, p. 100. The legal right stressed here was the same as the one on which the FCC based its FM shift seventeen years earlier, namely, the commission's legal power to assign frequencies to the various broadcast services.

[16] U.S. House, House Committee on Interstate and Foreign Commerce, *All-Channel Television Receivers*, House Report No. 1559, 87th Congress, 2nd Session (April 9, 1962), pp. 19–20. The deintermixture proceedings were officially terminated on September 12, 1962.

[17] Interview with Commissioner Lee, October 25, 1965. One might ask why Congress and the broadcasting industry felt a "deal" was necessary— why wasn't, for example, a prohibition of deintermixture considered in the absence of an All-Channel Receiver Bill? The answer seems to be that the events of the early 1960s—including the quiz-show scandals, reports of improper industry-commission contacts, and the general stir over Chairman Minow's criticisms of television—had put the broadcasting industry and its congressional allies on the defensive. Thus, a purely negative response to the commission's attempts to alleviate the problems of UHF television seemed untenable.

[18] "House Passes Set Bill," *Broadcasting*, May 7, 1962, p. 50.

[19] "All-Channel Sets Minow's Goal," *Broadcasting*, January 15, 1962, p. 28. Contrary to these predictions, however, retail prices did not increase at all or increased only $5 or $7 per set. Washington interview with Jack Wyman, staff director of Consumer Products Division, Electronic Industries Association, October 20, 1965.

[20] FCC, "Notice of Proposed Rule Making," Docket No. 14769, September 13, 1962.

[21] In an intriguing linking of the FM and UHF cases considerable effort has been made in the 1970s by FM interests to secure passage of all-channel (AM-FM) *radio* legislation to enhance FM's growth. In 1974 the Senate passed such a bill, but a similar bill introduced in the House that would have applied only to car radios failed to receive clearance by the House Rules Committee. However, the parallels are not exact. The all-channel radio legislation primarily seeks a solution to the need for an AM-FM receiver in car radios, since today's FM radios are separate but equal to AM receivers. The UHF tuners, nondetent, or without click-stop dialing, are more difficult to use and discourage viewers from tuning in a UHF station. Also, the economics of UHF-VHF are not comparable. This time, *Broadcasting* magazine editorialized *against* all-channel receivers in the name of free enterprise.

[22] There was one observer, a few years later, who viewed the All-Channel Receiver Television Law as a mistake and suggested that if the law were not repealed (an action which he saw as unlikely in view of FCC inflexibility), it at least should not be strengthened. Douglas W. Webbink, "The Impact of UHF Promotion: The All Channel Television Receiver Law," *Law and Contemporary Problems*, 34 (Summer 1969), 535–561. Webbink argued that the law's primary effect was to provide a considerable subsidy to UHF stations (paid by consumers and manufacturers) with comparatively minor returns in terms of new stations and diversity of UHF programing.

[23] John Serrao of Kaiser Broadcasting, a company that had large investments in UHF television, credited color and portable television with much of the growth of UHF television, but also said, "We wouldn't have gone into UHF without the all-channel bill." Quoted in Morris J. Gelman, "'Up' as in Upward," *Television Magazine*, October 1965, p. 56. In 1977 Kaiser withdrew from UHF broadcasting, selling most of its stations to Field Communications.

[24] Arbitron Television Census, Fall 1976. An analysis of the FCC's annual financial statistics showed that in 1976, 68.4 percent of the UHF stations affiliated with a network showed a profit, whereas 63.9 percent of independent UHF stations were in the black. UHF network-affiliated stations had total revenues of $210 million, expenses of $155 million, and income of $27 million. Independent UHF stations had $217 million in revenues and $143 million in expenses for a profit of $38 million. "1976: The Biggest by Far for TV," *Broadcasting*, August 29, 1977, p. 26.

7

The Commercial
Time Fiasco

In the preceding two cases the FCC was struggling with problems arising from the development of new broadcast services— innovations that promised to alleviate the scarcity of existing AM radio and VHF television facilities. The controversy examined in this chapter is rather different, for in proposing to limit broadcast commercial time, the commission was attempting not to expand program variety but to regulate a scarce commodity.

On March 28, 1963, the FCC announced it was contemplating policies designed to control the number and frequency of advertisements broadcast by radio and television stations. Although later conceded by Chairman E. William Henry to have been "a radical departure from previous regulation in terms of procedure,"[1] the commission's concern about advertising abuses was not new in substance. In its 1946 statements entitled *Public Service Responsibility of Broadcast Licensees* (popularly known as the "Blue Book"), the FCC stated that in issuing and in renewing the licenses of broadcast stations particular consideration would be given to program service factors relevant to the public interest, including the elimination of excessive ratios of advertising time to program time.[2] The commission recognized the broadcasting industry's efforts at self-regulation; however, it found "abundant evidence" that the codes of the National Association of Broadcasters were being flouted by some stations and networks.[3] As late as 1963 less than half of all radio stations and less than three quarters of all television stations were code subscribers.[4] And, since the FCC had not actively pursued its early interest in advertising practices in the years between 1946 and 1963,[5] the commission's decision in 1963 was widely considered an unprecedented involvement by the government in an area traditionally left to broadcasters.

In this connection it is interesting to recall that Secretary of Commerce Herbert Hoover had strongly opposed all broadcast advertising, telling the First Annual Radio Industry Conference in 1922, "It is inconceivable that we should allow so great a possibility for service . . . to be drowned in advertising chatter." The industry representatives at this conference responded with a resolution "that advertising . . . be absolutely prohibited and that indirect advertising be limited to the announcement of the call letters of the station and the name of the concern responsible for the matter broadcasted."[6]

The commission, in its public notice of March 28, 1963, had not indicated a specific approach to the problem of overcommercialization. Although all seven commissioners agreed on the need for action, they were split on whether to regulate advertising on a case-by-case basis or to institute rule-making proceedings.[7] They did try to reach agreement on "a program for action to be taken before [initiating] the more bloodthirsty approach"[8]; however, these attempts at consensus failed. Consequently, in May 1963 the commission proposed (by a narrow vote of 4 to 3) the adoption of rules requiring all broadcasting stations to observe the limitations on advertising time contained in the NAB Radio and Television Codes.[9] The commission announced that it wanted to receive a broad cross section of comments and specifically invited the comments of all organizations and members of the public concerned about the broadcasting of commercial advertising.

The commission's decision to adopt existing industry codes rather than set its own standards was an interesting one. By proposing standards that the industry claimed to be following, the commission could argue that it was only trying to do the industry a favor. As reported by *Broadcasting*: "One of the appeals the NAB Codes have for Chairman Minow and some others in the agency is that they were drafted and adopted by the broadcasting industry, not imposed by the government."[10]

The incorporation of private industry standards should have made the commission's task easier; instead, it led to an attack by the industry on the adoption of any code standards for advertising time. One of the major advantages of the code, in the eyes of the industry, was the flexibility it provided the broadcaster who could not live with the time standards; he could just stay out.[11] If the FCC made these standards universal, this flexibility would be lost. In attacking the code, *Broadcasting* magazine editorialized that "no fixed rules can successfully be written to cover all kinds of time periods on all kinds of stations."[12] Both *Broadcasting* and its then companion *Television* magazine called upon NAB to scrap all code time standards on advertising.[13] By proposing to regulate advertising time and suggesting the adoption of NAB Code standards, the commission had, in the words of one broadcaster, "opened a hell of a big can of worms."[14]

Opposition to the commission's plans continued to increase. In late June 1963 the NAB voted to oppose commercial time limitations and formed committees of broadcasters in each state to contact congressmen.[15] The commission scheduled hearings on its proposals for December 9 and 10; however, the Subcommittee on Communications and Power of the House Committee on Interstate and Foreign Commerce anticipated this by holding earlier hearings on November 6, 7, and 8 on a bill, introduced by Subcommittee Chairman Walter Rogers, to prohibit the commission from adopting any rules governing the length or frequency of broadcast ads.[16] Testimony highly critical of the FCC was offered at these hearings by some thirty broadcasting and four congressional witnesses. Their objections, briefly summarized, were: (1) The commission was not empowered to make such rules; (2) the proposed rules would entail an undesirable increase in regulation; and (3) uniform standards for all stations would be undesirable. Support for the commission came mainly from poorly organized sources such as the League Against Obnoxious TV Commercials and the National Association for Better Radio and Television.

The Rogers bill, H.R. 8316, was unanimously approved by the House Interstate and Foreign Commerce Committee on November 18, in the absence of one committee member who opposed it. (Earlier in November an Appropriations Subcommittee of the Senate Appropriations Committee had added injury to insult by cutting $400,000 from the commission's fiscal 1964 budget request, while criticizing the FCC for straying into policy areas not intended by Congress.[17]) The Rogers bill was then sent to the floor of the House where it waited while the FCC held its planned hearings on December 9 and 10. These events prompted *Broadcasting* to report on December 16 that "the FCC's controversial commercial-time standards reached the end of the road last week, battered and all but friendless."[18]

The membership of the FCC had shifted during this time. Lee Loevinger joined the commission on June 10, 1963, filling the spot made vacant when Commissioner Henry was made chairman (following Chairman Minow's resignation). Without Minow, the commissioners were deadlocked 3 to 3, and commissioner Loevinger held the deciding vote. "I knew I had the vote, but Henry kept it bottled up," he said. Because the chairman kept the proposal from coming to a vote, Loevinger explained, "the false impression was given that the withdrawal [of the FCC proposal] was due to the Rogers bill."[19] Without Loevinger's support for the proposals of March and May 1963, however, there was no hope for their adoption, and, on January 15, 1964, when the commercial proposal was finally voted upon, the FCC unanimously terminated the rule-making proceedings.[20]

The House continued its deliberations on the Rogers bill in order to make sure the commission fully understood its feelings. On February 24, 1964, the NAB dispatched memos to all broadcast stations marked "URGENT URGENT URGENT": "Broadcasters should immediately urge their Congressmen by phone or wire *to vote for* H.R. 8316. . . . [A] vote for the bill is a vote of confidence in the broadcasters in his district. A vote against the bill would open the door to unlimited governmental control of broadcasting."[21] Three days later the House passed the Rogers bill by a resounding vote of 317 to 43.

No actions occurred on this bill in the Senate, and, in fact, it has been suggested that the Senate Commerce Committee would not have favored it.[22] Nevertheless, the episode was conclusive for the FCC. As Commissioner Lee summarized it, "For all practical purposes we will not attempt anything such as this in the conceivable future."[23] The adoption of rules limiting advertising, then, seemed unfeasible, but the question remained: Could the commission still regulate ads on a case-by-case basis? In its action of January 15, 1964, terminating the rule making, the commission had expressed its intention to examine new and renewal applications for advertising excesses, and Chairman Henry, in a speech early in February, promised that the commission would build policy in this area on a case-by-case basis "so that you will know and we will know what the rules of the game are to be."[24] By July 1964, however, Chairman Henry had lost the control of the commission on this issue to Loevinger (by 4 to 3), and *Broadcasting* reported, "Indications are that only the most extreme cases of overcommercialization will be brought to the Commission's attention."[25] According to Chairman Henry, the campaign against excessive advertising "almost came to a halt . . . until Ford was replaced by Wadsworth [in February 1965]. . . . Now we are questioning new applicants and renewals."[26] The departure of Chairman Henry from the commission in May 1966 made Nicholas Johnson, a newly appointed commissioner in June 1966, the possible swing man between Lee, Cox, and Wadsworth, who favored case-by-case scrutiny of excessive commercialization, and Chairman Hyde, Bartley, and Loevinger, who opposed such activity.

By June 1967 the commission's scrutiny of individual renewal applications had led one participant to charge that the FCC had revived its use of NAB standards on a case-by-case basis. The direction of commission activity in the post–1966 period was heavily toward a case-by-case consideration of commercial time abuses, with the FCC taking great care to avoid any appearance of making general rules. At present, rather than adopting a formal policy or rule setting allowable limits on commercials, the FCC attempts to influence the commercial practices of broadcasters by the standards it uses in processing applications for new stations, transfers, and renewal of licenses. The FCC has delegated authority to its staff to grant applications which propose a normal hourly maximum of eighteen minutes of commercials for radio stations and sixteen minutes for television stations. The guidelines on delegations of authority also allow the FCC staff to grant applications which specify that these normal commercial limitations will be exceeded under certain special circumstances (such as during political campaigns).

The commission had tried in 1963 to institute a bold policy for the regulation of broadcasting.[27] That it failed to implement this policy, however, can be attributed not only to industry pressure and to the massive congressional opposition which developed but also to the inability of the initial majority of four in 1963 to convert any of the other three commissioners to their cause. Not one of these men shifted his position, and the policy initiative consequently lost following the presidential appointment of a fourth man, in the middle of 1963, who did not support the establishment of commercial time limits. The confusion over the legal authority exercised by the commission, the differing value preferences held by the major participants in the regulatory process, the very definite economic interests at stake in the regulation of advertising, and the opposition of a united industry and militant House added to the difficulties facing the proposed policy. Perhaps the clearest result of the commission's decision to abandon across-the-board rules on over-commercialization was the loss suffered by the FCC itself, not in terms of changes in its statutory authority, but in terms of a political reversal.

Notes

[1] Washington interview with Chairman E. William Henry, October 22, 1965.

[2] Federal Communications Commission, *Public Service Responsibility of Broadcast Licensees* (Washington, D.C.: U.S. Government Printing Office, 1946), p. 55.

[3] Ibid., p. 43.

[4] Newton N. Minow, *Equal Time: The Private Broadcaster and the Public Interest* (New York: Atheneum, 1964), p. 25.

[5] See Richard J. Meyer, "Reaction to the 'Blue Book'," *Journal of Broadcasting*, 6 (Fall 1962), 295–312; and his "'The Blue Book'," *Journal of Broadcasting*, 6 (Summer 1962), 197–207.

[6] Quoted in Murray Edelman, *The Licensing of Radio Services in the United States, 1927 to 1947: A Study in Administrative Formulation of Policy* (Urbana: University of Illinois Press, 1950), pp. 83–84. Historian Eric Barnouw writes that Herbert Hoover, when he was secretary of commerce, said that "'If a presidential message ever became the meat in a sandwich of two patent medicine advertisements, it would destroy broadcasting.' When Hoover died on October 20, 1964, NBC broadcast a tribute which was at once followed at its key station by a beer commercial, a political commercial and a cigarette commercial. The ex-President was triple-spotted into eternity." *Tube of Plenty, The Evolution of American Television* (New York: Oxford University Press, 1975), p. 357.

[7] Washington interview with Chairman Henry, October 22, 1965.

[8] Personal letter from former FCC Commissioner Frederick Ford, June 16, 1967.

[9] In 1962 a similar proposal to adopt the NAB Codes had been rejected by a 4 to 3 vote. Commissioners Minow, Henry, and Lee voted in the minority, and Commissioners Hyde, Bartley, Ford, and Craven in the majority. The replacement of Commissioner Craven by Cox in late March 1963 swung the vote in May the other way with Minow, Henry, Lee, and Cox now constituting the majority.

[10] "Commission May Put Ceiling on Commercials," *Broadcasting*, April 1, 1963, p. 84. However, Commissioner Ford contended that the FCC's adoption of the NAB Code would undermine the desire for self-regulation: "What would be the use of trying if Government is going to move in and make industry's efforts at self-regulation a matter of law? There would be no incentive, self-regulation would be destroyed, and the benefits of a very valuable regulatory tool would be lost." Speech before the Convention of the National Religious Broadcasters, January 23, 1963.

[11]*Broadcasting* stated that "some stations are known to have stayed out of the Code because they cannot command high enough rates to make a living from the number of commercials now permitted per program period." "Is This the Way Out of the Trap?" *Broadcasting*, June 17, 1963, p. 34.

[12]Editorial in *Broadcasting*, December 23, 1963, p. 78.

[13]Editorials in *Broadcasting*, June 3 and July 1, 1963; and *Television*, January 1964.

[14]Quoted in "Now a Crisis in the Radio-TV Codes," *Broadcasting*, May 27, 1963, p. 27.

[15]"NAB Boards Resolve to Fight Back," *Broadcasting*, July 1, 1963, p. 44.

[16]U.S. House of Representatives, House Committee on Interstate and Foreign Commerce, *Hearings on Broadcast Advertisements*, 88th Congress, 1st Session (November 6, 7, and 8, 1963). Robert Lewis Shayon of the *Saturday Review* noted: "Congressmen who want the FCC to handle limitation of commercials on a case-by-case basis know that the Commission is made least effective this way. Its standards become loose and lack uniformity." "Forecast for the FCC," *Saturday Review*, January 11, 1964, p. 51.

[17]"Where It Hurts," *Broadcasting*, November 11, 1963, p. 5.

[18]"FCC Unhorsed in Commercial Crusade," *Broadcasting*, December 16, 1963, p. 38.

[19]Washington interview with Commissioner Loevinger, October 25, 1965. Chairman Henry agrees with him that "the shift in personnel shifted the policy by a shift in votes—not Congressional action." Washington interview with Chairman Henry, October 22, 1965.

[20]Although the official vote was unanimous, it must be remembered that the sentiment of the commissioners was split 4 to 3. Washington interview with Phil Cross, legal assistant to Commissioner Robert T. Bartley, October 25, 1965.

[21]Quoted in Eric Barnouw, *The Image Empire: A History of Broadcasting in the United States*, vol. III—from 1953 (New York: Oxford University Press, 1970), p. 251.

[22]Washington interviews with Nicholas Zapple, counsel to the Senate Commerce Committee, October 21, 1965, and FCC Chairman Henry, October 22, 1965.

[23]Washington interview with Commissioner Robert E. Lee, October 25, 1965.

[24]Remarks of Chairman E. William Henry before The Advertising Federation of America, February 4, 1964 (mimeo), p. 4.

[25]"FCC Again Rebuffs Chairman," *Broadcasting*, July 27, 1964, p. 34.

[26]Washington interview with Chairman Henry, October 22, 1965.

[27]The initiation of the policy within the commission came from Commissioner Lee, who said that the idea for the proposed regulation came from a broadcaster. Personal letter from Commissioner Lee, June 14, 1967. In a broader view, however, the policy grew out of a perceived need—especially vivid to New Frontier commissioners such as Minow and Henry—to meet the problems of advertising excesses.

8

Comparative License Renewal Policies: The Nonindependence of an Independent Regulatory Agency*

Few broadcasting policy areas have been as turbulent in recent years as the one involving comparative broadcast renewal proceedings. Such hearings arise when, every three years, an established broadcaster asks the FCC to renew his license to run the station only to face opposition from a competitor applying for the same license.[1] (The FCC conducts licensing hearings in three types of situations: (1) when determining whether or not to renew the license of an existing television or radio station, even though that license is not being sought after by other parties [such hearings are not usual, since most licenses are renewed without hearing]; (2) when there are several competing applications for a *new* broadcast station; and (3) when there are competing applicants for an *existing* station—the area where most of the controversy has arisen.) Since only one party can broadcast on a given frequency, the FCC must make a difficult choice. Two FCC commissioners, borrowing from Sir Winston Churchill, referred to this choice, as it involves competing applicants for an existing station, as

> a riddle within an enigma within a conundrum. The riddle: by what standards is a renewal applicant to be measured. The enigma: by what standards is a renewal challenger to be measured. The ultimate conundrum of course is, even assuming the measurement of such respective

*We are grateful to Dr. Herbert A. Terry of the Department of Telecommunications, Indiana University, for his major assistance in the revision of this chapter.

standards, how can there be constructed a matrix which can be used to rationally measure and compare two largely unrelatable properties: an empirical property (an existing record) and an a priori property (a set of applicant pledges)?[2]

Prior to 1969 the riddle, enigma, or conundrum simply did not exist. That is not to say that there were no judicial or FCC precedents governing broadcast license renewal procedures. In 1945 the Supreme Court, in *Ashbacker Radio Corp.* v. *FCC*, held that constitutional due process requires an opportunity for all competing applicants for a *new* broadcast station to have a full comparative hearing before the FCC.[3] Then in 1949, in *Johnston Broadcasting Co.* v. *FCC*, the U.S. Court of Appeals for the District of Columbia ruled that the FCC must consider every material difference between two applicants in a comparative hearing.[4] However, the issue of competing applicants for an existing license was not an explicit issue in this case, nor was it in the Ashbacker case.

One of the earliest FCC policy statements governing competing applicants for an *existing* station was issued in 1951 when the commission voted to renew the license of WBAL, Baltimore. In the WBAL case the FCC reaffirmed its position that in a comparative hearing for an *existing* station the past performance of a broadcaster is the most reliable indicator of future performance.[5] A good past record is determinative, the FCC found, despite the newcomer's promise of a better showing on such factors as integration of ownership and management, local residence, and diversification.

In 1965 the commission issued a major policy statement on comparative hearings involving applications for *new* stations.[6] This statement stressed the importance of such factors as diversification, integration of ownership and management, and local residence. The FCC also stated that the past record of performance of a broadcast station that is one of the applicants in a comparative hearing for a new station would be of interest to the commission only if it was either "unusually good" or "unusually bad." Several months later the commission expanded this policy statement in a case in which two applicants had challenged the incumbent licensee. In the case of *Seven League Productions, Inc.*, the FCC decided that its policy statement on competing applicants for a *new* station should govern the introduction of evidence, though not the weight to be given particular factors, in proceedings where there is a competitive challenge to an existing station.[7]

This reliance on the incumbent's record of performance erected a barrier so formidable to potential competing applicants that the commission was forced to decide just one comparative renewal case between 1952 and 1969. In that case, involving the Wabash Valley Broadcasting Corp. (WTHI-TV), the commission did not even try to factor the incumbent's past performance into the overall comparative decision. Instead, the commission compared Wabash with its challenger on standard criteria but disregarded those criteria showing shortcomings in Wabash which were created by FCC policy shifts since Wabash had been licensed originally. Wabash won renewal largely upon its past broadcast record.[8] The wall protecting incumbent broadcasters from successful challenges by newcomers seemed as solid as ever.

That barrier was shaken, however, on January 22, 1969, when the FCC, by a vote of 3 to 1, refused to renew the license of Boston's WHDH-TV and instead gave the license to a competing applicant.[9] The decision aroused great anxiety in the broadcast industry. For the first time in its history the FCC had refused to renew the license of a broadcast station that had an "average" record of performance, and it had awarded the license to an applicant which, reportedly, would be more actively involved in the station's operation and would add to the diversity of control over mass communications media in the area.

Three years later the Herald-Traveler Corporation asserted before the Supreme Court that loss of its authority to operate WHDH would jeopardize the jobs of 2,600 employees of the Boston *Herald-Traveler* and would mean the death of the newspaper. In March 1972, after all legal appeals had been exhausted, the Herald-Traveler Corporation was forced to relinquish control of the station. A few months later the newspaper stopped publication and its assets were sold to a competitor.

The FCC's action was obviously of great consequence to the communications media in the Boston area, yet for the broadcasting industry it portended something far more threatening: Broadcasters holding immensely valuable licenses might lose them in competitive hearings at renewal time.

The initial reaction to the FCC's WHDH decision in 1969 was one of confusion and shock. The FCC vote itself—involving only four of the seven commissioners—was described by the trade press as "strange" and "weird."[10] The three-man majority consisted of

Commissioners Robert Bartley, Nicholas Johnson, and James Wadsworth (who was generally regarded as a moderate or a conservative). Commissioner Kenneth Cox, on the other hand, did not participate because he had dealt with the case when he was chief of the Broadcast Bureau. Commissioner H. Rex Lee was absent, visiting El Salvador on an educational television matter. Chairman Rosel Hyde abstained, issuing an unusual statement to the effect that he could not make up his mind![11] The position of Commissioner Robert E. Lee, however, was clear: He had provided the lone dissenting vote. Some industry observers, seeking a bright side to the decision, felt that the voting lineup was unique: "Hyde normally will vote to let [a] satisfactory operator keep [his] station; Wadsworth may revert to [a] similar view in other cases; no one knows which way Rex Lee might go; even Cox isn't absolutely rigid on this front—though he likes to keep pressure on licensees."[12]

Confusion also resulted from both the majority and the various concurring and dissenting statements in the WHDH case. The majority decision noted that the case was an unusual one, involving a challenge by three applicants against WHDH, which had never received a regular three-year renewal because of charges by the Department of Justice in the late 1950s and early 1960s of improper private conferences between the station's former president and the then chairman of the FCC. In his dissenting opinion, however, Commissioner Robert E. Lee commented that he was "very much afraid that this decision will be widely interpreted as an absolute disqualification for license renewal of a newspaper-owned facility in the same market. Competing applications can be anticipated against most of these owners at renewal time."[13] In a similar vein (but from the opposing viewpoint) Commissioner Johnson's concurring statement concluded: "The door is thus opened for local citizens to challenge media giants in their local community at renewal time with some hope for success before the licensing agency where previously the only response had been a blind reaffirmation of the present license holder."[14]

The WHDH decision was immediately attacked by those who feared that the stability of the broadcast industry would be threatened by license renewal challenges. Professor Louis L. Jaffe of Harvard Law School, for example, characterized the decision as a "desperate and spasmodic lurch toward 'the left'" which "overrules an administrative practice of at least eighteen years standing" and probably places "all licensees at hazard every three years, a proposition which would work a revolution in the industry and cause serious problems of financing."[15] In an article entitled "$3 Billion in Stations Down the Drain?" *Broadcasting* magazine asserted that the potential impact of the WHDH decision and related FCC proposals aimed at promoting greater diversity of control of mass media "could jeopardize broadcast holdings that, in the top 50 markets alone, are valued at more than $3 billion. . . . [T]he shockwaves of the losses would be felt by thousands of big and small stockholders alike, threatening the financial underpinnings of the broadcast industry and possibly swamping many small broadcast groups."[16] In an accompanying editorial *Broadcasting* commented that "Congress has become the broadcasters' only real hope for a restoration of order in an FCC that has clearly gone out of control."[17]

Whether the FCC had intended its decision with respect to WHDH to be a special case or the initiation of a broad new policy on license renewal challenges will not be discussed here. The importance of the precedent-shattering WHDH decision lies in the sequence of political events it triggered. It stimulated widespread controversy in the broadcasting industry, the Congress, the White House, and among citizens groups. A year later it led to the FCC's adoption, under pressure from Congress and the broadcasting industry, of a policy statement on license renewal challenges. (Seventeen months later, that statement itself would be overturned by the courts.) Most importantly, it provoked a whirlwind of lobbying and legislative activity intended to safeguard the interests of broadcast licensees.

Shortly after the release of the WHDH decision the National Association of Broadcasters began a lobbying campaign to obtain congressional passage of a bill that would prevent the FCC from considering competing applications when acting on the renewal application of a licensee. Senator John Pastore, chairman of the Communications Subcommittee and one of the most influential members of Congress in broadcasting matters, delighted broadcasters at the NAB convention in March 1969 by his remarks on harassment at license renewal time:

> It is my deep-seated conviction that public service is not encouraged nor promoted by placing the sword of Damocles over the heads of broadcasters at renewal time. The broadcaster must have reasonable assurance that if he does his job—and does it well—he's going to remain in business and not have his investment go down the drain.[18]

At the NAB convention, broadcasters met with Clay Whitehead and Abbott Washburn, then White House staff aides, and urged them to push for legislation on license renewal changes and the appointment of sympathetic commissioners to replace Rosel Hyde and Kenneth Cox.[19]

On April 29, 1969, Senator Pastore introduced S. 2004, which would amend Section 309 of the Communications Act to provide that the FCC could not consider competing applications for a license at renewal time unless it had first found, based on the licensee's renewal application, "that a grant of the application of a renewal applicant would not be in the public interest, convenience and necessity."[20]

By the time that the commission acted on requests for rehearing by the parties in the WHDH case, over fifty-five representatives in the House had introduced bills identical or similar to S. 2004.[21] In a decision on May 19, 1969, the FCC denied the rehearing requests but also emphasized that the WHDH proceeding was unique since, for reasons stemming from circumstances surrounding the original grant, the existing licensee of WHDH was "in a substantially different posture from the conventional applicant for renewal of broadcast license."[22]

In June 1969 *Television Digest* reported that, as a result of a massive lobbying campaign by the industry following the WHDH decision, the prospects were bright for congressional passage of S. 2004.[23] In addition to Pastore sponsors of S. 2004 included Senators Mike Mansfield, majority leader; Warren Magnuson, chairman of the Commerce Committee; Norris Cotton, ranking minority member on the Commerce Committee; and Hugh Scott, ranking minority member on the Communications Subcommittee.

Hearings on S. 2004 were held by the Senate Communications Subcommittee on August 5, 6, and 7, 1969. During the three days of hearings all but one of the witnesses testified in favor of S. 2004. Those supporting the bill included broadcasters from Rhode Island, Nebraska, Utah, and Pennsylvania, the President of the Federal Communications Bar Association, the General Manager of the American Newspaper Publishers Association, and the Dean of Temple University's School of Communications. Testifying in opposition was Earle K. Moore, general counsel of the National Citizens Committee for Broadcasting.

At this point, however, a combination of events and circumstances impeded the momentum of the broadcasters' campaign and raised doubts among many congressmen, including several sponsors of S. 2004, about the wisdom of the bill. During August the hearings were cut short because of the lengthy Senate antiballistic missile debate and the Senate's late summer recess. Other pressing business subsequently forced postponement of the resumption of hearings (which had been tentatively rescheduled for the middle of September),[24] and they were finally reconvened in December. During the intervening months minority groups were increasingly active in protesting the grant of license renewals of television stations which they contended cater almost exclusively to white, middle-class viewers. Also, articles appeared in the *New York Times*, *Harper's*, and *Time* magazine that were critical of S. 2004. An unsigned billboard appeared on Sunset Boulevard in Los Angeles:

> Watch for this coming subtraction!
> S. 2004
> Freedom's closing number brought
> to you by
> ABC, CBS & NBC Television.[25]

At the time of the Pastore hearings in August 1969 six of the seven FCC commissioners were opposed to S. 2004. However, in October 1969 President Nixon appointed to the commission Dean Burch, a former administrative assistant to Senator Barry Goldwater, and Robert Wells, a Kansas broadcaster, both favorable to this type of legislation. At the confirmation hearings for Burch and Wells, Senator Pastore said he was irked by the "cliché" that S. 2004 was tantamount to giving licensees a license in perpetuity. This cliché, he said, "sounds good, very dramatic, but I am surprised so many people are beginning to believe it. It was never intended as that."[26]

When congressional hearings resumed on December 1, 1969, members of Black Efforts for Soul in Television (BEST) were picketing NAB offices in Washington, New York, and Los Angeles and network-owned stations in Boston, Chicago, Philadelphia, and San Francisco to protest S. 2004 as a form of "backdoor racism," a "Congressional charade." The picketers read the following statement:

This bill represents backdoor racism because it is a subtle, and therefore more vicious, attempt to limit the efforts of the black community to challenge the prevailing racist practices of the vast majority of TV stations. . . . The Pastore bill . . . attempts to keep the media safely in the grips of monopolistic and politically selfish private white owners. It would deny black citizens the opportunity to demonstrate their ability to manage a TV station in a manner more consistent with the public interest than the station's present white owners. . . . Sen. Pastore seeks to protect the media barons who operate to satisfy their personal economic greed.[27]

The mood of the December hearings is perhaps best illustrated by one heated exchange between Senator Pastore and the audience. "When you say I introduced a racist bill you offend me," the senator shouted. "The one thing I don't want you people to do is go away and say this is a racist bill!" Blacks in the audience shouted back: "It is, it is!"[28] Senator Pastore was shocked and cited his strong civil rights record whenever a witness intimated that S. 2004 was a racist bill. "I'm not a patsy for the broadcasting industry. I'm nobody's patsy." Pastore also got into a shouting match with John Banzhaf, head of Action on Smoking and Health, who charged: "The bill which bears your name is unnecessary, unfair and unworthy of the support of any Senator . . . and even its consideration at this time is a waste of the Committee's time and a gross misallocation of its resources."[29] The lack of interest and support by other members of the subcommittee was evidenced by the fact that Pastore was often the only senator present at the December hearings.

On December 1, 1969, the FCC testified in opposition to S. 2004. Commissioner Robert Bartley, as the senior commissioner voting for the FCC's majority position, presented the majority statement, noting that it was originally adopted by a vote of 6 to 1 (before Burch and Wells succeeded Hyde and Wadsworth) but now could claim only a 4 to 3 majority. Bartley said that the commission did not support the bill because it "is unnecessary and would, in our opinion, have significant disadvantages to the public interest."[30] The majority statement emphasized that "the spur to a lagging broadcaster posed by the threat of competitors at renewal time is an important factor in securing operation in the public interest."

Concurring statements were delivered by Commissioners Cox, H. Rex Lee, and Johnson. In a forty-nine-page attack on S. 2004, Commissioner Johnson accused the "hear-no-evil-see-no-evil-speak-no-evil" leaders of the NAB of "taking the broadcasters themselves—jovial, prosperous, and martini in hand—down a jungle road into the longest ambush from an outraged citizenry ever unleashed upon an unsuspecting American industry." He questioned whether S. 2004 was constitutional since it would place "restrictions upon the ease with which individuals or groups could enter the field of broadcasting." Johnson contended that "S. 2004 may easily do more to continue racism in this country than any other single piece of legislation now pending before the Congress" and warned that "its passage will leave a frustrated people with no recourse except perhaps to engage in more violent protests and other actions that serve the interests of no one."

Dissenting statements were given to the subcommittee by Chairman Burch, Robert E. Lee, and Wells. Burch's testimony was significant because he suggested the following language as a substitute for the Pastore bill:

> In any comparative hearing within the same community for the frequency or channel of an applicant for renewal of a broadcast license, the applicant for renewal of license shall be awarded the grant if such applicant shows that its program service during the preceding license term has been substantially, rather than minimally, attuned to meeting the needs and interests of its area, and the operation of the station has not otherwise been characterized by serious deficiencies.

At the conclusion of the hearings the chances for S. 2004's passage seemed remote. Pressure was placed on the FCC to devise a way of avoiding legislative defeat for Senator Pastore, the twenty-two Senate cosponsors of S. 2004, and the more than one hundred sponsors in the House. The first hint of possible FCC action along this line came in the December 29, 1969, issue of *Broadcasting*, which predicted that the FCC's first action in January would be a "breakthrough in station licensing policy to alleviate [the] 'strike' application chaos triggered by WHDH-TV Boston revocation case" ("Burch Miracle," p. 5). (In commission usage, strike applications are those filed without any intention of operating a station, but solely to prevent another applicant from getting a license without a hearing. However, virtually all competing applications filed at renewal time have been submitted because of the applicant's desire to own and operate the challenged station.) *Broadcasting* indicated that the commission would adopt a policy whereby an applicant's license would be renewed following a comparative hearing if he demonstrated that his program service was substantially attuned to the needs and interests of his area.

Stimulated by these predictions in the trade press, the Citizens Communications Center (CCC) and Black Efforts for Soul in Television (BEST) filed a complaint on January 7, 1970, with the U.S. District Court for the District of Columbia. The complaint sought to enjoin the chairman and members of the FCC from "promulgating any policy, rule or interpretation or making any other change" in the standards applicable to comparative broadcast license renewal proceedings without first giving all interested parties notice and an opportunity to be heard. On the same day the complaint was filed, the court denied their request for a temporary restraining order and, shortly thereafter, dismissed the action for lack of jurisdiction.[31] The FCC attorney told District Court Judge Matthew McGuire that the two groups were simply "guessing" that the commission would take an action to which they would object and that they had no complaint until it did. The district court agreed with the FCC's contention that exclusive judicial review jurisdiction of the commission's action is vested in the courts of appeal under Section 402(a) of the Communications Act.

In another effort to dissuade the FCC from issuing a new policy statement on license renewal challenges, CCC and BEST, on January 9, filed a petition for rule making with the commission, urging that the issue of comparative hearings be dealt with in a formal rule-making proceeding. In addition, even though the FCC had not yet publicly announced any new policy, the United Church of Christ and the National Citizens Committee for Broadcasting issued statements opposing the adoption of a 'revised policy on license renewal challenges.[32]

These attempts to forestall FCC action failed. On January 15, 1970, the commission, by a vote of 6 to 1, issued its "Policy Statement on Comparative Hearings Involving Regular Renewal Applicants." Under the policy statement the renewal hearing was to be divided into two stages. In the first, the past performance of the applicant for renewal of a license would be examined. If the renewal applicant "shows that its program service during the preceding license term has been substantially attuned to meeting the needs and interests of its area and that the operation of the station has not otherwise been characterized by serious deficiencies . . . his application for renewal will be granted." If the examiner did not agree that the applicant's service had been so attuned, the hearing would continue into the second stage, in which the incumbent licensee would be deprived of any preference due to incumbency. The commission stressed that the policy of preferring an incumbent who had compiled a good broadcast record over a rival applicant whose promises were untested was firmly grounded in administrative precedent and was necessary to preserve industry stability.

In a dissenting opinion Commissioner Johnson said that the American people had been deprived of substantial rights by the commission's action. It would have been much wiser, he observed, for the commission to have used traditional rule-making procedures on such a controversial issue, but "there are legal and public relations considerations involved in issuing this statement as *fait accompli* rather than as proposed rule making for public comment." Johnson, in the closing paragraphs of his dissent, said that he could not avoid reference to the "significance of this necessary kind of compromise with broadcasting's power":

> The record of Congress and the Commission over the years shows their relative powerlessness to do anything more than spar with America's "other government," represented by the mass media. Effective reform, more and more, rests with self-help measures taken by the public. Recognizing this, the broadcasters now seek to curtail the procedural remedies of the people themselves. The industry's power is such that it will succeed, one way or another. This is sad, because—unlike the substantive concessions it has obtained from Government from time to time—there is no turning back a procedural concession of this kind once granted. Not only can the industry win every ball game, it is now in a position to change the rules.[33]

On the same day the policy statement was adopted the FCC, by a vote of 6 to 1, denied the petition submitted by CCC and BEST requesting the institution of a rule-making proceeding to codify standards for all comparative proceedings.[34] According to the commission the policy statement did not change existing law, and this area was simply not conducive to a formal rule. The commission also observed that

> parties may seek revision of the policy as cases come before the Commission, and may do so in the context of specific factual situations. Interested persons, such as petitioners, may seek to present their views in such cases as amicus curiae. If the requested policy changes are rejected, resort may be had to the courts if such rejection is believed unlawful, or to the Congress, if it is regarded as unsound policy. While, for all these reasons, we believe that further proceedings would not be helpful, it does serve the public interest to insure that our present policies, based largely on established precedents, are clearly stated. The policy statement does that.[35]

Senator Pastore praised the policy statement and stated that his subcommittee would not take any further action on S. 2004 until the policy had a fair test:

> I think the Commission ought to be given a chance. It's a step in the right direction. All I ever wanted to do right along was to make sure that a good licensee had a reasonable chance to stay in business, without harassment. The FCC policy doesn't eliminate competing applications, but in large measure it eliminates the element of harassment. It will have a salutary effect. It will discourage those engaged in piracy.[36]

Television Digest observed that the FCC's policy statement "has something for every Commissioner (except Johnson, who dissented)—and [the] truth is that implementation will be everything." Thus, in the future, both the toughest and most lenient commissioners would be able to rest their decisions solidly on material in the policy statement. *Television Digest* further observed that the document had received near-unanimous approval because most of the industry's critics on the commission infinitely "prefer this easily modified, flexibly interpretable policy—rather than imbedding into law the Pastore bill."[37]

On February 16, 1970, CCC and BEST filed with the FCC petitions for reconsideration and for repeal of the policy statement and a petition for reconsideration of the commission's denial of their petition for rule making. Other groups also seeking reconsideration of the policy statement were Hampton Roads Television Corporation and Community Broadcasting of Boston, Inc., two applicants for television channels in competition with renewal applicants in Norfolk, Virginia, and Boston.

On July 21, 1970, by a vote of 5 to 1 (with Commissioner Bartley absent), the FCC denied the various petitions for reconsideration, emphasizing that the policy statement was not a rule and was not intended to have the effect of a rule.[38] Again, only Commissioner Johnson dissented. He contended that the policy statement violated the Administrative Procedure Act, was an abuse of agency discretion, violated the hearing requirement specified by the Communications Act, and violated the First Amendment.[39] In view of the "political events" surrounding the adoption of the policy statement, he believed that the commission's position could not be considered reasonable or fair:

> The impact of citizen outrage measurably slowed the progress of S. 2004, and many Senate observers began to predict the Bill would never pass. Then, without formal rule making hearings, or even submission of

written arguments, the Commission suddenly issued its January 15, 1970 Policy Statement—achieving much of what Congress had been unable or reluctant to adopt.

There were many parties who had invested substantial time and money fighting the threatened diminution of their rights, and who no doubt would have opposed our January 15, 1970 Policy Statement on numerous grounds. In challenging S. 2004, many of these parties claimed to represent the interests of important segments of our population: the minorities, the poor, and the disadvantaged. By refusing even to listen to their counsels, this Commission reached a new low in its self-imposed isolation from the people; once again we closed our ears and minds to their pleas.[40]

On April 1, 1970, CCC and BEST submitted an appeal to the U.S. Court of Appeals for the District of Columbia Circuit challenging the legality of the policy statement. The two broadcasters who filed a petition for reconsideration of the policy statement (Hampton Roads and Community Broadcasting) joined CCC and BEST in the appeal. RKO General, Inc., and WTAR Radio-TV Corporation, the incumbent licensees in the Boston and Norfolk renewal proceedings, also intervened and filed briefs defending the policy statement. CCC and BEST argued that the policy statement deprives a new qualified applicant of his right to a comparative hearing and deprives emerging minority groups of equal protection of the laws:

Since the beginnings of broadcasting, Congress has repeatedly and expressly declared that a broadcast license shall not be a monopoly in perpetuity. Broadcasters for their part have sought to maintain in perpetuity the exceedingly valuable monopoly that is the exclusive privilege to broadcast on one of the limited number of radio or TV frequencies. The intent of the Congress remains in the silent statute books; the broadcasters daily whisper in the corridors of the Commission. The Policy Statement challenged in this appeal represents the FCC's final capitulation to the industry.[41]

During the summer of 1970, when the appeal was pending before the court, the FCC's policy statement became the subject of a study by the staff of the Special Subcommittee on Investigations of the House Committee on Interstate and Foreign Commerce. In a report released in late November 1970 the staff study charged that the policy statement "is not a policy but a flagrant attempt to repeal the statutory requirements and to substitute the FCC's own legislative proposal that a hearing is not required when it involves a license renewal proceeding having several competing applicants." The study further asserted that it "was not until now that any agency has had the temerity to usurp congressional power and by way of a 'policy statement' repeal a constitutional and statutory requirement in the interest of easing Commission workload requirements." The policy statement, the study concluded, "exemplifies both an unwarranted solicitude for the economic well-being of the licensee who enjoys a wealth-producing permit to use the public's precious airwaves and an indifference to the public interest including the right of viewers and listeners to have access to viewpoints and programs from diversified sources."[42]

The staff study was not endorsed by members of the subcommittee or its chairman, Harley Staggers, who merely forwarded the document to the FCC with a request that the commission submit a detailed legal opinion on the staff's conclusions by December 21, 1970. Acting with unaccustomed haste, the commission submitted a detailed response three days in advance of the deadline, declaring its innocence of the study's charges.[43]

On June 11, 1971, a three-judge panel of the court of appeals found the FCC's policy statement illegal and ordered that the FCC redesignate all comparative renewal hearings to reflect the court's judgment. In a decision written by Judge J. Skelly Wright, a Kennedy appointee, and supported by Judges George E. MacKinnon and Malcolm R. Wilkey, both recent Nixon appointees, the court said that its action "today restores healthy competition by repudiating a Commission policy which is unreasonably weighted in favor of the licensees it is meant to regulate, to the great detriment of the listening and viewing public." According to Judge Wright, the commission's suggestion that "it can do without notice and hearing in a policy statement what Congress failed to do when the Pastore bill . . . died in the last Congress is, to say the least, remarkable." The policy statement, Judge Wright observed, in effect administratively enacted the Pastore bill, and in his view the FCC's issuance of the statement without a prior public hearing raised additional serious questions.[44]

Judge Wright further held that "superior performance" should be regarded as "a plus of major significance in renewal proceedings" and that a new applicant had a heavy burden to produce sufficient evidence to displace an incumbent licensee in a comparative proceeding. He ordered the FCC to define both quantitatively and qualitatively what constitutes "superior programming service." Interestingly, the court of appeals decision relied heavily on language contained in the House Investigations Subcommittee staff study and the dissenting opinions of Commissioner Johnson.

The decision of the court of appeals was not welcomed by the industry. *Broadcasting* editorially condemned it as "a new prescription for anarchy in broadcast regulation," adding: "It is a formula for dismemberment of the system." The decision, *Broadcasting* asserted, "will create infinitely more chaos than prevailed in the year between the FCC's WHDH-TV decision and its adoption of the Policy Statement." The editorial concluded that the remedy must be found in Congress—"nothing less than survival is at issue."[45] Although most commissioners believed that the decision could lead to considerable instability in broadcast ownership, they agreed neither to seek a rehearing of the case by the full nine-judge panel of the court of appeals nor to ask for review by the Supreme Court for fear that further judicial review "might make things worse."[46]

The history of policy in the area of comparative renewal hearings after the Citizens Communications Center case is a convoluted one, involving all of the parties to the regulatory process. Almost from the day of the WHDH decision, "renewal relief"—usually combining protection from competing applications with other issues of the moment (most prominently, a longer license term)—has been a primary lobbying effort of broadcaster groups, including the National Association of Broadcasters.[47] Congress has struggled unsuccessfully with new legislation in the area, and citizens groups have lobbied in Congress to defeat that legislation.[48] The Ford White House even offered renewal legislation which represented a major departure from the "carrot and stick" approach of the Nixon administration.[49] The FCC has attempted to formulate policy while at the same time "motor[ing] right along,"[50] deciding comparative renewal cases on a case-by-case basis, but also producing long and discursive analyses of the comparative problem by articulate commissioners such as Nicholas Johnson, Richard Wiley, and Glen Robinson.[51] The courts have had to deal with numerous appeals of these FCC decisions, "laboring valiantly, sweep[ing] up behind," and producing caustic criticisms of the process on their own.[52]

The most immediate FCC response to the rebuff it received in the Citizens Communications Center case was to amend its Docket 19154 proceeding to inquire into the possibility of defining quantitatively the meaning of "superior" performance as called for in the Citizens case (although the FCC never did adopt the phrase "superior").[53] The commission amassed a substantial record, but it was years, as will be shown, before it did anything with the information and, when it did act, the commission simply decided not to adopt quantitative, percentage-based renewal standards after all.

Meanwhile broadcasters took their cause to Congress. In 1974, despite vigorous opposing testimony from representatives of the citizens movement, both the House and the Senate passed versions of a bill, H.R. 12993, that was regarded as acceptable by most in the broadcast industry. Both versions extended broadcast license terms, a longstanding industry objective, but more importantly from the industry's perspective, both provided for the celebrated two-step renewal process originally proposed in S. 2004. Under the new provisions the FCC would first have to determine that a licensee's operation had failed to meet properly ascertained community needs during the previous license term before accepting competing applications. Essentially, it would have to deny renewal before considering new licensees.

Unfortunately for broadcasters, House Interstate and Foreign Commerce Committee Chairman Staggers was angered when the House voted to increase the broadcast license term from three to four years. (The Senate also wanted a three-year term.) As a result Staggers refused to name House members to the conference committee formed to resolve differences between the House and Senate versions of the bill. Consequently, the 93rd Congress adjourned without passage of legislation that broadcasters wanted desperately.[54]

Broadcasting interests have not fared very well in Congress with respect to renewal relief since 1974. Without fiery Communications Subcommittee. Chairman John Pastore, the Senate has been slow in focusing on specific legislation. In the House in 1976 the Communications Subcommittee, chaired by Lionel Van Deerlin of California, embarked on a comprehensive review of the entire Communications Act of 1934. In May 1977 that House subcommittee published its "Option Papers," a staff document outlining the alternatives for reform before the staff of the subcommittee. The options under consideration included expanding the number of broadcast stations, requiring stations to allocate specific percentages of time to local programing, separating the networks from their owned and operated stations, and, most radically, adopting an entirely new concept of broadcasting based on leasing, public utility, or "public access." Such proposals did little to endear the reform project to the broadcasters.[55]

With inaction the most typical characteristic of Congress, broadcasters have looked to the FCC for possible relief, and, at least in specific cases, they have found it. Since 1969 the FCC has encountered several comparative renewal cases. Many have not yet been concluded.[56] Two of the most controversial cases that were decided were the commission's 1973 renewal of RKO General's KHJ-TV (Los Angeles) and consequent rejection of Fidelity Television's competing application,[57] and the much more recent renewal of Cowles Communications' WESH-TV (Daytona Beach).[58] The KHJ case has completed the inevitable appeals path, and the FCC has been sustained both by the U.S. Court of Appeals for the District of Columbia Circuit and, in effect, by the U.S. Supreme Court, which denied an application for review.[59] The long path of court review is just starting for WESH.

The 1973 challenge by Fidelity was one of those hard cases that rarely make good or clear law. It was, however, a victory for those who value industry stability over whatever benefits may accrue in replacing an existing "average" broadcaster with an untested competitor. Although the hearing examiner in the case characterized KHJ's past broadcast performance as "poor," he was equally unimpressed with Fidelity and particularly downgraded its plans to integrate ownership with inexperienced management. Nevertheless, he granted the license to Fidelity rather than to the incumbent, RKO General, Inc., then involved in a case alleging antitrust violations by its parent, RKO General Corporation. On appeal to the full FCC, however, the hearing examiner's decision was reversed, with RKO gaining renewal from a divided commission.[60] In this case there was no doubt that KHJ's performance could not be characterized as "superior" under the Citizens Communications Center standard. The best that the commission could do was to elevate the evaluation of the station from the hearing examiner's "poor" to "average," an elevation that made the difference.

The commission also was plagued with the issue of how to deal with the integration of ownership and management and the question of diversification. The FCC downplayed the latter by finding that KHJ was "one of many media outlets in the market" with nothing on the record to indicate that RKO's interest "had an adverse effect on the flow of information."[61] In essence, the commission managed to renew an incumbent, faced by a qualified challenger, without finding the past record of the station to be "superior," and it did this in a way that may have altered traditional commission policy on diversification and integration of ownership with management. Certainly Chief Judge David Bazelon thought that was what the commission had accomplished when, a few months later, he wrote a lengthy statement explaining why he voted to have the decision reviewed by the whole U.S. Court of Appeals for the District of Columbia Circuit.

According to Bazelon the FCC had simply failed to make a real comparison between RKO and Fidelity, opting instead for "pervasive result-oriented reasoning [removing] any veneer of rationality attaching to the comparative licensing decision."[62] He felt that the commission's determination to renew KHJ-TV led to violation—by the FCC and later by his judicial colleagues—of the standards of the Citizens Communications Center case; he also felt that it would set a new precedent on diversification and integration of management and ownership. There can be no doubt that Bazelon viewed the FCC decision, and the court decision affirming it, as totally unfounded.

However, the U.S. Supreme Court refused to review the Fidelity case, and it stood as precedent in June 1976, when the FCC acted on the renewal of Cowles-owned WESH, which was challenged by Central Florida Enterprises, Inc. The first decision in this case was not particularly controversial, although once again the commission divided sharply.[63] The majority opinion, written by Commissioner Charlotte T. Reid, joined by Commissioners Robert E. Lee, James Quello, and Abbott Washburn, changed Administrative Law Judge Chester Naumowicz's characterization of Cowles's past record from "thoroughly acceptable" to "superior" under the Citizens Communications Center standard, gave Cowles the associated "plus of major significance," and renewed Cowles's license.[64]

This proved to be too much for the other members of the commission—Chairman Wiley and Commissioners Robinson and Hooks. Each wrote a dissent. Hooks argued that the majority had not really tried to apply the 1965 policy statement on comparative hearings, as he believed the Citizens case required.[65] Wiley's personal inclination was to grant Cowles renewal, but he simply could not find its record "superior." Grudgingly, he voted to deny renewal, urging Congress at the same time to overhaul, and probably abolish, comparative renewal hearings.[66] Robinson's dissent, the longest of all, was a colorful criticism of the history of the FCC's comparative renewal policy ending with a plea for nearly automatic renewal for licensees who had substantially performed under commission policies and for an auction to decide among competitors for new stations.[67] After recounting the whole tortuous story from the WHDH through the Fidelity cases, Robinson provided a frank, but discouraging, description of the comparative renewal process as of late 1976:

> To the perceptive observer of the history of renewal contests, it will doubtless be apparent by now that there is less to such "contests" than meets the eye, that, in fact, it is not a real contest between two applicants but a pretend game played between the Commission and the public. The outcome of the game is predetermined; the art (and the sport) is to maintain interest until the inevitable outcome is registered. The Commission's role is to look judicious in pursuing a process that yields only one result; from the public the fun is watching the show and trying to anticipate how the Commission will finesse the result in the particular case. It rather resembles a professional wrestling match in which the contestants' grappling, throwing, thumping—with attendant grunts and groans—are mere dramatic conventions having little impact on the final result. Of course, wrestling fans know the result is fixed and generally in whose favor; still they fill the bleachers to see how it is done. So it is in the present case.[68]

In late 1976 the Cowles case seemed dormant. Appeals from the losing competitor were probable, but it appeared that the FCC majority had somehow managed to slip Cowles under the flexible umbrella of "superior" service as prescribed by the Citizens Communications Center case. Indeed, in September 1976 the FCC told Congress that "[n]o new major policy direction was set by the case,"[69] which was true for the time but hardly true in early 1977 when the commission—on its own and after the departure of Robinson—decided to "clarify" its earlier Cowles decision.

Somehow the commission had become troubled by its characterization of the Cowles record as "superior." Perhaps it was finally swayed by Chairman Wiley's dissent. In any event the FCC decided that "superior" wasn't quite the right word anymore and that, instead, it would describe Cowles's record—in language reminiscent of the old 1970 policy statement—as "sound, favorable and substantially above a level of mediocre service which might just minimally warrant renewal."[70] Ironically the commission's judicial support for this shift of language was the court of appeals decision in the

WHDH decision, which had helped create this policy crisis in the first place.[71]

The change in language was cheered by the broadcasting industry. *Broadcasting* magazine editorially praised the commission for "what could become the basis for a sound renewal policy."[72] The magazine encouraged the commission to formalize it quickly as a policy statement of general application and wondered if it wasn't "the next best thing to renewal legislation."[73]

The Citizens Communications Center, joined by the National Black Media Coalition and the National Citizens Committee for Broadcasting—almost the same parties that had challenged the 1970 policy statement—quickly filed a petition for reconsideration of the Cowles "clarification." Henry Geller, chairman of the Citizens Communications Center board and a former FCC general counsel, argued that the commission should conclude its longstanding inquiry on quantitative renewal standards and then use standards so established in that inquiry to determine "substantial" performance meriting a renewal plus.[74]

Also troublesome to the citizens groups was language in the FCC "clarification" that reworked the commission's treatment of diversification of media holdings and integration of ownership and management in the Cowles case. The original FCC decision in Cowles had given the competitor, Central, a "clear preference" over Cowles on the diversification issue because of Cowles's substantial media holdings outside Daytona Beach. The clarification tried to explain why this clear preference had not tipped the scales in favor of Central. In 1977 the commission found the answer in "the nature and management of Cowles' other mass media interests, the autonomy given local management, and most especially their remoteness from Daytona Beach." The commission saw "no evidence in the record that the dangers of concentration . . . exist in this case." With that, the preference for Central was relegated to the status of "little decisional significance."[75]

On the integration issue the FCC's clarification stressed that although management was not well integrated with ownership, "Cowles had accorded WESH-TV's local management team substantial autonomy in its operations." The commission thought it necessary to "make it clear . . . that this factor [the autonomy given WESH management] did serve to further diminish the preference accorded Central."[76] To support this interpretation of both the integration and diversification issues, the commission, not unnaturally, cited the court of appeals decision in the Fidelity case, which seemed to accept the FCC's treatment of RKO's Los Angeles media holdings; the commission held that its current treatment of Cowles's media holdings was similar. Geller's petition argued, unsuccessfully since the FCC eventually rejected it, that the concepts of "remoteness" and "autonomy" were at odds with commission and judicial precedent and that they undermined the multiple-ownership and minority-ownership policies of the FCC. On June 30, 1977, the commission, by a vote of 4 to 1, rejected Geller's petition for reconsideration, leaving further action, if any, up to the courts.[77]

The commission first claimed that the citizens groups lacked standing to challenge the Cowles clarification so late in the game. Graciously, however, it agreed to consider Geller's objections since, the FCC now admitted, the WESH clarification had announced "policies of general applicability to comparative renewal proceedings."[78] The commission reiterated its belief that Fidelity had met the FCC's standards for autonomy and remoteness, and disputed Geller's contention that those concepts really undermined other licensing policies. In addition, the commission argued that the request for quantitative standards had been rendered moot since the FCC had, since the filing of the petition for reconsideration, terminated its inquiry into such standards (Docket 19154) by deciding not to issue such standards. On that point the commission said, "Any continuing concern which petitioners might have in the matter of adopting quantitative standards should be confined to review proceedings which might be undertaken with respect to Docket 19154."[79]

That docket is the last remaining strand of this tangled story—at least as the story stands in late 1977. After over six years of consideration (the docket having been opened in February 1971), four notices of inquiry, and the compilation of a massive record including a survey of all commercial TV licensees in 1973, the FCC concluded, while keeping open its options to adopt such standards in the future, that establishing quantitative standards for local and informational programing "would not simplify the hearing process, and . . . could not offer a licensee any real assurance of renewal. They are a simplistic, superficial approach to a complex problem, and we will not adopt them."[80] Basically the commission feared that any quantitative standards would become artificial ceilings, encouraging stations to inflate their local and news and public affairs programing with no guarantee of quality. Geller, on behalf of the

National Black Media Coalition and the Committee for Open Media, San Jose chapter, filed a brief on August 31, 1977, with the U.S. Court of Appeals for the District of Columbia seeking reversal of the FCC decision not to adopt quantitative standards. The year neared its end with the policy vacuum nearly as absolute as before.

Two further questions seem worth raising: (1) Is the policy area as important as the parties contend and (2) can any settlement be expected, given the politics of broadcast regulation? As to the first, many outside observers believe that the broadcasting industry overestimates the dangers of losing licenses in comparative renewal hearings. Since the WHDH decision, the FCC still has not granted a TV license to a challenger when the incumbent had anything like a record of acceptable past service.[81] On the other hand, the industry is right in saying that defending (or bringing) competitive applications is an exceedingly costly business. It has been estimated that a challenger to WPIX-TV in New York City spent $2 million just to get through the initial hearing stage, and the incumbent spent an additional $1.5 million to the same point.[82] Court fees would boost those figures. Such high litigation costs doubtless mean that the interests of citizens groups, especially of minority groups who already have difficulty attracting capital, cannot be served by filing competing applications for broadcast stations. Indeed, citizen-filed competing applications are rare.[83] What tactics can the citizens movement effectively employ, then?

Henry Geller's petition for reconsideration of the Cowles clarification is one possible tactic, namely, the attempt to influence policy in this area by means of the commission's rule-making process, and if unsuccessful, by persuading the courts to reverse the FCC. Geller's concern is that loose renewal policies in cases where incumbents face qualified challengers will negate the statutory spur to substantial service and will affect the treatment of factors like diversification in general license renewal cases, where the more normal citizens group tactic, the petition to deny, is employed. The FCC, in 1976, took a diametrically opposite regulatory approach in recommending that Congress abolish the comparative renewal process. The commission stated that with the regular license renewal process at its disposal plus its ability to use the Fairness Doctrine on a case-by-case basis, the government's grip on broadcasters is so firm that the comparative license renewal process is both unnecessary and counterproductive.[84]

Any ultimate solution to this crisis over comparative renewal policy will come from one of two parties whose contributions to the politics of broadcast regulation are most durable—the courts or the Congress. If there is truly a constitutional aspect to ownership policy, as Judge David Bazelon argues,[85] then the final word will eventually have to come from the U.S. Supreme Court. If, on the other hand, the constitutional aspects are minimal, then final policy will have to come from the Congress, which, no doubt, will be buffeted by diverse lobbying efforts. It is obvious that no solution to this case study, which of all the cases presented most closely resembles a policy stalemate, can escape being formed by the political regulatory system.

Notes

[1] Although we shall try to restrict this chapter to comparative renewal hearings, it is almost impossible to divorce that subject from other FCC policy areas. Comparative hearings are also held among applicants for unoccupied broadcast channels, using procedures that may be criticized as inefficient [see Dissenting Statement of Commissioner Glen O. Robinson in *Cowles Florida Broadcasting, Inc.*, 60 F.C.C. 2d 372, 435–448 (1976)] but are nonetheless clearer than the procedures that are followed when one applicant is an incumbent. This policy area is also entangled with media ownership policy and integration of ownership with management, as will be shown in the WHDH, Fidelity, and Cowles cases described in this chapter.

[2] Separate Statement of Commissioners Benjamin Hooks and Joseph Fogarty in *Report and Order in Docket 19154*, F.C.C. 74-204, released April 7, 1977.

[3] *Ashbacker Radio Corp.* v. *F.C.C.*, 326 U.S. 327 (1964).

[4] *Johnston Broadcasting Co.* v. *F.C.C.*, 175 F. 2d 351, 359 (C.A.D.C., 1949).

[5] *Hearst Radio, Inc. (WBAL)*, 15 F.C.C. 1149 (1951).

[6] *Policy Statement on Comparative Broadcast Hearings*, 1 F.C.C. 2d 393 (1965).

[7] *Seven League Productions, Inc.*, 1 F.C.C. 2d 1597 (1965).

[8] *Wabash Valley Broadcasting Corp. (WTHI-TV)*, 35 F.C.C. 677 (1963).

[9] *WHDH, Inc.*, 16 F.C.C. 2d 1 (1969).

[10] "The Strange Ch. 5 Decision," *Television Digest*, January 27, 1969, pp. 1, 2.

[11] "On the first round I voted against WHDH, Inc. On the second round, in light of certain changed circumstances, I cast my vote for WHDH, Inc. This is now the third round and it is no less difficult for me to choose among those competing applicants. In view of my previous participation and

finally the fact that my vote is not essential to resolution of the matter, I have simply abstained." *WHDH, Inc.*, 16 F.C.C. 2d, pp. 23-24. The FCC's decision in the WHDH case was affirmed by the courts. *Greater Boston Television Corporation* v. *F.C.C.*, 444 F. 2d 841 (1970), certiorari denied, 403 U.S. 923 (1971).

[12] *Television Digest*, January 27, 1969, p. 2.

[13] 16 F.C.C. 2d, p. 27.

[14] Ibid., p. 28.

[15] Louis L. Jaffe, "WHDH: The FCC and Broadcasting License Renewals," *Harvard Law Review*, 82 (1969), 1693, 1700.

[16] "$3 Billion in Stations Down the Drain?" *Broadcasting*, February 3, 1969, p. 19.

[17] Editorial, "Boston Stake: $3 Billion," *Broadcasting*, February 3, 1969, p. 84.

[18] "Ironics of TV Spotlighted at NAB," *Television Digest*, March 31, 1969, p. 3.

[19] "The White House Looks into FCC's Future," *Broadcasting*, March 31, 1969, p. 36. The term of Rosel Hyde expired on June 30, 1969, but President Nixon asked him to continue as chairman until a successor was confirmed. Commissioner Cox's term expired on June 30, 1970.

[20] "Pastore Submits Antistrike Bill," *Broadcasting*, May 5, 1969, p. 58.

[21] William H. Wentz, "The Aftermath of WHDH: Regulation by Competition or Protection of Mediocrity?" *University of Pennsylvania Law Review*, 118 (1969), 368.

[22] 17 F.C.C. 2d, p. 872.

[23] "July Hearings on Renewals," *Television Digest*, June 9, 1969, p. 3.

[24] Wentz, "The Aftermath of WHDH," p. 395.

[25] Nicholas Johnson, *How to Talk Back to Your Television Set* (New York: Bantam, 1970), p. 205.

[26] "Pastore Hits Renewal-Bill Opposition," *Television Digest*, October 20, 1969, p. 2.

[27] "Picket Lines Due," *Broadcasting*, December 1, 1969, p. 10.

[28] "Pastore & Blacks Clash on 'Racism'," *Television Digest*, December 8, 1969, p. 2.

[29] Ibid., p. 4.

[30] The excerpts quoted from the statements of the FCC majority and each of the commissioners are contained in *Hearings Before the Communications Subcommittee on S. 2004*, 91st Congress, 1st Session, Part 2 (December 1, 2, 3, 4 and 5, 1969), pp. 375-412.

[31] "A Return to Order in Renewals," *Broadcasting*, January 12, 1970, p. 36.

[32] "Renewal Protection—Program Performance," *Television Digest*, January 12, 1970, p. 3.

[33] 22 F.C.C. 2nd 430 and 433 (1970). In hearings on S. 3434, before the Subcommittee on Administrative Practice and Procedure, Senate Committee of the Judiciary (July 2, 1970), Johnson claimed that the commission had worked with White House approval in adopting the policy statement.

[34] 21 F.C.C. 2d 355 (1970).

[35] Ibid., p. 357.

[36]"FCC Renewal Policy Supplants Pastore Bill," *Television Digest*, January 19, 1970, p. 1. The policy statement did in fact discourage competing applications. In 1969 when the WHDH decision was announced, eight renewal applicants were challenged. However, during 1970, not one renewal application was challenged.

[37]Ibid., p. 2.

[38]24 F.C.C. 2d 383 (1970).

[39]Ibid., p. 386.

[40]Ibid., p. 389.

[41]Brief of CCC and BEST, Case No. 24,471, p. 5.

[42]"Analysis of FCC's 1970 Policy Statement on Competitive Hearings Involving Regular Renewal Applicants." Staff Study for the Special Subcommittee on Investigations of the House Committee on Interstate and Foreign Commerce, 91st Congress, 2nd Session (November 1970).

[43]"FCC Disputes Hill Report on Renewals," *Television Digest*, December 21, 1970, p. 2.

[44]*Citizens Communications Center* v. *F.C.C.*, 447 F. 2d 1201 (C.A.D.C., 1971). Judge Wright's opinion appears on pages 1202–1215.

[45]Editorial, "Life or Death?" *Broadcasting*, June 21, 1971, p. 108.

[46]"No More Appeal on Renewal Policy," *Broadcasting*, July 5, 1971, p. 44.

[47]A rival group, the National Radio Broadcasters Association, has occasionally tried to separate the renewal problems of television stations from the generally less disputed area of radio by proposing radio-only renewal relief bills. In this effort it has had some support from the NAB.

[48]See H.R. 15168, 94th Congress, 2nd Session (1976), introduced by Representative Richard Ottinger (D.-NY), which contained a shopping list of citizens group reform issues attached to a license renewal proposal.

[49]The phrase was used by Dr. Clay T. Whitehead, former head of the Office of Telecommunications Policy, in a speech to the Indianapolis chapter of Sigma Delta Chi, December 18, 1972. See "The Dust Hasn't Settled After Speech by Whitehead," *Broadcasting*, January 1, 1973, p. 18.

[50]Statement of Chief Judge David Bazelon in *Fidelity Television, Inc.* v. *F.C.C.*, 515 F. 2d 684, 726, (C.A.D.C., 1975).

[51]See the dissenting opinion of Commissioner Nicholas Johnson in *Moline Television Corp.*, 31 F.C.C. 2d 263, 277–288 (1971); the dissenting statement of Chairman Wiley in *Cowles Florida Broadcasting, Inc.*, 60 F.C.C. 2d 372, 430–433 (1976); and the dissenting statement of Commissioner Robinson in the same case on pages 435–448.

[52]See statement of Chief Judge David Bazelon in *Fidelity Television, Inc.* v. *F.C.C.*, 515 F. 2d 684, 726 (C.A.D.C., 1975).

[53]*Further Notice of Inquiry in Docket No. 19154*, 31 F.C.C. 2d 443 (1971).

[54]"Renewal Relief Dies on Hill: What Chance of Reincarnation?" *Broadcasting*, December 16, 1974, pp. 19–20.

[55]"Option Papers," Subcommittee on Communications, Committee on Interstate and Foreign Commerce, U.S. House of Representatives, 95th Congress, 1st Session (May 1977). The paper on broadcasting by subcom-

mittee counsel Harry (Chip) Shooshan, III, is on pages 35–91, and in the appendices.

[56] In September 1976 the FCC told Congress that there were then twelve comparative renewal cases before the commission, four of them at least four years old. *Report of the Federal Communications Commission to the Congress of the United States re: The Comparative Renewal Process*, September 20, 1976 (mimeo), p. 48. Other cases decided by the commission were still under review by the courts.

[57] *RKO General, Inc. (KHJ-TV)*, 44 F.C.C. 2d 123 (1973).

[58] *Cowles Florida Broadcasting, Inc.*, 60 F.C.C. 2d 372 (1976), clarified in *Cowles Florida Broadcasting, Inc.*, 62 F.C.C. 2d 953 (1977). See also *Moline Television Corp.*, 31 F.C.C. 2d 263 (1971).

[59] See particularly *Fidelity Television, Inc. v. F.C.C.*, 515 F. 2d 684 (C.A.D.C., 1975); reconsideration and rehearing denied, dissenting statement by Chief Judge Bazelon, 515 F. 2d 705 (1975); certiorari denied, 423 U.S. 926 (1975).

[60] The vote was in essence 3 to 2, nearly as fragmented and incomplete as the WHDH decision four years earlier. Commissioners Wiley and Hooks did not participate. Commissioners Robert E. Lee and Charlotte Reid wrote a joint opinion favoring KHJ, although Reid had not participated in the oral argument. Chairman Burch concurred in the result without further statement. Commissioners Johnson and H. Rex Lee dissented, Johnson calling this "the worst decision of this Commission during my term of seven years and five months." *RKO General, Inc.*, 44 F.C.C. 2d 123 (1973).

Nearly two years later Chief Judge David Bazelon agreed with Johnson. See *Fidelity Television, Inc. v. F.C.C.*, 515 F. 2d 705 (C.A.D.C., 1975).

[61] *RKO General, Inc.*, 44 F.C.C. 2d 123, 134 (1973).

[62] *Fidelity Television, Inc. v. F.C.C.*, 515 F. 2d 684 (C.A.D.C., 1975).

[63] *Cowles Florida Broadcasting, Inc.*, 60 F.C.C. 2d 372 (1976).

[64] Ibid., pp. 1539–1544. Commissioner Robinson acidly commented:

One might think it important to know what constitutes "superior performance." The answer I derive from the Commission's opinion is that "superior" means whatever the licensee has done, providing the licensee has not seriously misbehaved. . . . This evidently is the Commission's version of the Court of Appeals' "hard look" requirement: it looks hard until it finds what it is after.

Ibid., pp. 441–442. The licensee of WESH-TV has filed an appeal of the FCC's decision with the U.S. Court of Appeals for the D.C. Circuit.

[65] Ibid., p. 434.

[66] Ibid., pp. 430–433.

[67] Ibid., pp. 442–448.

[68] Ibid., p. 439. Robinson further called Fidelity

a tour de force, accomplishing even more than the Commission had purported to accomplish with its ill-fated 1970 Policy Statement. In 1970, the Commission merely purported to guarantee renewal to an incumbent which demonstrated "substantial" service. In Fidelity, it managed to grant renewal to an incumbent who demonstrated "average service," who was actually the weaker candidate on one major comparative criterion, and not materially better on the others (integration and local ownership).

Ibid., p. 438.
[69]*FCC Report to Congress*, p. 40.
[70]*Cowles Florida Broadcasting, Inc.*, 62 F.C.C. 2d 953, 955 (1977). The 1970 policy statement had provided, in part, that "[the commission] is not using the term 'substantially' in any sense of partial performance in the public interest. On the contrary, as the discussion within makes clear, it is used in the sense of 'solid,' 'strong,' etc. . . . performance as contrasted with a service only minimally meeting the needs and interests of the area."
[71]*Greater Boston Television Corp.* v. *F.C.C.*, 444 F. 2d 841 (1970), certiorari denied, 403 U.S. 923 (1971).
[72]"Start of Something Big," *Broadcasting*, January 10, 1977, p. 82.
[73]"The Next Best Thing to Renewal Legislation?" *Broadcasting*, January 10, 1977, p. 20.
[74]Petition for Reconsideration, February 3, 1977, pp. 7-10.
[75]*Cowles Florida Broadcasting, Inc.*, 62 F.C.C. 2d 953, 956-957 (1977).
[76]Ibid., p. 956.
[77]*Cowles Broadcasting, Inc.*, 40 RR 2d 1627 (1977).
[78]Ibid., p. 1628.
[79]Ibid., p. 1630.
[80]*Report and Order in Docket 19154*, F.C.C. 77-204, released April 7, 1977.
[81]Two possible exceptions should be noted. In *Star Stations of Indiana, Inc.*, 51 F.C.C. 2d 95 (1975), Don Burden eventually lost five radio station licenses in a proceeding that started out as a comparative renewal hearing. However, the hearing raised serious questions about Burden's character, and he was, personally, eventually determined unfit to continue as a licensee. In the KORK-TV (Las Vegas) proceeding Donrey Media faces loss of a license due to fraudulent billing, lack of candor, and misrepresentation. Once again the proceeding began as a comparative renewal hearing, but if Las Vegas Valley Broadcasting Company, the competitor, is ever awarded the license, it will probably not be because of Donrey Media's past broadcast record. In any event, broadcasters are concerned about changes in policy based on changes in the composition of the commission.
[82]See Dissenting Statement of Commissioner Glen O. Robinson in *Cowles Florida Broadcasting, Inc.*, 60 F.C.C. 2d 372, 447, n. 34 (1976).
[83]But consider the case of United Broadcasting Co., which, since 1975, has faced a challenge from Public Communicators, Inc. (PCI) for its KBAY-FM station in San Jose, California. PCI proposes a commercial operation, but with a far less than normal concern for profit and a far greater emphasis upon public affairs and direct-access programing. This is in sharp contrast to KBAY's present "Beautiful Music" format, which sharply reduces news. PCI has succeeded in getting several unique issues added to the proceeding. See particularly *United Broadcasting Co. (KBAY)*, 59 F.C.C. 2d 1412 (1976). By acting without counsel PCI probably has substantially reduced the cost of

participating in the comparative process but may also have reduced its chance for an eventual victory.

[84]*FCC Report to Congress*, p. 32.

[85]Statement of Chief Judge Bazelon in *Fidelity Television, Inc.* v. *F.C.C.*, 515 F. 2d 725–726 (1975).

9

CB Radio: The National Party Line Overwhelms the Regulators

Citizens band (CB) radio has proven to be the major economic, social, cultural, and technological force for change in communications in the 1970s. From its spectacular takeoff in 1974 CB radio has rapidly grown to a $2 billion industry[1] involving at least 20 million CB users[2] competing for space on forty CB channels. The FCC has found itself struggling with a massive overload of CB license applications (5 to 8 million a year), as well as with complaints of CB interference (over 100,000 a year), and has been able to do little more than make interim decisions and responses to immediate uses and needs. Meanwhile, the availability of simple, relatively low-cost, two-way communications has for the first time provided millions of Americans with the opportunity to engage in personal communications, often not just to one selected party but to anyone listening. As one widely used advertisement has put it, when you've got a CB radio, "You've got the world by the ears."[3]

CB service actually started in January 1949, when the FCC established a "business and communications" band of UHF frequencies. This allocation, however, was relatively little used; as of 1958, for example, only 40,000 licenses had been granted by the commission.[4] In 1958, the FCC tried once more to develop a land-mobile citizens radio service—this time with greater success. The commission established twenty-three "class D" radio channels in the 27 megahertz band, a region of the spectrum shared with garage door openers and model aircraft remote-control transmitters.[5]

"Class D licensees," as citizens band users were referred to by the FCC, were limited, as today, to a maximum power output of 4 watts, which gave them a range from fifteen to thirty miles. Most American equipment manufacturers showed little initial interest in producing transceivers for this new service. As a result early CB equipment was largely the province of smaller, less well-known American companies and importers of Japanese-made equipment. The major initial users were farmers, small businessmen, and, later, truckers, who found CB radio a useful means of communication while on the open road.[6]

The FCC was quite specific about what CB radio was not to be: "A Citizens radio station shall not be used: for engaging in radio communications as a hobby or diversion, i.e., operating the radio station as an activity in and of itself."[7] This 1964 statement was upheld in a 1965 court challenge,[8] even as forces were growing that would transform CB into the very diversion prohibited in 1964.

Late in the 1960s CB radio became increasingly common in truck cabs. Drivers found that CB radio not only lessened the monotony of the long haul by providing verbal companionship with fellow truckers but also provided a direct link to others in case of breakdown, severe weather, or other emergency conditions. Further, the CB link provided an operator with a way of beating "Smokey"—the highway policeman—by warnings flashed up and down interstate roads from truck to truck. For example, "There's a Bear in the weeds taking pictures at the seventeen-mile marker" meant that a police car is at the side of the road at highway marker seventeen with a radar unit.

Events of 1974 added to the appeal of CB not only to truckers but also to automobile users. The Arab oil embargo resulted in a period of widespread gasoline station closings, so that supplies were often difficult to find in many areas at night and on Sundays. CB operators—in cars as well as trucks—found information on open stations readily available from other helpful CBers.

Another dramatic and highly publicized use of CB radios in that year further enhanced their appeal. This was the use of CB radio as a means of communication and coordination by truckers engaged in slowdowns and strikes in Pennsylvania and Ohio to protest the scarcity of truck fuel. Mobile CBs came to be seen as useful information and communications devices for citizens—a method of communication complete with its own language and codes, which would allow the car driver to share in the "trucker's aura."[9]

The 1 million licenses issued in 1974 were to be only the start of exceedingly rapid CB growth in the next few years. By the end of 1976 the number of CB licenses had increased more than seven times over the 1974 figure. In early 1977 applications poured into the commission at a rate exceeding 670,000 a *month*.[10] As of the end of February 1977 the FCC reported that it had issued a total of 8,818,815 CB licenses.[11] One projection estimated that the likely total of CB licenses at the end of 1977 would be 15 million, or one out of every fourteen American citizens.[12] Since the commission allows members of a license holder's family to use the licensee's radio, it is difficult to determine the number of actual CB users, but the FCC estimates this total as over twice the number of its licensees, or more than 20 million operators as of February 1977.[13] There are also many illegal, unlicensed CB operators. Their number is impossible to estimate, but they swell by millions any estimate of CB users.[14] In short, CB operation is a mass activity of the American people, one which has dramatically developed since 1974 to enormous proportions.

CB also is a big business. In both 1974 and 1975 sales of CB sets doubled over the preceding year. Reports by the Electronic Industries Association (EIA) for 1976 and estimates for 1977 both total about 10 million transceivers. John Sodolski, vice-president of the EIA, estimated early in 1977 that there might be 30 million more sales in the next three years before market saturation was reached at about 55 million sets.[15] Other analysts have spoken of a possible 75 million total market, with a stable replacement market, on a five-year life cycle, of some 15 million sets yearly.[16]

Recently, electronic giants such as Texas Instruments, General Electric, Motorola, Panasonic, Hitachi, and RCA have entered the CB field, threatening the numerous smaller companies which pioneered CB radio. Although some observers fear a flood of CB equipment resulting from new corporate competition, others stress that the market probably will eliminate rapidly those manufacturers with weak distribution and promotional networks, leaving a limited number of companies dominant in the perhaps $2 billion CB market.[17] One must keep in mind that all of this citizen, government, and corporate activity is focused upon a band of frequencies which, through the end of 1976, would fit into the band spread of *one* television station.[18]

A number of factors help explain the appeal of CB broadcasting. W. I. Thomas, president of CB manufacturer Pathcom Corporation, stresses the social appeal of CB radio: People like to talk, and they want to be heard. "The concept of CB is a party-line concept."[19]

There is also a spirit of camaraderie expressed in the standard CB greeting of "Hey good buddy," as well as in CB institutions such as the "eyeball" or coffee break at the local Donutland, the regular meeting of a local CB club, or the audio-only friendship of CBers who just pass on interstate roads.[20] At the height of the craze for CB radios the President's wife, Betty Ford, operated her own CB equipment under the name of "First Momma."

Besides allowing for an extension of self, CB radio is also attractive because of its mystique and implicit fringe illegality. A "secret" language is used, complete with dictionaries, which is "middle-South in dialect but utterly national in its imaginative vocabulary and idiom."[21] Handles such as Salty Charlie, Sugar Cookie, Curly Dog, or Spider replace personal names—and usually even FCC-required call letter identification. A popular use of CB radio is to warn against a lurking "Smokey" who might give you a ticket unless you "ease up on the hammer to the double nickel [55 MPH]."[22]

Along with the proliferation of CB radios have come undesirable CB users—and uses. CBers have found themselves engaged in forceful oral—and even physical—arguments over the proper use of channels. In late September 1976 the Associated Press reported that an argument over a CB channel between CBers "Blue Rover" and "Bear Track" led to their meeting in a parking lot near Lincoln, Nebraska, for an "eyeball." The result: Bear Track was run over by Blue Rover's pickup truck. In December 1976 an argument between "Dirty Bird" and "Blue Goose" on a freeway near Haltom City, Texas, resulted in the shooting death of Blue Goose.[23]

Besides violence CB has resulted in some social innovations. In 1976 antibusing rioters in Boston were reported to be coordinating their activities by CB radio.[24] Michael McCormack, president of the American CB Radio Association and publisher of *CBers News*, asserts that some CB channels in the South are now de facto segregated: "By the articulation and language you can detect who owns the channel." McCormack also reports that "in Oregon, there's a channel taken over by about 20 lesbians who work as tree planters."[25]

CB has been put to illicit use as well. In February 1977 the Associated Press reported that coffee thieves in San Francisco advertised over CB radio the availability of 12,000 pounds of stolen coffee at discount prices.[26] And, according to the *Wall Street Journal* (as well as other sources), enterprising businesswomen such as

"Shady Lady" of Louisville, Kentucky, and "Love Machine" of West Virginia have added new CB lingo definitions to terms such as "pit stop."[27]

The FCC has proved remarkably inept in regulating or shaping this rapid development of CB radio. One reason has to do with the sheer volume of CB radio demands upon the commission. With license applications pouring in at well over 20,000 a day, the FCC has not been able to keep up with issuing the licenses themselves, much less reviewing them in any fashion. Complaints concerning CB interference with neighborhood TV and stereo systems have also overwhelmed the FCC. The 100,000 officially recorded complaints in 1976 are expected to double by the end of 1977.[28] This figure, of course, represents only those willing to take the effort to complain to the commission about occasional raucous voices on their clock radio at 7 A.M. Moreover, lodging official complaints is not easy. A study of phone calls to one FCC field office found that 90 percent of the 13,000 callers received only a busy signal and were unable to get through.[29] And those whose calls were answered usually got a tape recording urging them to put any complaint in writing, presumably in case the one hundred or so field agents nationwide should have time someday to look into it.[30]

Besides coping with the paperwork demands of CB operation, the commission has also had to set policy for the new service. An initial requirement, discussed above, was that CB radio should not be used as a hobby or for idle chitchat. The increase in use of CB radios for that express purpose finally compelled the FCC to drop this regulation on September 15, 1975.

Another regulation still in existence requires CBers to identify their station by their call sign at the beginning and close of each conversation. This simply is not the CB practice today. As one CB handbook notes, "If you listen to most CB conversations . . . you will rarely hear call letters being used at any time in the conversation."[31]

Many CB operators do not use call letters because they are unlicensed. With the suspension of all fees for CB licenses in December 1976,[32] a license is now free as well as virtually automatic (although it may be many months in coming). Yet one consequence of the no-cost license is to downplay its significance and necessity, especially in light of the general nonuse of license call letters and nonenforcement of FCC regulations. Increasingly CB radio has been seen as a citizen's right for anyone who can afford the equipment, not as something to be regulated by the government.

With regard to channel use the commission's presence has also seemed remarkably limited, but in this instance largely because of self-imposed modesty. The FCC officially designated Channel 9 as the emergency channel but has otherwise been unable to designate specialized uses for other channels. At one point it proposed, but then abandoned, Channel 11 as a national calling channel,[33] with contacts once initiated on Channel 11 then being shifted to other channels. The commission has at times referred to Channel 19's unofficial use as a road information channel by truckers. It has mentioned severe problems on Channel 9 because of "bleeding" from the heavy use of Channels 8 and 10. And it has called for some type of "volunteer cooperation" concerning channel use by conventional AM CBers and incompatible, more advanced, single sideband CB users. In effect, the commission has proved unable or unwilling to impose any sort of rational system of use for a very limited number of CB channels. Each user or type of user is free to operate on all but Channel 9 in whatever way he wishes—or can.[34]

Another problem of CB radio lies in the very proliferation of CB operators. With over 20 million CB users jammed onto only forty channels (only 23 channels until January 1, 1977), congestion and interference are the natural results. According to one observer, "Normally, only about half the transmissions one hears on a given channel are intelligible; the rest sound like the speaker was shaving with an electric razor while munching granola."[35]

This problem, an extremely severe one in crowded urban or suburban areas, is compounded greatly by the use of illegal equipment designed to boost broadcast power and range beyond the allowed limits. Linear amps, with charming trade names such as "Afterburner," "Band Blaster," and "Powerhouse," can raise the power of CB radios from the legal 4 watt limit to 100 watts or even more. They are widely available and have even been advertised in CB magazines, although their use for CB radio is strictly illegal.[36] Part of the difficulty in regulating linear amps lies in the fact that they are legal and even necessary for ham radios, including those that operate in the 28 to 30 megahertz frequencies. This equipment, however, is also usable for CB radios that operate in the 27 megahertz band. To control this CB problem the FCC, by a vote of 7 to 0 on February 19, 1977, took action to prohibit sales of *any* linear amp that focuses its amplification between 24 and 30 megahertz—which would include ham radio equipment. Despite this commission action, a disastrous loophole opened up for linear amp CBers. Linear amps *can* be sold, though not for CB operation, if they are broadband and do not focus upon the 20 megahertz band. Such equipment is both cheap and "dirty," for their use (illegally) by CBers also amplifies strongly CB second and third harmonics, which cause interference to plague TV Channels 2 and 5.[37]

A related problem has to do with a phenomenon called "skip," the daytime propagation of CB radio far beyond its customary range by reflection off the F_2 layer of the ionosphere. This phenomenon, fascinating to the CBer in Georgia who finds himself talking to a CB operator in Mexico City,[38] is also the source of enormous interference problems for local CBers trying to get a road report.

Skip is greatly dependent on sunspot patterns and is liable to become more prevalent in the next two or three years, starting in 1978, as the eleven-year cycle for sunspot activity approaches its peak. A warning as to the serious problems liable to result was given in a 1976 report by Donald L. Lucas, assistant director of the Office of Telecommunications of the Department of Commerce in Boulder, Colorado, who indicated: "Long-range interference from other CB stations can severely limit the useful ground-wave range of CB users. . . . Based on conservative estimates of parameters . . . the effect may be much more than cited."[39]

The response of the FCC to these fears has been rather hesitant and uncertain. One FCC commissioner's office stated: "Yes, we do know that sunspots are supposed to increase in 1978, but there are several schools of thought about it. Not only CB, but other telecommunications will be affected. The FCC has been looking for another band in which to locate CB in place of the 27 megahertz band or in addition to it."[40]

Interference is also a problem because it affects television sets, radios, and stereo equipment. The problem is an immediate one for TV viewers who find their picture dissolving into a herringbone pattern whenever their "good buddy" neighbor fingers his mike. Stories abound of unintended CB reception on television sets, stereo systems, and even on such unlikely receivers as public-address systems in churches. The Reverend Joseph Gorsuch of the Church of St. Helen in Eloy, Arizona, reported, "We'd hear things like: 'I'm coming home, warm up the bean pot' during funerals."[41] One woman is said to have received CB calls via the oven of her electric range as she was cooking dinner.[42]

The most persistent form of CB interference has been with TV reception. Television interference (TVI in CB jargon) is due largely to CB second harmonics appearing on TV Channel 2 and third harmonics interfering with TV Channel 5.[43] Although these problems sometimes arise from the illegal use of linear amps which blast their way into neighborhood home electronic equipment, even legal CB broadcasts—especially those from base stations with highly efficient antenna systems—also frequently result in electronic interference. To a degree the fault may lie in inadequate shielding of television sets and inexpensive home electronic equipment, but, of course, those sets were not designed with the thought that they would have to contend with a broadcasting station one hundred yards away. Filter traps for affected equipment are available and sometimes alleviate the problem. However, the installation and adjustment of such devices usually require a technician, at considerable cost and bother. Low-pass filters to control spurious harmonics on the CB transceiver itself are more effective, but they may cost the CBer dearly.

The attitude of the FCC until late 1976 was to blame TVI largely on inadequate shielding in the affected TV, radio, or stereo equipment. More recently the commission has started to stress the problem of the CB transceiver. As Robert A. Luff, engineering assistant to Richard E. Wiley, former chairman of the FCC, put it: "When CB radio took off, it caught the manufacturers as well as ourselves by surprise. Everyone started cutting corners for mass production and lowered their quality control."[44] As a result of renewed emphasis on the cause of CB interference rather than its effect, the commission declared in 1976: "If an individual [CB] licensee causes interference to a neighbor's television reception on television channels 2, 5, or 6 because of insufficient harmonic attenuation, he will have to obtain additional suppression by the insertion of a low-pass filter."[45]

In 1976 the FCC also acted to tighten specifications for the new forty-channel CB models that were to be introduced in January 1977. Existing CB sets had been approved by the commission if they radiated no more than 49 decibels of harmonic radiation.[46] Television interests, including the Association of Maximum Service Telecasters and the American Broadcasting Company, requested in 1976 that the FCC require harmonic suppression of 105 decibels for the new CB sets. On July 27, 1976, the commission announced that it was settling for suppression of 60 decibels (which represents a power ratio of one million to one), an only modest improvement on the existing 49-decibel requirement. The FCC explained that this was only an "interim" requirement, established at 60 decibels so as not to unduly delay the engineering of new forty-channel CB equipment.[47] By this decision the commission had bowed to severe pressure from CB users and manufacturers to allow for the speedy development of the promised seventeen new channels. It decided to set technical standards for the new forty-channel equipment at a modest additional 11-decibel harmonic suppression, despite the predictable increased incidence of electronic interference resulting from expanded CB radio use. CB operators and financial interests had proven themselves a formidable political force which the commission had to placate. Delay in the authorization of expanded CB service, especially in the face of overwhelming demand, was unthinkable, even if it meant modest "interim" interference standards. Protests by the Association of Maximum Service Telecasters and the American Broadcasting Company were ignored[48] and forty-channel CB radio became a reality on January 1, 1977. The FCC approval of forty channels was made easier by considerable congressional pressure, responding to CB constituent views, for the speedy expansion of CB radio. However, the commission did resist CB constituent pressures in one regard: It refused to allow owner "add-on" conversion of existing CB sets to forty channels by the purchase of a converter. The FCC based its decision on the belief that the quality of the resulting hybrid equipment would be highly variable in terms of harmonic interference.[49]

The decision to add seventeen new CB channels was itself the conclusion of commission deliberations started in 1973. On June 12, 1973, the FCC issued a Notice of Inquiry and Proposed Rule Making concerning a possible shift of all CB radio from the existing 27 megahertz band to a VHF band of 224 to 225 megahertz, currently in military and ham radio use. This proposal would have entailed, of course, the obsolescence of all existing CB equipment, as did the FM shift twenty-eight years earlier.[50] The plan faced immediate objections from the military, ham broadcasters, as well as from Canada, and it was quickly dropped.[51] Although a shift might have avoided sunspot-generated skips and offered some additional channel space, it also might have caused CB harmonic interference with TV

Channels 11, 12, and 13.[52] Long-range thinking more recently has tended to center around possible eventual CB use of frequencies above 900 megahertz, although it is conceded that present technology and economics would not currently allow for this.[53] CB radio thus remains locked into an exceedingly narrow band of frequencies, highly sensitive to the skip phenomenon, with a possibility of some day being wholly or partially uprooted to entirely new frequencies.

Curiously, there is already in existence one technical development in CB broadcasting which would in effect immediately double the number of available CB channels—single sideband CB, or SSB CB. This set operates by taking the main carrier (or signal), as used in existing conventional AM CB, and dividing it into an upper-sideband channel and a lower-sideband channel. Instead of forty CB channels, SSB CB has eighty effective channels in the same frequency space.[54]

SSB CB radio is currently available and is, in fact, used by some operators in CB broadcasting. However, it is considerably more expensive (sets start at about $200) and slightly more complex (one more knob) than existing AM CB equipment.

Even more crippling to SSB is its complete incompatibility with the predominant AM CB. SSB operators are unable to participate in AM CB communications activity, including traffic and Smokey reports on Channel 19 and emergency assistance on Channel 9, unless they invest in even more expensive combination AM-SSB units.

One possible solution to the problem for SSB users would be the official reservation of certain CB channels for the exclusive use of SSB.[55] For rather unclear reasons the commission has declined to do so.[56] Instead, the 8 to 10 percent of CB operators who use SSB[57] must rely on luck to find each other in the babble of forty channels and millions of AM CB users.

As inexpensive, mass-produced AM equipment proliferates and swamps SSB use in the open warfare of channel use, one might assume that SSB CB will quietly fade away. Possibly its technological superiority, together with informal channel usage patterns, will allow for its continuation and even further development. More likely, however, it will disappear because of its higher costs (which have not been lowered by mass production), inability to secure exclusive channel haven, and utter incompatibility with predominant AM CB.

The commission has been able to approach CB policy making largely without severe external constraints arising from an activated Congress or White House or a highly organized industry. Congressional concern about CB has been limited almost entirely to complaints about FCC procedural inadequacies in handling CB license applications or questions as to whether a CBer should even be required to have a license.[58] Only in September 1977 did a congressional committee focus its attention solely upon the larger policy problems arising from CB growth. This "Panel Discussion on Personal Radio," as it was called, generally was viewed as not only unique but also unlikely to lead to ongoing congressional policy-making pressures concerning CB radio.[59]

The White House also has kept out of CB issues, except for discussions in 1975 and 1976 concerning spectrum allocations.[60] The Office of Telecommunications Policy did convene a user conference at one point, but White House interest has been extremely limited nevertheless; it has been directed almost solely to the question of how to open up more spectrum space to meet multimillion user demand.[61]

Industry interests are represented by a number of different voices. CB users are represented by several more or less self-appointed national user organizations, most of which are commercial companies that publish magazines. These efforts at representation in Washington are viewed by many as limited and amateurish.[62]

CB manufacturers themselves are represented individually by Washington attorneys and somewhat collectively by the Citizens Radio Section of the Electronic Industries Association. This association, however, has to speak with two tongues, since another major EIA division, the Consumer Electronics Group, represents TV manufacturers who want CB regulated to reduce TV interference. There is no separate national CB industry association to provide an unequivocal collective voice.[63]

The FCC, then, generally has been free of the more constraining external pressures outlined in the preceding case studies. Initiatives within the commission have themselves come not from individual commissioners but almost entirely from the staff, most notably from the new Personal Radio Planning Group, established in February 1976, as well as from the Chief Engineer's Office and the Safety and Special Services Bureau.[64] Thus the FCC has had the luxury of relative freedom from massive external pressure in CB policy evaluation.[65] Its success in creating viable CB policy has not been particularly notable, however.

The commission completely failed to anticipate the spectacular growth of CB radio starting in 1975, and it allocated additional channels only when the existing twenty-three channels were sinking under the weight of 20 million users. The commission failed to assess the interference problems that would be generated by CB omnipresence and has provided few realistic means of relief for the individual plagued by television interference or stereo system CB reception. It has failed to maintain workable standards for CB operators in terms of station identification, power limitations, channel differentiation, or proper use. And it has failed to act to allow for the long-term growth of CB radio by creating an adequate number of permanently assigned channels, perhaps multiplied by the use of SSB CB.

Instead, the FCC has allowed CB radio to develop through its own momentum, to set its own functions (increasingly centering around idle chatter), and to police itself (often with disastrous results). It has permitted AM CB to overwhelm the more efficient SSB CB and has provided new frequencies only when the CB band was collapsing under the pressure of overuse.

Perhaps the FCC should be forgiven because of the severe burdens placed upon it by the rapid growth of CB radio. Nevertheless, commission policy—or more precisely, nonpolicy—toward CB radio since 1974 raises important questions concerning the FCC's ability to deal with rapidly developing innovations. The FCC has been criticized often in terms of its ineptness or even negligence in responding to technological change in broadcasting.[66] The overwhelming of the FCC by the development of CB radio raises additional questions concerning the broadcast policy-making process. Specifically, with respect to CB radio, a report to the Office of Telecommunications Policy noted:

> The first and perhaps the most fundamental issue is whether the FCC should allow the existence of a service that it is unable to regulate by virtue of the fact that the size and nature of the service are beyond the practical reach of enforcement measures. Should such a service be expanded without rectifying this deficiency? The CB radio licensee deserves some protection when he purchases his transceiver, EIA standards are not adequate, and it is unreasonable to expect manufacturers to be self-regulating. Should we develop longer range policy

guidelines for our FCC spectrum management instead of continuing to play it by ear?[67]

Citizens band radio has provided enormous and unprecedented opportunities for individual communication. One can only hope that in the immediate years ahead the politics of broadcast regulation will evolve appropriate and even possibly wise answers to the unresolved regulatory and policy questions concerning citizens band radio.

Notes

[1] *U.S. News and World Report*, March 7, 1977, p. 76.

[2] *FCC News* (official news bulletin of the FCC), March 15, 1977. According to some estimates CB users numbered over 30 million as of September 6, 1977. Washington interview with Carlos Roberts, Office of Plans and Policy, FCC, September 6, 1977.

[3] CB radio was, of course, originally intended specifically for point-to-point communication (e.g., between a baker and his fleet of delivery trucks). A major change in CB radio in the 1970s has been its transformation into a less selective communications service (although still two-way), with CBers often indicating their wish to talk to anyone listening.

[4] Mark J. Meltzer, "Chaos on the Citizens Band—Regulatory Solutions for Spectrum Pollution," *Hastings Law Journal*, 26 (January 1975), 797. For additional discussion of the history of CB radio see Carlos Valle Roberts, "Two-Way Communication Systems for Use by the General Public" (Masters thesis, Department of Electrical Engineering, University of Colorado, 1975), especially pp. 4–8; and Carolyn Marvin and Quentin J. Schultz, "CB in Perspective: The First Thirty Years," *Journal of Communication*, 27 (Summer 1977), 104–117.

[5] In January 1977 this class D citizens radio service was officially renamed by the FCC as the "citizens band radio service." The most complete account of the FCC's actions concerning CB radio between 1945 and 1977 can be found in Marvin and Schultz, ibid., 106–114.

[6] For useful summaries of the early history of CB radio see Marvin and Schultz, ibid., 104–117; David A. Loehwing, "No Bucket Mouth: A Shakeout May Be Coming in Citizens Band," *Barron's*, May 31, 1976, pp. 3–11; and Michael Harwood, "America with Its Ears On," *New York Times Magazine*, April 25, 1976, pp. 28ff.

[7] 47 C.F.R. 95.83(a) (1) (1973).

[8] *Lafayette Radio Electronics Corporation* v. *U.S.*, 345 F. 2d 278 (2d Cir., 1965). More generally, see Meltzer, "Chaos on the Citizens Band," 808–809. The 1964 rule was finally repealed by the FCC on September 15, 1975.

[9] For further discussion, see Loehwing, "No Bucket Mouth." One might note, in addition, that two of the major hit records of 1976, "Convoy" and "The White Knight," were based on CB trucker experiences.

[10] *FCC News*, March 24, 1977. The rate of FCC license applications dropped somewhat in the later months of 1977, suggesting a possible leveling off of rapid CB growth. Washington interviews with Carlos Roberts and Tom Keller, Washington attorney and former general counsel of the White House Office of Telecommunications Policy, September 6, 1977.

[11] Ibid.

[12] *U.S. News and World Report*, March 7, 1977, p. 76.

[13] *FCC News*, March 15, 1977.

[14] One study reports, without any supporting evidence, that perhaps one in two of all truckers, one in seven of all recreational-vehicle owners, and one in twenty of all automobile owners with CB radios are unlicensed. Harwood, "America with Its Ears On." See also the discussion of unlicensed CBers in Roberts, "Two-Way Communication Systems," pp. 17–19.

[15] *Wall Street Journal*, February 3, 1977, p. 1.

[16] Loehwing, "No Bucket Mouth," p. 8. For an earlier analysis of the economic impact of CB radio, see Roberts, "Two-Way Communication Systems," pp. 21–24.

[17] Loehwing, "No Bucket Mouth," p. 8. Some of the new CB equipment uses microcomputer technology consisting of miniature electronic chips or integrated circuits, automatic available channel selection, and keyboard-type controls. "CB Break," syndicated column by Mike Wendland, June 26, 1977.

[18] The growth of CB radio has not been limited to the United States. Considerable CB activity has occurred in West Germany, Sweden, France, Italy, and Holland (although in Europe it is generally illegal except for business use). Sales there are estimated at 1.5 million sets as of early 1977, and operating conditions are reported as chaotic. See *Business Week*, March 21, 1977, pp. 47–48; and *Washington Post*, January 1, 1977, p. 136. Canada and Mexico also have considerable CB activity, despite the fact that in Mexico it is completely illegal. The *New York Times* reports that some 10,000 sets are operating illegally in Mexico City alone, with some residents, in addition, buying CB car antennas for 75 pesos ($3.50) because it makes them look influential. *New York Times*, February 10, 1977, p. 3.

[19] Quoted in the *Washington Star*, September 20, 1976. One eighty-two-year-old recent convert to CB radio states, "I live by my CB now. My vision is 90 percent gone but I get everything that goes on in the world. If I can't sleep, I get up and talk on the CB to the truck drivers. CB is kinda like the old time party line. People meet and talk on it and get to be friends even though they might never see each other." Quoted by Dale N. Hatfield, chief of the FCC Office of Plans and Policy, in remarks before the Harvard University Program on Information Resources Policy Seminar, March 14, 1977.

[20] A 1977 study of CBers by the Axiom Market Research Bureau found that the typical CB user "listens to Hank Snow and Dolly Parton records on the radio, watches 'Baa Baa Black Sheep' on television, would rather see a

roller derby than a movie, reads *Hustler* and *Car & Driver* and is about twice as active as the average person." It concludes that "compared to the rest of the population, CBers have a robust, energetic lifestyle with heavy participation in outdoor and sports activities." Quoted in *Washington Post*, August 5, 1977, p. D14.

[21] Harwood, "America with Its Ears On," p. 28. For discussions of CB lingo from the point of view of communications theory, see Jon T. Powell and Donald Ary, "CB in Perspective: Communication Without Commitment," *Journal of Communication*, 27 (Summer 1977), 118–121; and W. Dale Dannefer and Nicholas Poushinsky, "CB in Perspective: Language and Community," *Journal of Communication*, 27 (Summer 1977), 122–126.

[22] In fairness one should note many CB law-supportive activities, such as private-volunteer monitoring of the emergency Channel 9 by members of REACT, a private association of 1,200 teams made up of some 40,000 individual members. See Jethro Lieberman and Neil S. Rhodes, *The Complete CB Handbook* (New York: Avon, 1976), p. 183. In addition many state policemen have been allowed to equip their police cars with CB "ears," and they find Channel 19 traffic reports and accounts of accidents of considerable value in their duties.

[23] Associated Press stories of September 24, 1976, and February 28, 1977. For a discussion of CBers as a social stratum, see Roberts, "Two-Way Communication Systems," pp. 12–14.

[24] *Media Industry News*, August 23–30, 1976, p. 7.

[25] Associated Press story, February 28, 1977.

[26] Associated Press story, February 26, 1977. The coffee thieves were arrested, however, by the FBI, who apparently "had their ears on."

[27] *Wall Street Journal*, March 8, 1977, p. 1; *Washington Post*, November 30, 1976, p. C2; *Washington Star*, February 28, 1977, p. D1. According to a 1977 survey by the Axiom Market Research Bureau, "CB owners are four times more likely to read *Hustler* and three times more likely to read *Oui* than the average person." *Washington Post*, August 5, 1977, p. D14.

[28] *U.S. News and World Report*, March 7, 1977, p. 76.

[29] Burt Schorr, "Crossed-Band Woes Are Unlikely to Ease Despite FCC Moves," *Wall Street Journal*, August 23, 1976.

[30] *U.S. News and World Report*, March 7, 1977, p. 77.

[31] Lieberman and Rhodes, *The Complete CB Handbook*, p. 27. See also Dannefer and Poushinsky, "CB in Perspective," 123–124, and Roberts, "Two-Way Communication Systems," p. 9.

[32] The FCC acted in December 1976 to suspend fees for all commission licenses, including those for CB radio, in response to a court of appeals decision striking down its entire fee structure. At the time the CB license fee was $4; prior to mid-1975, it had varied between nothing and $20.

[33] The national calling channel use for Channel 11 was proposed by the FCC in September 1975 but dropped by 1977.

[34] *FCC News*, March 15, 1977. Various informal channel stake-outs have been reported across the country. Channel 8 reportedly is being used in some areas by farmers, Channel 13 in other areas by fishermen and CB boaters; some truckers are moving to Channel 20, and some single sideband (SSB) users are attempting to establish exclusive SSB use for Channels 15,

16, 17, or the new Channels 36 to 40. These arrangements are, of course, purely unofficial and often are maintained only by vigorous persuasion over the air by "channel chasers" or even by some self-appointed vigilante group in an area operating under a name such as "CB Channel Control." See "CB Break," syndicated column, by Mike Wendland, January 23, 1977, for a discussion of some of these unofficial channel stake-outs.

[35] Loehwing, "No Bucket Mouth," p. 6.

[36] Meltzer, "Chaos on the Citizens Band," 810. According to some estimates perhaps 15 percent of CB operators use illegal linear amps. This practice is quite distinct from the entirely legal use of "modulation" or "power" mikes, which keep microphone volume at a relatively high level.

[37] *Washington Star*, February 19, 1977, p. B6; confirmed by the Washington interview with Carlos Roberts, September 6, 1977.

[38] Officially this would be illegal since FCC rules prohibits using skip to contact anyone more than 150 miles away.

[39] Quoted in *Media Industry Newsletter*, August 23–30, 1976, p. 5. The sunspot-caused problems with skip have been blamed directly on the commission's action in 1958 establishing CB radio in frequencies susceptible to sunspot effects. See Marvin and Schultz, "CB in Perspective," 108–109.

[40] *Media Industry Newsletter*, August 23–30, 1976, p. 5.

[41] Quoted in the *Washington Star*, January 23, 1977.

[42] *New York Times*, January 23, 1977, p. 1. This article provides an interesting and useful account of CB interference problems. Sometimes the content of CB broadcasts causes other special problems. In 1976 CBer Lewis L. Simpson ("Sly Fox") of Indianapolis became the first CB operator to be convicted of using indecent language on the air. Apparently his broadcasts had been widely received on area televisions, radios, and even telephones. Associated Press story of January 2, 1977. The U.S. Court of Appeals for the 7th Circuit subsequently overturned the conviction on July 29, 1977.

[43] Engineers have expressed concern that the new seventeen channels added to the already existing twenty-three channels on CB radio will create additional TV interference on TV Channel 6. *Broadcast Engineering*, October 1976, p. 4; and December 1976, p. 4.

[44] Quoted in the *New York Times*, July 10, 1976, p. C13.

[45] David Lachenbruch, "Stay Off My TV, Good Buddy," *TV Guide*, October 23, 1976, p. 26.

[46] The FCC has required equipment manufacturers to submit transceivers to the commission for acceptance only since November 22, 1974.

[47] *Broadcasting*, October 25, 1976; *Washington Star*, February 9, 1977, p. A3; Schorr, "Crossed-Band Woes Are Unlikely to Ease." This interim requirement still remained as policy over a year later as the commission continued to consider harmonic radiation standards. The FCC has instituted a rule-making proceeding on a proposal to require that CB transmitters provide at least 100 decibel suppression of harmonic frequencies. Current thinking, as of late 1977, was that the FCC might eventually settle for 75 decibel suppression, an increase over the "interim" assignment, but far below the 1976 AMST–ABC request for 105 decibel suppression.

[48] Radio broadcasters have also become increasingly concerned about

the growth of CB radio, not because of technical interference but rather because of a significant decrease in the size of the car radio audience— radio's prime commercial audience. *Billboard*, October 2, 1976, p. 55.

[49] Ibid.

[50] The comparison between proposals to shift CB and FM was noted in *Media Industry Newsletter*, August 23, 1976, pp. 5-7.

[51] Meltzer, "Chaos on the Citizens Band," 812. The total uprooting of CB radio to a new home now looks extremely unlikely, but *supplementary* CB assignments in the range of 200 megahertz or other bands are still under consideration.

[52] Loehwing, "No Bucket Mouth," p. 10.

[53] Ibid. The director of the White House Office of Telecommunications Policy, Thomas J. Houser, was quoted in October 1976 as raising the possibility of CB radio's further expansion in the 27 megahertz band, perhaps using 27.54 to 28 megahertz. *Washington Star*, October 19, 1976, p. A2.

[54] Because SSB CB focuses its transmitter power in a narrow band, it also has more range. The 4 watts allowed CB turns into an effective 12 watts in SSB, and the maximum thirty-mile range of AM CB becomes an SSB range of up to fifty miles. For further discussion, see Mike Wendland, *CB Update* (Kansas City: Sheed, Andrews, and McMeel, 1976), p. 23.

[55] This had been generally assumed as recently as 1976 as likely to occur. Ibid., p. 73.

[56] In March 1977 the FCC announced that it had no plans to designate any channels for exclusive, or even predominant, SSB use; it called for "voluntary cooperation" between AM and SSB CBers over channel sharing. *FCC News*, March 15, 1977, p. 1.

[57] Estimate by Washington attorney Rick Brown, who represents major CB manufacturers. Washington interview, September 6, 1977.

[58] Washington interviews with Roberts and Keller, September 6, 1977; and Washington interview with Robert Booth, Washington attorney and general counsel, American Radio Relay League, September 6, 1977.

[59] Washington interviews with Roberts, Keller, and Booth, September 6, 1977; and telephone interview with Bryan Moir, counsel to the Subcommittee on Communications, House Commerce Committee, September 6, 1977. This panel discussion was held by the subcommittee and was part of a much larger subcommittee reevaluation of the entire Communications Act of 1934.

[60] Ibid.

[61] Ibid.

[62] Ibid.

[63] Washington interviews with Roberts and Keller, September 6, 1977. The National Association of Broadcasters has also involved itself in CB questions but only in a limited manner over the issues of TV interference and the loss of car radio audiences.

[64] Ibid. The Personal Radio Planning Group has been the mechanism for longer-range planning; the other offices have dealt with more immediate matters.

[65] Many individuals at the commission, however, are aware that they are dealing with what may be a sleeping giant. Raymond Spence, FCC Chief Engineer, recently commented: "There are 12 million CB licensees. Can you imagine what kind of lobby they would have if they were organized? They'd be bigger than anything else." "Citizen Band: The Complaints Are Beginning to Catch Up with the Sets," *Broadcasting*, October 24, 1977, p. 55.

[66] Especially relevant to the question of technological assessment is Don R. LeDuc, *Cable Television and the FCC: A Crisis in Media Control* (Philadelphia: Temple University Press, 1973), especially chap. 2. LeDuc notes: "Factors of custom, innate conservatism and limited analytical ability all operate to create an initial bias against any group seeking to change the established procedures of a regulated industry, with the degree of hostility modestly related to the magnitude of the change" (p. 28).

[67] Quoted from a study of CB radio by the consulting firm of Arthur D. Little, undertaken for the White House Office of Telecommunications Policy; the quote was reprinted in *Media Industry Newsletter*, August 23-30, 1976, p. 7. See also *Billboard*, October 2, 1976, p. 55. In response to these criticisms the FCC, in 1976, established a personal radio planning group made up of three engineers and an economist charged with the responsibility of studying the problems of CB radio and evaluating its future role. See Lionel Van Deerlin, "Updating Federal Regulation—At Last," *Television Quarterly*, Spring, 1977, pp. 39-42. See also Ronald S. Stone, "Personal Radio Planning at the Federal Communications Commission" (unpublished FCC paper, 1977).

A Closing Look: Reflections on Broadcast Regulation

The preceding chapters have taken the reader beyond organization tables and formal procedures in an effort to provide the flavor and detail of what we have called the politics of broadcast regulation. In this closing chapter we propose to examine that political process as a totality—to provide the connecting links between the analytical and theoretical material in the first four chapters and the specific facts of the five case studies.

The Case Studies Analyzed

Emmette S. Redford has suggested that three questions are central to evaluating the regulatory process: "What fashioned this decision?" "What has fashioned the subsequent lines of policy?" "Who got what out of the process?"[1] Like Harold Lasswell he sees the politics of administrative decision making in terms of "who gets what, when, and how" (see Introduction, page 2). Along similar lines we shall pose the following questions to compare the five case studies just presented:

> Who initiated the policy proposal?
> Why?
> What determined involvement in the dispute?
> Who won?
> Why?
> What were the ultimate results of the policy—who really won?

Table 2 analyzes the five case studies in terms of these common questions. Table 3 carries this comparative analysis one step further by summarizing who was on which side in each case.

Certain generalizations emerge from a study of Tables 2 and 3. The FCC initiated all five of the policies under consideration. In four of the cases the FCC succeeded in having its desired policy implemented. However, most of the cases were not clear-cut victories for the commission. In one the commission had to pay the price—albeit a modest one—of dropping deintermixture to obtain passage of the All-Channel Receiver Bill. The "win" in the FM shift controversy turned out to be a hollow victory indeed, for while the commission achieved its immediate goal of reestablishing FM in a higher band, it failed to accomplish its professed objectives. The "victory" in the renewal policy statement was short-lived since the court of appeals struck down the policy statement less than six months after its adoption and controversy continued. Only in the forty-channel CB decision did the FCC achieve a clear "win," and yet in this policy case, the commission was responding to events and CB pressures more than taking the lead. The key role of the FCC in initiating regulatory policy is evident, but the case studies underscore that the fate of such policy is determined by the struggle among various participants for control or influence over the policy-making process. In most instances involvement in a policy conflict is a direct result of perceived economic threats or benefits from the proposal.

Division and Alliance Among Participants. Division among any of the participants severely weakens the FCC's effectiveness. For example, the dissenting opinions in the controversies over advertising time and the license renewal policy statement contributed measurably to the ultimate ineffectiveness of the FCC on these issues. The degree of broadcasting industry unanimity is no less important. If the industry is divided, as is frequently the case, a policy which favors the most powerful groups is likely to fare better than a policy which is opposed by these groups. In the FM and all-channel receiver cases, for instance, groups with long-established working relationships with Congress and the FCC were better able to persuade the commission to adopt their views than were the newer groups. In the CB case the new CB industry was successful not only because of the merits of its argument (that forty channels were crucial) but also because of the very size of its constituency along with the nearly undeniable need for growth. CB industry support for new channels further enhanced commission willingness to respond to CB user demands, while ignoring television industry concerns.

Table 2. Comparison of the Five Cases

	1945 FM Shift	1961–1962 All-Channel Receiver Bill	1963–1964 Advertising Limits	1970 License Renewal Policy Statement	1976 Forty-Channel CB
1. Who initiated the policy proposal?	Commission (unanimous)	Commission (unanimous)	Commission (split)	Commission (split)	Commission (unanimous)
2. Why?	(1) To develop technically superior FM; (2) to make available low-frequency space for more critical needs	To meet need for diversity of programming through development of UHF	To meet problems of advertising excesses	To calm fears of broadcasters raised by the WHDH decision	To meet immediate demand for more CB channels
3. What determined involvement?	Economic interests—although clothed in terms of technical debate	Economic interests; opposition to deintermixture and desire to block it through the All-Channel Receiver Bill	Economic interests; fear of potential implications of such regulation	Economic interests in terms of costs of litigation, devaluation of investments, and possible loss of license	Economic and user interests: CBers wish for more channels, CB industry desire for set sales, TV industry concern over interference, and other user concerns over allocation

4. Who won?	FCC (in part only); established interests	FCC; UHF interests	Broadcasting industry; Congress	Broadcasting industry; FCC	CB users and interests; FCC
5. Why?	Technical character of dispute; unquestioned legal authority of commission; power of dominant interests	Fear of deintermixture; need to take some positive action	Split in commission; strong industry and congressional pressure; confusion over commission's authority; economic issues potentially at stake	Major industry concern; key congressional support for a compromise agreement	Strong CB industry economic interests and numerous CB users; clear urgent demand and need
6. What were the results—who really won?	TV interests and others opposed to FM growth	FCC; UHF interests; those VHF interests threatened by deintermixture	Broadcasting industry; Congress	As a result of a subsequent ruling of the court of appeals, citizens groups and critics of broadcasting industry won temporary victory; policy stalemate since 1971	CB users and industry—unless sunspot skip grows to plague CB radio

Table 3.   Who Sided with Whom in the Five Cases

	For the Proposal	Against the Proposal	Result
FM Shift in 1945	United FCC; TV and certain AM interests; manufacturers; and prospective broadcasters	FM backers; RTPB Panel 5; Television Broadcasters Association (very late)	Implemented
The All-Channel Receiver Bill in 1961–1962	United FCC; generally united industry (when coupled with deletion of de-intermixture); President Kennedy	Electronic Industries Association	Implemented
Regulation of Commercial Time in 1963–1964	Split FCC (4–3)	United industry; House of Representatives	Not implemented
Licenses Renewal Policy Statement in 1970	Split FCC (6–1); industry; key congressmen	Citizens groups; House Committee staff report	Implemented (but later struck down by court of appeals)
Forty-Channel CB in 1976	United FCC; CB users and CB industry	Television interests concerned about interference and other actual or potential users of the proposed space for CB	Implemented

The case studies also demonstrate that, in order to initiate and implement a policy successfully, the FCC needs support from either industry or Congress; if the commission itself is divided, it needs support from both. Since Congress will generally oppose FCC policy only when the united industry does, the commission can usually satisfy Congress by satisfying the industry. Because of this possibility of neutralizing two participants by neutralizing one, the process of interaction among industry, Congress, and the FCC would appear to have a built-in bias toward industry consultation and mollification.

In recent years, however, the increasing involvement of the courts and of citizens groups has tended to weaken the effects of congressional support for the broadcasting industry. In effect, the politics of broadcast regulation has shifted from a simple tripartite system of industry, Congress, and commission to a more complex set of interrelationships which includes the White House, the courts, and citizens groups. The Congress, the courts, and the FCC have devised ways to encourage greater citizen participation in the regulatory process, and this has further expanded the number of possible participants on any side of a given controversy.

The all-channel receiver case, in which an FCC request resulted in widely supported legislation, suggests the potential for constructive cooperation between Congress and the commission. The success of the FCC in this case, as well as its failure to regulate commercial time or to implement policy-restricting license renewal challenges, may conceivably have "conditioned" the commission to limit itself to politically acceptable types of policies and means of policy introduction. It should be noted, however, that the courts remain in an effective position to thwart an FCC-congressional alliance.

Under various circumstances, one or more of the six major participants in broadcast regulation may appear to wield considerable power. As pointed out in chapter four, however, none has hierarchical control over the policy-making process. The FCC was able to succeed in its policy initiative in the all-channel receiver case, and to prevail (at least initially) in three other cases, *only* because of significant support from other participants. And, although industry and Congress were able through a united struggle to block the commission's proposed regulation of advertising time, neither could unilaterally dominate the policy-making process.

Mutual Adjustment of Conflicting Goals.   In chapter four we noted that although the participants in broadcast regulation seek different goals—and feed conflicting demands and supports into the system— the prevalent pattern in such controversies is one of mutual adjustment or compromise. Throughout the all-channel television proceedings, the commission sought to ensure greater diversity in programing—a goal little shared by the VHF television broadcasters. Final policy development took the form of a compromise proposal: no disruption of existing VHF channels through deintermixture and long-term strengthening of UHF broadcasting through the required manufacture of all-channel television receivers. This resolution had the considerable advantage of not immediately affecting existing VHF broadcasters while holding out hope for the future prospects of UHF. Similarly, the commission authorized forty-channel CB while at the same time, as a sop to the broadcast industry, slightly increasing the rigor of its standards concerning interference.

The goals of the FCC and the industry most clearly clashed in the advertising time controversy—the commission asserting its authority to outlaw broadcasting excesses and the industry equally determined to retain freedom of action. Here no mutually adjusted solution was found. Rather than allowing the commission some means of gracefully modifying or withdrawing its rule-making proposal, the broadcasting industry and the House of Representatives insisted on censuring the FCC politically.

Why was mutual adjustment not the pattern in this case? The answer lies partly in the political weakness of the commission, which had initiated the rule by only a one-vote majority. In addition, the FCC's proposal was seen by many broadcasters as a threat to the very lifeblood of commercial broadcasting. Some quickly concluded that the same rationale might be used to justify regulation of programing or—even worse—of such vital matters as rates and profits. These industry fears that symbolic legal or ideological rights could be violated aroused a fierce protectiveness in Congress, and the FCC was sternly rebuked.

Goals and Strategies in FCC Policy Making

In the diagram of the input-output system for broadcast regulation (see Figure 2, chapter four), the FCC occupies a crucial position as the principal (although by no means the most powerful) agent in the regulatory process. Because of its key relationship to authoritative outputs and also because the future of broadcast regulation in the United States is squarely in the commission's lap, it is worthwhile to extract from the case studies some aspects of the modus operandi which have characterized the FCC's actions and procedures over the last forty-four years of its existence.[2]

Modest Change. The FCC strives generally for only modest change—some acceptable level of goal accomplishment short of maximization. Charles Lindblom has described the strategy of opting only for modest change as one which "satisfices" (satisfies and suffices) rather than maximizes. This strategy evolves naturally out of certain structural and attitudinal features of the regulatory process—namely, the limited resources of the regulatory body (the FCC) and the conflicting goals of the participants.

Throughout the all-channel television case the FCC was aware that UHF's prospects might be significantly improved by the development of an all-UHF television service. However, it never seriously considered this policy because of the high economic—and political—costs entailed in uprooting all existing VHF stations. The commission had no stomach for imposing upon VHF television broadcasters or set owners the kind of disruption it had earlier forced upon FM. But, while all-UHF was rejected as too drastic, the All-Channel Receiver Bill did not go far enough to provide substantial relief for UHF interests. Although the bill required new sets to receive all eighty-two VHF and UHF channels (which was helpful), it did not require these sets to have click-stop (detent) tuners for the UHF channels. Consequently, even though the sets could receive UHF programing, many viewers were discouraged from watching UHF because of tuning difficulties.

Similarly, the FCC did not, in 1963, suggest the regulation of commercial content, placement, or frequency—problems often noted. Instead it limited itself to proposing the adoption of industry-established standards governing the maximum total minutes of commercial time per hour. It is clear that many affected interests considered this proposal extreme; nevertheless, a good case can be made for its modesty. In nonprime-time television, for example, an acceptable total of advertising time according to these standards would be 27.2 percent. More than sixteen minutes of commercials in each hour have been sanctioned as broadcasting in the public interest.

The principle of modest change also was operative in the commission's decision on license renewal policies in comparative hearings. In this case the FCC did not try to adopt the provisions of the Pastore bill, which would have prohibited the filing of a competing license application at renewal time unless the FCC first found that a grant of the renewal application would not be in the public interest. Instead, the FCC endorsed the compromise approach originally suggested by Chairman Dean Burch at Senate hearings on S. 2004. In adopting the policy statement the FCC emphasized that the policy of preferring an incumbent who had compiled a good broadcasting record over a rival applicant whose promises were untested was firmly grounded in prior commission precedent and did not change existing law. (The court of appeals, however, later overturned the FCC policy statement.) In 1976 the commission had several options open to it: establishing rigorous interference standards for new forty-channel CB radio, moving it entirely to some new frequency band more free from sunspot-generated skip and less prone to television interference, or establishing means for the gradual phasing in of SSB CB as an alternative to and even replacement for existing AM CB. Instead it opted for modesty: It authorized forty-channel CB as an expansion of existing frequency space despite the consequent problems of skip and electronic interference, and it took a hands-off attitude toward the development of SSB CB radio.[3]

Flexibility and Sensitivity to Feedback.   One advantage of modest change is that it can usually be reversed—if necessary—more easily than sweeping innovations. Thus, the FCC attempts to remain flexible in its policy choices so as not to make irreversible decisions; in short, it values the second chance.

The shift of FM in 1945, however, was essentially an irreversible decision, based on questionable technical data and made under the pressure of time. Similarly, the commission issued the renewal policy statement suddenly—apparently in response to pressures from Congress and the industry to act—without waiting for the submission of written or oral arguments by interested parties. Yet this is not the typical pattern. Much of the history of broadcast regulation can be described in terms of FCC vacillation and indecision.

In the all-channel television case, the FCC requested that Congress act to relieve UHF's problems. Throughout this case, the tentative commitment of the commission to all-channel television legislation was evident. The FCC frequently indicated that it considered such legislation to be the best immediate solution. However, it reserved the right to reconsider, after suitable time, the consequences of the legislation.

The forty-channel CB decision of 1976 was seen by the FCC as reversible. In fact, the commission formally termed both the modest interference standards and the frequencies assigned as "interim," subject to continued review and reconsideration.

In the advertising time controversy, however, the commission got caught in a politically costly policy initiative from which it could not extract itself in time to avoid punitive action. The FCC had left open the escape hatch of dropping its proposed rule-making proceeding; however, internal inertia prevented it from responding quickly enough to avoid industry condemnation and the House approval of the Rogers bill. In this case the necessary flexibility was lacking.

In the FM shift, advertising time, and license renewal cases, the commission, under the pressure of time, initiated proposals that later proved to be irreversible. In these same cases the commission, for various reasons, did not have time to make substantive changes in policy in response to feedback. The effectiveness and flexibility of the FCC, then, seem to be partly a function of the time it had for policy development. Sufficient time to collect adequate data on which to base policy choices—and sufficient time to respond to political reactions to these choices—are usually necessary for successful policy making.

Focus on Short-Range Ills—Breaking Bottlenecks. Given limited resources for the accomplishment of its goals, the FCC is forced to direct its attention to those problems which give the greatest promise of resolution with the least amount of difficulty for the agency. For this reason the commission tends to focus on short-term problems—to deal with the immediate rather than with the interminable. In the CB case, for instance, the FCC sought to deal with the immediate, and in so doing, it ignored the serious. The commission expanded CB channels from twenty-three to forty without any expectation that forty channels would be able to accommodate 20 to 30 million CB users. It established 60-decibel limits on interference because the figure could be engineered quickly into CB equipment. And it failed to act to distinguish CB channels, thereby assisting SSB CB, probably because of the difficulty of enforcing any commission designation of channel use.

The clearest instance of a short-term focus on policy bottlenecks occurred in the all-channel television case. In the 1950s the development of UHF television seemed to depend upon making television markets either all VHF or all UHF. When this proved politically unfeasible, the commission turned its attention in 1961 to the problem of ensuring at least a potential audience for UHF programing. Unable to reach most existing sets, few UHF license holders were prepared to broadcast—and few advertisers were prepared to buy—commercial time.

The policy which the commission finally developed in 1962 to assist UHF broadcasters was primarily a short-range solution directly aimed at this significant bottleneck. The commission was of the opinion that the desire to broadcast and to advertise on UHF frequencies would result from wider distribution of all-channel sets. With about 90 percent of all television sets now able to receive UHF, its prospects have become considerably brighter. Further obstacles to UHF prosperity—tuner problems, programing difficulties, and competition from cable—are now under active consideration by the commission, but the established approach to breaking such bottlenecks is to approach only one problem at a time.

Similarly, the renewal policy statement was adopted in response to the short-term, immediate problem of the increased filing of competitive applications at renewal time. Confronted with the complex problem of formulating standards for comparative renewal proceedings, the FCC chose a policy that would obviate the need for a hearing in most situations as long as the renewal applicant had shown that its program service during the preceding term had been substantially attuned to community needs and interests and that its operation had not been marred by serious deficiencies.

The policy statement was designed to discourage the filing of competing applications at renewal time and thereby to alleviate the concern of broadcasters about the stability of their licenses. It did not, however, deal with the larger problem of standards to be applied to renewal applicants and challengers in competitive renewal hearings. The staff report of the House Investigations Subcommittee in effect criticized the FCC's focus on policy bottlenecks by charging that the statement usurped congressional power and repealed "a constitutional and statutory requirement in the interest of *easing Commission workload requirements.*"[4]

Sequentialism and Incrementalism. As discussed in chapter four, short-range, sequential policies are less likely to violate the existing ideological and legal consensus, and they therefore make policy acceptance easier. This is probably why the FCC sees its policy making as serial or sequential—a never-ending process of successive steps in which continual nibbling is a substitute for a good bite.

Reviewing the case studies in the light of this hypothesis, it is at first difficult to see the FM and advertising disputes as part of a sequence of gradual, incremental steps. There was certainly nothing moderate in the effects of these policies upon key participants. Yet the FCC had been concerned for some time with the efficient use of the lower frequencies, and it doubtless regarded the lengthy hearings and collection of relevant data as logical steps leading to the final decision to shift FM upstairs in the spectrum.

In the same way the regulation of advertising time had at least a general precedent—the commission's long concern, in its determination of the public interest, with the overall performance of broadcasters. All that was really new in 1963 was that the FCC's expectations about commercialization were formalized and the proposal was made that they be imposed upon licensees as a definite requirement.

FCC sequentialism is best illustrated by the all-channel receiver bill and by the commission's policy making concerning CB radio. The all-channel receiver approach was a policy which evolved step by step amid an agony of indecision, as a means for dealing with a given problem: the intermixture, on an unequal technical, economic, and programing basis, of VHF and UHF stations. FCC policy toward rapidly emerging CB radio has also taken the form of an evolutionary series of steps as the commission has tried to discover modest means of dealing with CB problems. Because sequentialism is essentially in the eye of the beholder, however, all of the case studies actually fit the sequential model. What seems to the FCC to be only incrementally different from existing policy may be vigorously condemned by industry or citizens groups as violating established legal or ideological taboos, opening up or eliminating new avenues of regulation and control, or foretelling different and harsher procedures.

When the commission majority proposed a policy that was not clearly incremental (such as making a voluntary industry advertising standard compulsory), the commissioners may have felt they were "only trying to do industry a favor" by regulating overcommercialized stations. But the method and substance of the proposal failed to communicate this benevolence to the industry. Similarly, in the renewal policy statement, the six commissioners favoring the policy may have regarded their action as merely a codification of existing policies and prior precedent. In both instances the commission apparently did not expect the intense reactions to its proposals that rapidly appeared.

A Broader View of the "Public Interest"

In an effort to encourage the ventilation of contrasting viewpoints, the FCC has recently been holding public hearings and panel discussions of outside spokesmen on major policy issues, including cable television, communications satellites, children's programing, minority ownership of broadcast stations, and the Fairness Doctrine. During the administration of Chairman Richard Wiley the commission held ten regional meetings that were open to members of the public and conducted monthly meetings to which various public groups were invited to make presentations. Direct confrontation and robust debate provide FCC commissioners with a wider perception of the public interest. Moreover, public proceedings are useful in the commission's relations with other institutions such as the courts and the Congress. Former Chairman Burch acknowledged that one of the objectives of the Fairness Doctrine inquiry—which included the filing of voluminous comments by interested parties, oral argument, and panel discussions before the full commission—was to improve the FCC's position before the courts by showing that the agency had the benefit of all shades of opinion and could demonstrate that it had agonized over the issues.[5]

We have seen that the commission usually seeks modest goals, is flexible in its policy choices and sensitive to feedback, directs its attention to immediate problems in a series of serial or sequential steps, focuses on bottlenecks, and limits its consideration to proposals which are, in its view, only incrementally different from existing policies. One of the deficiencies of this type of approach is that the FCC tends to be reactive rather than innovative and to adopt short-term measures rather than long-range solutions. The basic issues in each of the case studies—fostering the full growth of FM and UHF, the form of advertising restrictions, the standards for judging renewal applicants against challengers, and the future use and standards of CB radio—remain unresolved and are still perplexing the commission today. To enlarge its focus from bottlenecks to broad policy questions, the commission, in 1967, established a Research and Policy Studies Program to provide guidance on complex policy questions and technical issues. In 1973 the FCC created the Office of Plans and Policy (OPP) to recommend research blueprints and projects to the commission and to evaluate and analyze proposals made by other offices and bureaus. However, it has a small staff of professionals (eight in 1977) and a research budget in fiscal year 1977 of only $400,000. The efforts of OPP have not been entirely successful.[6] There is a need to strengthen to a considerably greater degree the commission's capabilities to study alternative policies, to evaluate the submissions of outside parties, and to conduct its own independent research.

One of the questions traditionally posed about the FCC and other independent regulatory agencies is "Why doesn't the commission regulate the industry more vigorously?" Such a question assumes that the public interest will be furthered by greater regulation. However, the history of such regulated industries as transportation has shown that stricter governmental controls may in fact disserve the public interest. Moreover, calls for the imposition of more restrictive regulations by the FCC usually do not take into account the highly complex, politically sensitive, and rapidly changing character of the communications industry. Under the system of regulation established by the Congress, the FCC has operated within a sequential, bargaining policy-making process. America's stake in broadcasting is too fundamental and precious to be subjected to drastic or politically unpopular actions which do not allow the FCC to modify policies without excessive loss if new information indicates unexpected troubles.

A more relevant question might be "Does the FCC operate in the public interest?" Although an agency which seems preoccupied with incremental or marginal changes may seem less than heroic, this approach does tend to raise the level of competence of policy decisions. Such a strategy concentrates the commission's analysis on familiar, better-known experience and reduces the number and complexity of factors it has to analyze. The commission, moreover, is much more than an "inert cash register" whose actions are dictated by the most politically powerful forces. As a policy maker the commission does have the ability to affect the forces which seem to limit sound public policy. By testing certain regulatory possibilities, other means of accomplishing the same ends may develop. The very act of proposing regulation may reveal hidden or unknown defects. Attempts to initiate unpopular policy need not be merely an exercise in futility, for they may lead to the eventual establishment of different and more effective policy.

The communications regulatory policies fashioned by the FCC

are not abstract theories. They are, rather, real world political decisions allocating material rewards and deprivations—decisions, in Laswellian terms, concerning who gets what, when, and how. The development of policy in this manner is not easy. Before any proposal can emerge as public policy, it must survive trial after trial, test after test of its vitality. The politics that govern broadcast regulation offer no escape from that imperative.

Notes

[1] Emmette S. Redford, "Perspectives for the Study of Government Regulation," *Midwest Journal of Political Science*, 6 (February 1962), 2.

[2] The following discussion is an extension and application of hypotheses developed by Charles E. Lindblom in "Strategies or Dodges," *The Policy-Making Process* (Englewood Cliffs, N.J.: Prentice-Hall, 1968), pp. 24–27.

[3] In establishing forty-channel CB radio, the FCC was attempting to extend existing policies: Citizens band radio should be free to operate essentially in a laissez-faire manner with only minimal commission attempts to establish channel use, to regulate operator practices, or even to control interference to neighborhood home electronic equipment.

[4] "Analysis of FCC's Policy Statement on Comparative Hearings Involving Regular Renewal Applicants," staff study for the Special Subcommittee on Investigations, the House Committee on Interstate and Foreign Commerce, 91st Congress, 2nd Session (November 1970), p. 111.

[5] "Chance to Get Fairness Under Control," *Broadcasting*, April 10, 1972, p. 62.

[6] See *Interim Report and Recommended Courses of Action Resulting from The Hearings on Telecommunications Research and Policy Development*, prepared by the staff of the Subcommittee on Communications, House Committee on Interstate and Foreign Commerce, 94th Congress, 1st Session (Washington, D.C.: Government Printing Office, 1976), pp. 8–11.

Annotated Bibliography

General Works on Regulatory Agencies

Although the literature on independent regulatory commissions is immense, the number of studies dealing with the political aspects of regulation is very limited. Three works which provide insights into the politics of regulation are Merle Fainsod's essay, "Some Reflections on the Nature of the Regulatory Process," in Carl J. Friedrich and Edward S. Mason, eds., *Public Policy: 1940* (Cambridge, Mass.: Harvard University Press, 1940); the study by Samuel P. Huntington, "The Marasmus of the Interstate Commerce Commission: The Commission, the Railroads, and the Public Interest," *Yale Law Journal*, 61 (April 1952); and the work by William W. Boyer, *Bureaucracy on Trial: Policy Making by Government Agencies* (Indianapolis: Bobbs-Merrill, 1964). A study by William L. Cary, *Politics and the Regulatory Agencies* (New York: McGraw-Hill, 1967) illuminates many aspects of the regulatory process but only partially defines the political context of the problems he encountered as chairman of the Securities and Exchange Commission.

Valuable background material on independent regulatory commissions may also be found in the classic studies by Robert E. Cushman, *The Independent Regulatory Commissions* (New York: Oxford University Press, 1941) and Marver H. Bernstein, *Regulating Business by Independent Commission* (Princeton: Princeton University Press, 1955). A helpful book of readings edited by Samuel Krislov and Lloyd P. Musolf, *The Politics of Regulation* (Boston: Houghton Mifflin, 1964), emphasizes the interrelations of social interests and regulatory outcomes. *A New Regulatory Framework: Report on Selected Independent Regulatory Agencies* (Washington, D.C.: Government Printing Office, 1971) contains recommendations by the President's Advisory Council on Executive Organization for restructuring regulatory agencies as well as a selected bibliography of articles, books, reports, and studies useful for understanding the regulatory process. A thoughtful evaluation of the Advisory Council's report is Roger G. Noll, *Reforming Regulation* (Washington, D.C.: Brookings Institution, 1971). For a handy annotated guide to the agencies and literature of communications regulation in the United States and Canada, see "A Guide to Government Policy-Making Bodies in Communications, *Aspen Handbook on the Media: 1977–1979 Edition* (New York: Praeger Special Studies, 1977).

The regulatory process has been the subject of increasing attention by the Congress in the mid-1970s. A 749-page study, *Federal Regulation and Regulatory Reform*, a report by the Subcommittee on Oversight and Investigations, House Committee on Interstate and Foreign Commerce, 94th Congress, 2nd Session (Washington, D.C.: Government Printing Office, 1976), provides a detailed review of the FCC and eight other regulatory agencies. In July 1975 the Senate Committee on Government Operations (later renamed the Committee on Governmental Affairs) was directed to conduct a comprehensive study of federal regulation in order to assess the impact of regulatory programs and the need for change. Following eighteen months of study the committee issued six volumes addressing the following major regulatory problem areas: Volume I, *The Regulatory Appointments Process*; Volume II, *Congressional Oversight of Regulatory Agencies*; Volume III, *Public Participation in Regulatory Agency Proceedings*; Volume IV, *Delay in the Regulatory Process*; Volume V, *Regulatory Organization and Coordination*; and Volume VI, *Framework for Regulation, and Case Studies in Federal Regulation*. (The first four volumes were published by the Government Printing Office in 1977 and the two remaining volumes are expected to be published in early 1978.)

In recent years economists have turned their attention increasingly to the analysis of the regulatory process. This rich literature tends to focus on two sets of questions. The first involves the economic effects of regulation—who benefits and who is hurt by regulatory policies. An excellent overview of this topic may be found in Clair Wilcox and William G. Shepherd, *Public Policies Toward Business*, 5th ed. (Homewood, Ill.: Irwin, 1975), especially chap. 16, "Regulation of Communications." Also, virtually every issue of the *Bell Journal of Economics and Management Science* carries articles on the subject. The second type of question economists have tended to ask about the regulatory process concerns why regulators do what they do in adopting policies which favor some interests (often established) and hurt others. A pathbreaking study by George J. Stigler, "The Theory of Economic Regulation," *Bell Journal of Economics and Management Science*, 2 (Spring 1971), analyzes what has been labeled the "economic theory of regulation"; the theory explains how and why economic regulation favors the interests of politically powerful interests in terms of the market forces of supply and demand. This theory has been advanced by economist Richard A. Posner as well in "Theories of Economic Regulation," *Bell Journal of Economics and Management Science*, 5 (Autumn 1974), with a bibliography on pp. 356–358. A collection of essays by Professor Stigler is contained in a useful paperback: George J. Stigler, *The Citizen and the State: Essays on Regulation* (Chicago: University of Chicago Press, 1975). The *Bell Journal of Economics* continues to publish important new research in this area. Those interested in the economic regulatory literature would do well to subscribe to the journal, which will be sent free upon request by writing to the Journal Manager, *Bell Journal of Economics*, AT&T, 195 Broadway, Room C1800, New York, New York 10007.

Literature on Broadcast Regulation

No definitive work exists on the political problems of the Federal Communications Commission, although two recent studies offer useful evaluations of the commission's role in the regulatory process as a controller of technological innovation: Vincent J. Mosco, *The Regulation of Broadcasting in the United States: A Comparative Analysis*, and Richard Berner, *Constraints on the Regulation Process: A Case Study of Regulation of Cable Television* (both 1975 publications of the Harvard Program on Information Technologies and Public Policy, Cambridge, Massachusetts). Walter B. Emery's *Broadcasting and Government: Responsibilities and Regulations*, rev. ed. (East Lansing, Mich.: Michigan State University Press, 1971) offers a comprehensive (albeit dated) study of the legal aspects of broadcast regulation. Emery's study provides useful insights into the backgrounds of commissioners, the various governmental agencies concerned with broadcasting, and commission-congressional relationships. A fascinating study of the manner in which appointments were made to the FCC and the Federal Trade Commission during a twenty-five-year period appears in the work of Washington lawyers James M. Graham and Victor H. Kramer, *Appointments to the Regulatory Agencies: The Federal Communications Commission and the Federal Trade Commission (1949–1974)*, published as a Committee Print for the Senate Committee on Commerce, 94th Congress, 2nd Session (Washington, D.C.: Government Printing Office, 1976).

Considerable material concerning broadcast regulatory policy prior to 1948 is contained in the published doctoral dissertation of Murray Edelman, *The Licensing of Radio Services in the United States, 1927 to 1947: A Study in Administrative Formulation of Policy* (Urbana, Ill.: University of Illinois Press, 1950). A well-written case study of *ex parte* influences in TV assignments is Victor G. Rosenblum's "How to Get into TV: The Federal Communications Commission and Miami's Channel 10," in Alan F. Westin, ed., *The Uses of Power: 7 Cases in American Politics* (New York:

Harcourt Brace Jovanovich, 1962). A valuable discussion of the role of Congress during the 1920s and 1930s is contained in the study by Carl J. Friedrich and Evelyn Sternberg, "Congress and the Control of Radio-Broadcasting," *American Political Science Review*, 37 (October, December 1943). An analysis of the role of Congress in formulating broadcast regulatory policy during the early 1970s appears in an article by Erwin G. Krasnow and Harry M. Shooshan, III (counsel to the Subcommittee on Communications, House Interstate and Foreign Commerce Committee), "Congressional Oversight: The Ninety-Second Congress and the Federal Communications Commission," *Harvard Journal on Legislation*, 10 (February 1973); reprinted in *Federal Communications Bar Journal*, 26 (Issue No. 2, 1973).

Participant-oriented material on the FCC can be found in several first-person books. Bernard Schwartz's *The Professor and the Commissions* (New York: Knopf, 1959) is a controversial account, by a New York University law professor who was hired by the House Committee on Interstate and Foreign Commerce in 1957 to study the regulatory commissions, of abuses at the FCC. Schwartz claimed that he was fired by the committee in 1958 after he proposed to expose violations of the *ex parte* rules and other laws that were politically embarrassing to the FCC, certain congressmen, and the administration. Another first-person account based on experiences at the FCC, Charles S. Hyneman's *Bureaucracy in a Democracy* (New York: Harper & Row, 1950), is a thoughtful examination of government regulation. A collection of Newton Minow's speeches when he was chairman of the FCC appears in a book edited by Lawrence Laurent entitled *Equal Time: The Private Broadcaster and the Public Interest* (New York: Atheneum, 1964). *How to Talk Back to Your Television Set* (Boston: Little, Brown, 1970; reissued with added bibliography and an index by Bantam Books, 1970) is a lively, readable synopsis of Commissioner Nicholas Johnson's views on various regulatory issues which gives practical advice on how to change television programing. Perceptive articles on the regulatory process by Commissioner Lee Loevinger are cited in chapter two of this book. And a recent book by Barry G. Cole, a former consultant to the FCC, and Mal Oettinger, who had been a reporter for *Broadcasting* magazine, *The Reluctant Regulators: the FCC and the Broadcast Audience* (Reading, Mass.: Addison-Wesley, 1978) provides a behind-the-scenes account of the commission's handling of such issues as license renewal and children's television. For insights into the theory and application of First Amendment principles to broadcasting, two books merit special attention: Fred W. Friendly, *The Good Guys, the Bad Guys and the First Amendment: Free Speech vs. Fairness in Broadcasting* (New York: Random House, 1976), and Benno C. Schmidt, Jr., *Freedom of the Press vs. Public Access* (New York: Praeger Special Studies, 1976).

The economic literature on regulation has focused increasingly on broadcasting. In addition to the books and articles mentioned above, three works are recommended as a starting place for those interested in reading about various economic theories of regulation: Roger G. Noll, Morton J. Peck, and John McGowan, *Economic Aspects of Television Regulation* (Washington, D.C.: Brookings Institution, 1973); Bruce M. Owen, Jack H. Beebe, and Willard G. Manning, Jr., *Television Economics* (Lexington, Mass.: Lexington Books, 1974); and Bruce M. Owen, *Economics and Freedom of Expression: Media Structure and the First Amendment* (Cambridge, Mass.: Ballinger, 1975).

Textbooks. There are several excellent textbooks which provide background for the historical, economic, technical, sociological, and regulatory aspects of broadcasting. Perhaps the best is Sydney W. Head's *Broadcasting in America: A Survey of Television and Radio*, 3rd ed. (Boston: Houghton Mifflin, 1976). A work edited by communications lawyer Scott H. Robb, *Television/Radio Age Communications Coursebook* (New York: Communications Research Institute, 1977), meets a long unfulfilled need for a looseleaf textbook; the *Coursebook* will consist of annual editions supplemented by four updates during the year. Broadcast law textbooks focusing on regulation of programing, multiple ownership, and other legal issues include Donald M. Gillmor and Jerome A. Barron, *Mass Communication Law: Cases and Comment*, 2nd ed. (St. Paul: West, 1974); Harold L. Nelson and Dwight Teeter, Jr., *The Law of Mass Communications: Freedom and Control of Print and Broadcast Media*, 2nd ed. (Mineola, N.Y.: Foundation Press, 1973); William K. Jones, *Cases and Materials on Electronic Mass Media* (Mineola, N.Y.. Foundation Press, 1976); Harvey L. Zuckman and Martin J. Gaynes, *Mass Communications Law in a Nutshell* (St. Paul, Minn.: West, 1977); William E. François, *Mass Media Law and Regulation* (Columbus, Ohio: Grid, 1975); Don. R. Pember, *Mass Media Law* (Dubuque, Iowa: William C. Brown, 1977); and Marc A. Franklin, *Cases and Materials on Mass Media Law* (Mineola, N.Y.: Foundation Press, 1977).

History. A rich and fascinating social history of American broadcasting is the comprehensive three-volume work by Erik Barnouw: *A Tower in Babel: A History of Broadcasting in the United States to 1933; The Golden Web: A History of Broadcasting in the United States, 1933–1953;* and *The Image Empire: A History of Broadcasting from 1953* (New York: Oxford University Press, 1966, 1968, and 1970, respectively). Each volume contains a chronology, the text of major laws relating to broadcasting, and an extensive bibliography. A more recent book by Professor Barnouw, *Tube of Plenty: The Evolution of American Television* (New York: Oxford University Press, 1975), condenses material dealing with television found in the first three volumes and provides about five years of updating. Christopher H. Sterling and John M. Kittross, *Stay Tuned: A*

Concise History of Broadcasting (Belmont, Calif.: Wadsworth, 1978) details trends in broadcast regulation against a context of radio-television development.

Other useful books on various aspects of the history of broadcasting include Llewellyn White's *The American Radio: A Report on the Broadcasting Industry in the United States from the Commission on Freedom of the Press* (Chicago: University of Chicago Press, 1947; reissued by Arno Press, 1971); Sydney W. Head's *Broadcasting in America*, cited above; and Robert S. McMahon, *The Regulation of Broadcasting: Half a Century of Government Regulation of Broadcasting and the Need for Further Legislation*, a detailed account of congressional consideration of laws on broadcast regulation written for the Committee on Interstate and Foreign Commerce, U.S. House of Representatives, 85th Congress, 2nd Session (Washington, D.C.: Government Printing Office, 1958). The McMahon study is supplemented in "A Legislative History of Broadcast Regulation," which appears on pp. 93–226 of the *Option Papers* prepared by the staff for use by the Subcommittee on Communications of the House Committee on Interstate and Foreign Commerce, 95th Congress, 1st Session (Washington, D.C.: Government Printing Office, 1977). "A Selected Bibliography on the History of Broadcasting," prepared by Barry G. Cole and Al Paul Klose, appears in the Summer 1963 issue of the *Journal of Broadcasting* (vol. 7).

The FCC's *Annual Reports* constitute excellent background material from the commission's perspective; reports for the years 1935 through 1955 were reissued by Arno Press in 1971. A collection of landmark legal documents affecting broadcasting (with helpful introductory notes) is contained in Frank Kahn, ed., *Documents of American Broadcasting*, 3rd ed. (Englewood Cliffs, N.J.: Prentice-Hall, 1978); (New York: Appleton-Century-Crofts, 1973). An anthology by Lawrence W. Lichty and Malachi C. Topping, eds., *American Broadcasting: A Sourcebook on the History of Radio and Television* (New York: Hastings House, 1975), includes ninety-three documents and articles on various aspects of broadcasting, ranging from network programing to government regulation.

Primary Sources. The following publications of the U.S. Government Printing Office in Washington, D.C., contain copies of the basic laws, rules, and decisions pertaining to broadcast regulation: the *United States Code*, all federal laws (the Communications Act of 1934 appears in Title 47); the *Federal Register*, daily materials on rule-making proceedings by governmental agencies; the *Code of Federal Regulations* (Title 47 includes FCC rules and regulations in four volumes), an annual compilation of rules and regulations adopted by such agencies; and the *Federal Communications Reports*, decisions, notices, and reports of the FCC. The standard comprehensive reference work in the field of broadcast regulation is *Pike & Fischer Radio Regulation*, a commercial publication which includes (1) the text of broadcast laws; (2) legislative histories of such laws and rules proposed and adopted by the FCC; (3) decisions, reports, and other rulings of the commission; and (4) decisions of courts and other governmental agencies directly affecting radio and television. Another commercial publication, *Media Law Reporter*, a weekly looseleaf service published by the Bureau of National Affairs, provides the text of court and agency decisions of significance to the electronic and print media.

Bibliographies. An excellent annotated bibliography of major published works dealing with the background, structure, function, content, and effects of the communications media is Eleanor Blum, *Basic Books in the Mass Media: An Annotated, Selected Booklist Covering General Communications, Book Publishing, Broadcasting, Film, Magazines, Newspapers, Advertising, Indexes, and Scholarly and Professional Periodicals* (Urbana: University of Illinois Press, 1972). The subtitle accurately describes the bibliography's contents. The following bibliographies supplement and update the Blum review: Oscar H. Gandy, Jr., et al., *Media and Government: An Annotated Bibliography* (Stanford, Calif.: Institute for Communication Research, Stanford University, 1975), and Christopher H. Sterling, *Broadcasting and Mass Communications: A Survey Bibliography* (Philadelphia: Temple University, 1978). *Mass Media Booknotes*, edited by Professor Sterling, is a monthly review of recent books on broadcasting and other media.

Several journals (*Journal of Broadcasting, Federal Communications Bar Journal, Journal of Law and Economics*, and *Public Telecommunications Review*) regularly publish articles on various aspects of broadcast regulation. The Summer 1970 issue (vol. 14) of the *Journal of Broadcasting* contains "A Selected Bibliography of Works on the Federal Communications Commission" by Robert Sperry, which is a highly selective list of articles, books, pamphlets, dissertations, and congressional documents. This bibliography is supplemented by Sperry in an article appearing in the Winter 1975 issue (vol. 19) of the *Journal of Broadcasting*, "A Selected Bibliography of Works on the FCC and OTP: 1970–1973." The Winter 1969–1970 issue (vol. 14; Part 2) of the *Journal of Broadcasting* includes "A Bibliography of Articles About Broadcasting in Law Periodicals, 1956–1968," prepared by Kenneth Gompertz, which is an index—by title, subject, and author—of 497 articles on administrative law and the regulation of broadcasting culled from American law journals. This issue also features an analysis of 526 articles published during the preceding thirty-five years entitled "An Annotated Bibliography of Articles on Broadcasting Law and Regulation in Law Periodicals, 1920–1955." See also John M. Kittross, comp., *Theses and Dissertations in Broadcasting: 1970–1972* (Philadelphia: Broadcast Education Association, 1977), a computer-indexed listing.

The Five Case Studies. Surprisingly little useful research has been published concerning the five case studies in chapters five, six, seven, eight, and nine. What literature exists tends to be either highly impressionistic and one-sided accounts or journalistic reports scattered through issues of various periodicals such as *Broadcasting*. The footnotes in chapters five through nine provide citations to the pertinent FCC, judicial, and congressional documents. Detailed contemporaneous accounts of FCC actions in the five cases (as well as other aspects of broadcast regulation) are reported weekly in *Broadcasting*. Although *Broadcasting* is the best known of the trade journals for the broadcasting industry, *Television Digest* and *Variety* offer informative accounts of FCC actions each week, frequently from a less industry-oriented perspective. (Both *Broadcasting* and *Television Digest* publish annual indexes.) Another useful source of information on FCC actions, frequently containing interviews with and articles by commissioners and broadcast executives, is a biweekly publication, *Television/Radio Age*. Monthly reports on FCC matters from the perspective of various citizens groups can be found in *access* magazine, published by the National Citizens Committee for Broadcasting.

The FM Shift. No single concise account exists of the FM shift decision, with the exception of an earlier version of chapter five by Lawrence D. Longley, "The FM Shift in 1945," *Journal of Broadcasting*, 12 (Fall 1968). Useful material on FM broadcasting may be found in W. Rupert Maclaurin, *Invention and Innovation in the Radio Industry* (New York: Macmillan, 1949, reissued by Arno Press, 1971), and in chapter five of Vincent Mosco's *The Regulation of Broadcasting in the United States: A Comparative Analysis*, cited above. A lively account of FM's early history, full of detail but undocumented, is contained in a book, reprinted in paperback, by Lawrence Lessing, *Man of High Fidelity: Edwin Howard Armstrong* (New York: Bantam, 1969). Probably no better introduction exists to the development of FM broadcasting—or to the life of a truly towering figure—yet the reader must keep in mind Lessing's obviously deep admiration of the man and his profound distrust of Armstrong's opponents. An alternate and briefer introduction to much of the same material (and with similar biases) can be found in the anonymous article, "Armstrong of Radio," *Fortune*, 37 (February 1948). Another account of Armstrong's role is contained in an emotional book by Don V. Erickson, *Armstrong's Fight for FM Broadcasting: One Man vs. Big Business and Bureaucracy* (University, Ala.: University of Alabama Press, 1973).

A useful study of the economic characteristics of the radio spectrum and of the roles played by various participants in the allocation of spectrum is Harvey J. Levin's *The Invisible Resource: Use and Regulation of the Radio Spectrum* (Baltimore: Johns Hopkins Press, 1971). Professor Levin examines the interplay between competition and regulation in spectrum allocation and advocates a modified free market for spectrum allocations. This is the theme examined by many economists in the economic literature discussed above.

The FM shift is also covered, although rather briefly, in the appendix of Elmer E. Smead's book, *Freedom of Speech by Radio and Television* (Washington, D.C.: Public Affairs Press, 1959); in Murray Edelman's *The Licensing of Radio Services in the United States*, cited above; and in the unpublished doctoral dissertations of Avard Wellington Brinton, "The Regulation of Broadcasting by the FCC: A Case Study in Regulation by Independent Commission" (Harvard, 1962), and Christopher H. Sterling, "Second Service: A History of Commercial FM Broadcasting to 1969" (University of Wisconsin, 1969). (Copies of the dissertations noted here may be obtained from University Microfilms, Ann Arbor, Michigan.) The bright new future which the development of FM might bring is glowingly predicted in a book written in the 1940s by Charles A. Siepmann, *Radio's Second Chance* (Boston: Little, Brown, 1946). Finally, two articles by Christopher H. Sterling, "Second Service: Some Keys to the Development of FM Broadcasting," *Journal of Broadcasting*, 15 (Spring 1971), and "Decade of Development: FM Radio in the 1960's," *Journalism Quarterly*, 48 (Summer 1971), establish a most useful context for understanding the events of the late 1940s and their impact on the subsequent development of FM broadcasting.

The All-Channel Receiver Bill. A comprehensive account of the deintermixture policies of the FCC during the 1950s and the events leading up to the All-Channel Receiver Bill in 1962 is available in an article written by the student editors of the *Harvard Law Review*, "Notes: The Darkened Channels: UHF Television and the FCC," *Harvard Law Review*, 75 (June 1962). Although limited because of its heavy reliance on formal statements and legal briefs, this is an excellent overview. Two dissertations cover the commission's early deintermixture efforts: John Michael Kittross, "Television Frequency Allocation Policy in the United States" (University of Illinois, 1960), includes a sound discussion (in chapter six) of UHF television and deintermixture in the 1950s; and Avard Wellington Brinton, "The Regulation of Broadcasting by the FCC: A Case Study of Regulation by Independent Commission" (Harvard, 1962), which reviews some of the events surrounding the deintermixture controversies in the course of trying to show the limitations of independent regulatory commissions.

Virtually without exception, the economic literature cited above criticizes the FCC for its vacillation and uncertainty in promoting the growth of UHF television. A perceptive critique of the commission's UHF policy may be found in chapter six of Vincent Mosco's *The Regulation of Broadcasting in the United States: A Comparative Analysis*, cited above. A 1976 report prepared by the House Subcommittee on Oversight and Investigations, *Federal Regulation and Regulatory Reform*, cited above, which draws upon the material in the first edition of *The Politics of Broadcast Regulation*, is quite critical of commission policy in this area. Some of the specific events surrounding the passage of the 1962 All-Channel

Receiver Act are discussed in chapter six, "All-Channel Television," of Newton N. Minow's *Equal Time: The Private Broadcaster and the Public Interest* (New York: Atheneum, 1964). Douglas W. Webbink analyzes this legislation in his critique, "The Impact of UHF Promotion: The All-Channel Receiver Law," *Law and Contemporary Problems*, 34 (Summer 1969). In fact, the relatively brief discussion by Minow and the criticism by Webbink constitute the entirety of significant materials published specifically on the 1962 legislation—with the exception of an earlier version of this chapter by Lawrence D. Longley, "The FCC and the All-Channel Receiver Bill of 1962," *Journal of Broadcasting*, 13 (Summer 1969).

The Commercial Time Proposal. The only published material which systematically examines events surrounding the commercial time fiasco is an early version of chapter seven, written by Lawrence D. Longley, "The FCC's Attempt to Regulate Commercial Time," *Journal of Broadcasting*, 11 (Winter 1966–1967). A criticism of the commission's 1963 initiative on legal and constitutional grounds was published at that time by Douglas A. Anello and Robert V. Cahill, attorneys with the National Association of Broadcasters, "Legal Authority of the FCC to Place Limits on Broadcast Advertising Time," *Journal of Broadcasting*, 7 (Fall 1963). One interested in the genesis of the commission's concerns should also examine the famous 1946 FCC "Blue Book," *Public Service Responsibility of Broadcast Licensees* (Washington, D.C.: Government Printing Office, 1946, reprinted by Arno Press in 1974), as well as two articles discussing this landmark document: Richard J. Meyer, "The Blue Book," *Journal of Broadcasting*, 6 (Summer 1962), and his "Reactions to the 'Blue Book'," *Journal of Broadcasting*, 6 (Fall 1962). A discussion of the FCC's policies on commercials following the abortive attempt in 1963 is contained in an article by Carl Ramey, "The Federal Communications Commission and Broadcast Advertising: An Analytical Review," *Federal Communications Bar Journal*, 20 (1963).

Competing Applications at Renewal Time. Sterling "Red" Quinlan's *The Hundred Million Dollar Lunch* (Chicago: J. Philip O'Hara, 1974) is a colorful account of the WHDH hearing, written in the style of a novel. A detailed chronology of events leading to the WHDH decision and its aftermath (as of 1973) and a listing of significant sources are contained in an article by Robert R. Smith and Paul T. Prince, "WHDH: The Unconscionable Delay," *Journal of Broadcasting*, 18 (Winter 1973–1974). A number of law review articles have focused on the legal issues posed by the WHDH decision. Some of the more insightful of these articles are: Louis Jaffe, "WHDH: The FCC and Broadcasting License Renewals," *Harvard Law Review*, 82 (1969); Hyman Goldin, "'Spare the Golden Goose'—The Aftermath of WHDH in FCC License Renewal Policy," *Harvard Law Review*, 82 (1969); "Comment, The Federal Communications Commission and Comparative Broadcast Hearings: WHDH as a Case Study in Changing Standards," *Boston College Industry and Commerce Law Review*, 10 (1969); and William H. Wentz, "The Aftermath of WHDH: Regulation by Competition or Protection of Mediocrity?" *University of Pennsylvania Law Review*, 118 (1970). An analysis of the development of the FCC's comparative renewal policy based on the model used in *The Politics of Broadcast Regulation* can be found in a doctoral dissertation by Stanley D. Tickton, "Broadcast Station License Renewals Action and Reaction: 1969 to 1974" (University of Michigan, 1974).

A study entitled *Licensing of Major Broadcasting Facilities by the Federal Communications Commission*, which was prepared by Professor William K. Jones for the Administrative Conference of the United States, is an excellent volume for general background reading on the FCC's processing of renewal applications and its standards in comparative hearings. The study was reprinted in U.S. House of Representatives, Subcommittee No. 6, Select Committee on Small Business, 89th Congress, 2nd Session, *Activities of Regulatory and Enforcement Agencies Relating to Small Business*, Part 1, A103–A112, A165–A174 (Washington, D.C.: Government Printing Office, 1966). A detailed review and analysis of the commission's standards in comparative proceedings are contained in an article by Robert A. Anthony, "Towards Simplicity and Rationality in Comparative Broadcast Licensing Proceedings," *Stanford Law Review*, 24 (1971). For analysis of the renewal process from the viewpoint of citizens groups, see John Grundfest, *Citizen Participation in Broadcast Licensing Before the FCC* (Santa Monica, Calif.: Rand Corp., 1976).

Citizens Band Radio. Virtually no literature exists on the regulatory problems created by the development of citizens band radio other than a law review article by Mark J. Meltzer, "Chaos on the Citizens Band— Regulatory Solutions for Spectrum Pollution," *Hastings Law Journal*, 26 (January 1975). For an excellent review of the history and development of CB broadcasting, see Carolyn Marvin and Quentin J. Schultze, "The First 30 Years," *Journal of Communication*, 27 (Summer 1977). For a discussion of the technical problems of CB radio and an evaluation of some alternative two-way communications systems, see Carlos Valle Roberts's unpublished masters thesis, "Two-Way Communications Systems for Use by the General Public" (University of Colorado, 1975).

This is not to suggest that newspapers and magazines have ignored the rise of CB radio; the large number of articles on this subject appearing in the *Washington Post*, the *New York Times*, the *Washington Star*, and the *Wall Street Journal* and cited in chapter nine illustrate the degree to which CB radio has caught journalistic attention. Similarly, a wide variety of handbooks on citizens band radio is available at bookstores and newsstands. For example, see Jethro Lieberman and Neil S. Rhodes, *The*

Complete CB Handbook (New York: Avon, 1977), revised and reissued yearly. Such books cover CB equipment selection, installation, and operation; CB lingo and codes; commission regulations; and unofficial CB practices. Nevertheless, little literature exists, as of 1977, that systematically assesses the technological, social, and economic impact of this phenomenon. Three partial efforts along these lines might be mentioned, however: Michael Harwood "America with Its Ears On," *New York Times Magazine*, April 25, 1976; Burt Schorr, "Crossed-Band Woes Are Unlikely to Ease Despite FCC Moves," *Wall Street Journal*, August 23, 1976; and David A. Loehwing, "No Bucket Mouth: A Shakeout May Be Coming in Citizens Band," *Barron's*, May 31, 1976.

INDEX